Ghosts in the Gallery
at Cooperstown

ALSO BY DAVID L. FLEITZ

Louis Sockalexis: The First Cleveland Indian
(McFarland, 2002)

Shoeless: The Life and Times of Joe Jackson
(McFarland, 2001)

Ghosts in the Gallery at Cooperstown

Sixteen Little-Known Members of the Hall of Fame

by David L. Fleitz

McFarland & Company, Inc., Publishers

Jefferson, North Carolina, and London

LIBRARY OF CONGRESS CATALOGUING-IN-PUBLICATION DATA

Fleitz, David L., 1955–
    Ghosts in the gallery at Cooperstown : sixteen little-known members
of the Hall of Fame / by David L. Fleitz.
      p.   cm.
    Includes bibliographical references and index.

    ISBN 0-7864-1749-8 (softcover : 50# alkaline paper) ∞

    1. Baseball players— United States— Biography.   2. Baseball
players— United States— Statistics.   3. National Baseball Hall of Fame
and Museum.   I. Title.
GV865.A1F54   2004
796.357'092'2 — dc22   2003026012

British Library cataloguing data are available

Cover photograph: Kid Nichols (National Baseball Hall of Fame Library,
Cooperstown, N.Y.)

Manufactured in the United States of America

McFarland & Company, Inc., Publishers
  Box 611, Jefferson, North Carolina 28640
  www.mcfarlandpub.com

For my parents

◆ ACKNOWLEDGMENTS ◆

I would like to thank a few people without whom this book would not have been possible.

As always, Bill Burdick at the National Baseball Library in Cooperstown, New York, offered helpful assistance in rounding up photographs for this book, and the Eugene C. Murdock collection of baseball books and materials at the Cleveland Public Library was invaluable. So was the SABR (Society for American Baseball Research) Lending Library, my source for microfilmed copies of *The Sporting News* and *Sporting Life*. I also made great use of the library at Bowling Green State University in my hometown of Bowling Green, Ohio, especially for microfilm of the *Cleveland Plain Dealer* and *The New York Times*. Eric Enders, of Triple E Productions in Cooperstown, New York, provided excellent information.

I would also like to thank my wife, Deborah, for her editing skills and her moral support.

◆ Contents ◆

♦ PREFACE ♦

I made my first pilgrimage to the Baseball Hall of Fame in Cooperstown, New York, during the summer of 1992.

My first order of business, upon entering the museum, was to go directly to the spacious display room that houses the plaques of the more than 200 members of the Hall of Fame. Al Kaline, my favorite player when I was growing up, was represented there, as were many others that I was fortunate enough to see in person such as Henry Aaron and Johnny Bench. However, there seemed to be many unfamiliar names mixed in with the more recognizable ones. Though I was a lifelong baseball fan, with more than a passing interest in the game's long history, I had to admit that I had never heard of some of the recipients of baseball's highest honor.

Other visitors that day expressed similar sentiments as they strolled past the bronze plaques that line the walls of the museum. Everyone knew about Babe Ruth, Mickey Mantle, and Willie Mays, but most did not recognize the names of Elmer Flick, John Clarkson, and Jake Beckley. Wasn't Roger Bresnahan the man who introduced shin guards for catchers, someone asked, and is that the reason he's here? Did Arthur (Candy) Cummings really invent the curveball, as his plaque claims, and how was pitcher Eppa Rixey elected when he won only 15 more games than he lost in his 22-year career? If men like John Clarkson and Roger Connor were great players, why were they not admitted to Cooperstown until nearly 70 years after their careers ended? Pete Rose and Shoeless Joe Jackson are not in the Hall of Fame, but Jake Beckley and Morgan G. Bulkeley are? How did that happen?

It became clear to me that, although the institution is called the Hall of Fame, many of its honored players are not famous at all. In fact, a good number of these all-time greats of the game, especially those who played long ago, are virtually forgotten men.

1

My walk through the display room also made me aware of a glaring gap in my baseball knowledge. At the time, there were 11 men who had gained election to the Hall of Fame on the basis of their play in the Negro Leagues before the integration of the sport in 1947. I knew of Satchel Paige, but names such as Ray Dandridge and Cool Papa Bell were complete mysteries to me. Five years later, when Willie Wells gained his place in the museum, I had no idea who he was or what position he played.

I decided to learn more about these obscure Hall of Famers, though it proved to be a daunting task. There are literally dozens of biographies available on Ted Williams, Mickey Mantle, and others of the better-known Hall members, but none at all for men such as Frank Selee and Vic Willis. The Society for American Baseball Research has produced valuable reference books with short biographies of these nearly forgotten greats, but nowhere did I find in-depth detail on any of them. Many played more than 100 years ago, and little documentation survives of their baseball careers save for their statistics. However, they each hold a place of honor among the greatest players of all time, and somebody, somewhere along the line, thought that these men belonged in Cooperstown beside Ruth and Mays.

We have the Hall of Fame Veterans Committee, in its several incarnations, to thank for the presence of these men in the museum. When the Hall was founded in the 1930s, the Baseball Writers Association of America was charged the task of electing members. However, Commissioner Kenesaw M. Landis found it necessary to appoint a special board to select 19th-century players and contributors. This panel, initially meant to be temporary, survives to the present day and has evolved into a second-chance method of entry to the Hall of Fame for those whose candidacies were previously rejected by the baseball writers. This has led many people to consider selection by the Veterans Committee as an inferior type of honor, though officially all Hall members enjoy equal membership. The Veterans Committee choices through the years have tended to focus on more obscure and little-known players, and this secondary panel selected all 16 of the men profiled in these pages.

This book is the result of my quest to learn more about these stars of the past — who they were, why they were considered great players, and how they gained their places in Cooperstown. I also wanted to see what kind of people they were on a personal level, so I combed through books, newspapers, and magazines, as well as the Hall's own files, to find quotes from each player and, whenever available, information about their families.

My research into their baseball careers was made more difficult by the discovery that, for long-ago players, four different reference books may list four different sets of statistics. In recent years, baseball researchers and experts in sabermetrics (the study of baseball statistics) have re-examined box scores and game accounts from the 19th century and published new totals and averages for almost all of the stars of the past. Roger Connor is credited, in different publications, with as few as 131 and as many as 138 home runs, while Bid McPhee's career batting average ranges from .271 to .281 and Vic Willis' win total from 243 to 249. I solved the problem by relying on the statistics posted for each player on the Baseball Hall of Fame web site, which are provided by the Elias Sports Bureau and have been essentially unchanged for many years. All stats in this book, for consistency's sake, are those that are accepted as fact by the Hall of Fame.

All of these obscure stars of Cooperstown are long deceased, some for 80 years or more, and are now remembered (if at all) with rows and columns of numbers detailing their batting averages, hits, and games won. I have tried my best to tell the stories behind the numbers. In the course of writing this book, I discovered something that I had long suspected — that athletes, as people, are far more interesting than their statistics. These 16 men are, paradoxically, not famous despite their presence in the Hall of Fame, but their lives and careers proved every bit as remarkable as those of their better-known brethren. These men have interesting stories, and those stories deserve to be told.

David L. Fleitz
December 2003

1

♦ MORGAN G. BULKELEY ♦

Baseball isn't the game that it was when I was a boy, or when I was president of the National League. I know that it is a better game in many ways because it has developed from the good start we gave it. What I like about it is that it has not departed so much from the old way of playing that I cannot enjoy it. — Morgan G. Bulkeley, 1922[1]

When the National Baseball Hall of Fame and Museum was created in the mid–1930s, Commissioner Kenesaw M. Landis gave the right to select honored players to the Baseball Writers Association of America (BBWAA). He did so, understandably, because most people took it for granted that the sportswriters would be the ones who were most knowledgeable about the game. It soon became apparent, however, that the writers were not cognizant enough about the past generations of baseball. Some sports columnists across the country criticized the Hall of Fame electors for ignoring the contributions of early players and executives. In response, Landis created a panel to select 19th-century players and pioneers of the game for induction.

In mid–1937, Landis appointed a committee consisting of himself, the two league presidents, a retired league president, and the president and chairman of the minor leagues. This panel, called the Centennial Commission, was charged with the task of electing 19th-century players and builders of the game to the Hall. The committee met for the first time on December 7, 1937, and elected five men to the Hall of Fame.

One of the five electees was Byron Bancroft (Ban) Johnson, the founder and first president of the American League, and logic dictated that the Centennial Commission would select Johnson's National League counterpart as well. However, the founder of the National League and its first president were two different people. William Hulbert, who led a revolt among dissatisfied club owners in the spring of 1876 and convinced them to dissolve the weak National Association and form a new circuit, was the true creator of the league. For political purposes, Hulbert asked Morgan G. Bulkeley, a wealthy and prominent Connecticut businessman and politician, to serve as president of the new league for one year only. Bulkeley accepted the offer and served merely as a figurehead, leaving the decision-making to Hulbert. In December 1876, with the league on solid footing, Bulkeley stepped down as president and returned to his business and political pursuits in Connecticut.

Therefore, the members of the Centennial Commission faced a dilemma — should they elect Hulbert or Bulkeley to the Hall of Fame? Hulbert created the National League, but Bulkeley was its first president, and so the commission selected Bulkeley. Though he held office for only ten months and made no important decisions, Morgan Bulkeley gained baseball's highest honor, while William Hulbert was relegated to obscurity by baseball fans and historians.

Morgan Gardner Bulkeley was the scion of one of Connecticut's wealthiest families. He was born the day after Christmas in 1837 to Eliphalet and Lydia Bulkeley in the town of East Haddam. Both of Morgan's parents were descended from passengers on the *Mayflower*, which arrived at Plymouth more than two hundred years before. Eliphalet Bulkeley was a judge, a state senator, and one of the founders of the Connecticut Republican Party. The family relocated to Hartford in 1846, where Eliphalet Bulkeley founded and served as the first president of the Aetna Life Insurance Company. Morgan played the various forms of bat-and-ball games enthusiastically as a child, including One Old Cat and Two Old Cat, games in which there were one or two bases depending upon the number of players available.

Morgan attended high school in Hartford and earned a dollar a day sweeping offices at Aetna, but he left school at age 15 to work as a clerk in a store owned by his uncle in Brooklyn. He was a baseball fan even then. "I remember with great distinctness the early struggles in Brooklyn, New York between the two rival clubs, the Atlantics and the Excelsiors, and later the Stars with [Jim] Creighton as pitcher," said Bulkeley years later.[2] This would have been in the late 1850s and early 1860s.

Before long, Morgan became a partner in his uncle's firm, though his path to business success was interrupted by the Civil War. Many a wealthy man avoided military service by paying a substitute to serve in his place, but the Bulkeley family was firmly patriotic. Morgan abandoned his business pursuits and enlisted in the 13th New York Volunteers, where he served under General George McClellan and saw action in the Peninsular Campaign. Morgan's brother Charles also joined the Union army and was killed in action at Alexandria, Virginia.

Bulkeley resumed his business career in Brooklyn at war's end, but when his father died in 1872 he returned to Hartford and entered the family business as a director of the Aetna Life Insurance Company. He also helped establish the United States Bank of Hartford, and through the bank he became involved in charitable and community pursuits. From these community activities came his brief association with baseball.

The first professional baseball league, the National Association, began play in 1871 with teams in ten cities, though several of them failed to finish the season. The circuit was weakly governed, and power in the Association was concentrated in the hands of the players, as shown in 1872 when Brooklyn third baseman Bob Ferguson was elected league president. Any team could join the Association by posting a ten-dollar entry fee, and in early 1872 a team from Middletown, Connecticut paid its way into the circuit. The Middletown nine disbanded in August, but the following season a club from a similarly small city, Elizabeth, New Jersey, joined the league as well.

Hartford was, and still is, the capital of Connecticut, and local businessmen and civic boosters figured that if Middletown could enter a team in the Association, then Hartford could do so more successfully. Morgan Bulkeley, already emerging as a civic leader and political force in Hartford, headed a group that applied for, and received, membership in the Association for the 1874 season. By then Bulkeley had gained election to a seat on Hartford's city council, and a leadership role with the local baseball team promised to add luster to his name and draw public attention to a man who was already mapping out the course of his future political career.

The team was named the Dark Blues, and the team owners determined to avoid the mistakes that doomed the Middletown nine to failure. The first order of business was to secure a playing field. Bulkeley and his fellow investors bought a piece of land in the industrial section of the city at the corner of Wyllys Street and Hendricxsen Avenue, a few blocks from the Colt revolver factory, and built a ballpark with 2,000 seats. They called it the Hartford Baseball Grounds.

In choosing players for the team, Bulkeley followed the example of the newly re-assembled Chicago White Stockings, who dropped out of the league after most of Chicago was destroyed by the Great Fire of October 1871. Both the new White Stockings and the Dark Blues signed experienced professional players to fill their rosters, hoping for immediate success in the standings. However, the Chicagoans cornered the market on the best available players. Hartford signed a former Baltimore slugging star, center-fielder Lip Pike, who led the league in doubles and slugging percentage, but none of the other acquisitions made much of a contribution. With Pike as manager of the club, Hartford finished its first season with a 16–37 record, good for seventh place in the eight-team league.

The new ballclub managed to survive its first season, unlike the Middletown nine two years before, but the attendance disappointed Bulkeley and the other investors. The Hartford ballpark was located more than a mile from the nearest train station, and few of the team's home games drew more than a few hundred fans. Still, Bulkeley, who was named team president in early 1875, plowed ahead with plans. The team signed star third baseman Bob Ferguson away from Brooklyn and appointed him manager, and scored a coup by signing pitcher Arthur (Candy) Cummings to a contract.

Cummings was probably the smallest man ever to play major league baseball on a regular basis. He stood five feet eight inches tall and weighed a mere 120 pounds, but was widely known as the inventor of the curve ball. The pitch was still a novelty in 1875, and Cummings made many batters flail aimlessly at the unusual delivery. Cummings' presence alone turned the on-field fortunes of the Dark Blues around, and his 35–16 record vaulted the Hartford team into a respectable third-place finish. However, attendance remained stagnant at the Hartford Baseball Grounds, and some onlookers expressed the belief that the city of Hartford could not adequately support a team in the nation's highest professional league.

The National Association experienced many other problems in its short existence. Small-town teams, like those in Troy, Elizabeth, or Hartford, could not hope to compete financially with teams from bigger cities like Chicago or Boston. Players were virtual free agents and jumped from one team to another each season. Candy Cummings played for four different clubs in four years from 1872 to 1875, and actually signed contracts with three different clubs in 1872 before the league forced him to honor one of them. Some of the more prominent teams found no need to complete their schedules after dropping out of the pennant chase, and the league was powerless to force them to play their remaining games.

The thorniest problem of the mid–1870s was the specter of "hippo-droming," or throwing games at the behest of gambling interests. Many players received offers from gamblers to withhold their best efforts, and at least some of them accepted bribes to do so. Since the players were now professionals, mostly with no local ties to their teams, many felt no loyalty to the communities in which they played. "Instead of the best youths of the land striving in honest rivalry with parents and friends as witnesses of their skill," complained the *Hartford Courant* in 1873, "hired hands of trained players scour the country, followed by crowds of gamblers and pick pockets."³ When the league suspended John Radcliff of the Philadelphia Athletics in 1874 for attempting to bribe an umpire, it decreed that the offender was banned for life. However, Radcliff played for another Philadelphia team, the Centennials, the following season, and the league possessed no power to stop him.

William Hulbert, president of the Chicago White Stockings, wanted to strengthen the National Association, but by the end of the 1875 campaign he decided on a more radical course of action. On February 2, 1876, Hulbert called a meeting of eight National Association club presidents, including Hartford's Morgan Bulkeley, and laid out a plan for a new league. The National League, proposed Hulbert, would replace the weakly managed Association with a much stronger administration with power centered in the clubs and not the players. The league would limit each major city to one team, and decide for itself which teams might enter championship play (and do away with the Association's ten-dollar entry fee). In short, the new National League would police its members, insist upon the sanctity of contracts and schedules, and become the custodian of professional baseball in the nation.

The Chicago club president was not merely acting out of selflessness. His ballclub had raided the Boston and Philadelphia teams of several of their best players, including a 23-year-old first baseman and catcher named Adrian C. Anson, and there were more than a few clubs in the National Association that would have liked to expel Hulbert and his White Stockings from the league. Instead, Hulbert outsmarted them in what the *New York Clipper* called "a startling *coup d'etat*," building his own league on the ruins of the old one. "I have a new scheme," said Hulbert to his star pitcher, Albert G. Spalding. "Let us anticipate the eastern cusses and organize a new association before the March meeting, and then see who will do the expelling."⁴

Hulbert also intended to gain the upper hand in dealings with the players by driving down salaries and restricting player movement, a stance that soon led to the adoption of the reserve clause. "It is ridiculous to pay ballplayers $2,000 a year," Hulbert once said. "Especially when the $800 boys often do just as well."⁵ This attitude appealed to Morgan Bulkeley and other conservative Eastern businessmen, as did Hulbert's stated goal of outlawing gambling and drinking in the ballparks and banning Sunday games. These ideals were well received by the public, though there was a financial consideration involved in the campaign to "clean up" the game. Hulbert, by assuring the people of baseball's integrity, hoped that the fans could be convinced not only to support their local teams, but also to pay 50 cents admission instead of the prevailing 25-cent charge.

Hulbert and his Chicago club had clashed several times with the Eastern team owners, and a certain amount of tension had existed in the Association between the eastern and western clubs since the White Stockings reentered the league in 1874. To hasten the acceptance of his plans, Hulbert offered the presidency of the new league to the wealthy Easterner, Morgan G. Bulkeley. Hulbert knew that the backing of such an influential personage would greatly influence the skeptical Easterners to join the new circuit and bring respectability to the league. Albert G. Spalding, who was present at the meeting, later recalled that Bulkeley balked at Hulbert's offer, but Hulbert "urged his acceptance as a tribute due to the East, where baseball had its origin and early development," whereupon Bulkeley accepted the post.[6]

Upon assuming the presidency of the new league, Bulkeley made it clear to Hulbert that he intended to serve for only one year. Some reports state that Bulkeley became president because Hulbert pulled his name out of a hat, but that scenario seems unlikely. Hulbert needed Eastern support in order for the National League to succeed, and Bulkeley's assumption of the presidency was an important element of Hulbert's overall plan. Hulbert, however, kept all the power and even named the new circuit himself. "Let us get away from the old, worn-out title, 'The National Association of Baseball Players,' and call it 'The National League of Professional Baseball Clubs,'" said Hulbert to his right-hand man Spalding.[7]

During the 1876 season, Bulkeley served as president of the National League in name only, while Hulbert made all the important decisions. Bulkeley primarily concerned himself with the Hartford team, of which he remained president, and with his burgeoning political career. He was elected as a Republican to the city's council of aldermen in 1876, and had already set his sights on higher office. Bulkeley was forced to handle a controversy on his own team in late 1876, when Hartford pitcher Tommy Bond accused manager Bob Ferguson of throwing games. Following an investigation, Bulkeley decided to back Ferguson, and the team board of directors suspended Bond for the remainder of the season. Bond had supplanted Candy Cummings as Hartford's main pitcher, but Cummings resumed his former position and finished the season strongly for the Dark Blues.

The National League survived its first campaign, but not before it deflected a potentially fatal blow in the season's last month. The league's two most prominent eastern teams, the New York Mutuals and the Philadelphia Athletics, fell out of the pennant race and refused to embark on their final western road trips and complete their schedules. The matter came to a head on December 7, 1876, when the other National League owners met at Cleveland's Kennard House hotel and made two crucial decisions. They elected Hulbert as the second president of the league, succeeding Morgan Bulkeley, and they expelled New York and Philadelphia from the circuit. Bulkeley was not present at the gathering, but he stepped down from the league presidency with the appreciation of the other club owners.

The Hartford Dark Blues finished in second place behind Chicago in 1876, finishing the campaign with nine straight wins, but attendance proved disappointing once again at the Hartford Baseball Grounds. Bulkeley and his fellow investors finally accepted the fact that Hartford could not support a National League team, and, since many of the players on the ballclub (as well as manager Bob Ferguson) came from Brooklyn, Bulkeley moved the team's home to Brooklyn's Union Grounds. Bulkeley also had to find a new starting pitcher when Tommy Bond refused to play for Ferguson and Candy Cummings jumped to a new league, the International Association. He signed Terry Larkin, a righthander who pitched for the New York Mutuals in 1876 and became a free agent when the Mutuals were expelled from the league that December.

Larkin posted a 29–25 record as the Hartford/Brooklyn contingent finished a respectable third in the six-team league in 1877, 10 games behind the Boston pennant winners, but the crowds remained small and the team continued to lose money. By July 1877 Bulkeley was hinting to Hulbert that he wanted to get out of the baseball business, and at season's end the owners of the Hartford/Brooklyn ballclub simply vacated the franchise and abandoned it to the league.[8] With that, Morgan Bulkeley withdrew from the game of baseball.

The National League prospered in the next several decades, and so did Morgan Bulkeley. In 1879 he took over as president of the Aetna Insurance Company, a post that he held for the remainder of his life, and in 1880 he was elected mayor of Hartford. Like many successful men, he waited until he was well satisfied with his financial prospects before he took a wife. He married Fannie Briggs Houghton in 1885, when Bulkeley was nearly 50 years old, and the couple produced three children.

He won re-election as mayor three times, each by a bigger margin than the previous election, and in 1888 the state Republican Party nominated him for the governorship of Connecticut. He lost the popular vote, but because of the presence on the ballot of several minor candidates, neither Bulkeley nor the Democratic candidate won an electoral majority. As a result, Bulkeley was elected to the governor's office by the state legislature,

Morgan G. Bulkeley, in a photograph taken during his term in the United States Senate (1905–1911). (National Baseball Hall of Fame Library, Cooperstown, New York)

which in Connecticut is called the General Assembly. He took office for a two-year term in January of 1889.

Bulkeley declined to run for re-election in 1890, but he spent two more years in the governor's chair anyway. Connecticut's gubernatorial election of 1890 was rife with charges and counter-charges of fraud and ballot irregularities, and in a bizarre foreshadowing of the 2000 Presidential election, the General Assembly fought over the counting of damaged and "speckled" ballots. Judge Luzon B. Morris, the Democratic candidate, appeared to have won the election by only 26 votes, but the ballot-counting controversy cast that margin into doubt, and no clear winner emerged. The General Assembly was bitterly divided between the Democratic Senate and the Republican House, and neither side budged as the Assembly fell into deadlock.

The Senate declared Morris the victor, while the House stood firm behind the Republican candidate Samuel E. Merwin, and by inauguration day no winner had yet been determined. Bulkeley interpreted the state constitution to read that he, as outgoing governor, should remain in office until a successor had been selected. This he did, to the outrage of Connecticut Democrats and the astonishment of the rest of the nation. Judge Morris appeared at the governor's office to demand recognition as Bulkeley's successor, but Bulkeley, "with courtesy and dignity," refused to relinquish his position.[9]

The state controller, a Democrat, defied Bulkeley and padlocked the governor's office in the state capitol building, but Bulkeley attacked the obstacle in his usual direct way. He procured a crowbar and pried the lock off the door himself, taking possession of his office once again. For the rest of his life, Morgan Bulkeley was known as the "Crowbar Governor." Though Governor David Hill of New York refused to transact business with Connecticut so long as Bulkeley held office, and although the Democrats in the General Assembly refused to provide funds to pay for the governor's staff and other expenses, Bulkeley held on to the post. Eventually, the state Supreme Court allowed Bulkeley to remain in office, though for two years the Democratic Senate refused to appropriate funding for the governor's expenditures. Bulkeley paid for the operation of his office with personal and Aetna funds, which were reimbursed by the state after his elongated term expired.

He finally stepped down as governor after the 1892 election. Conservative Republicans were impressed with his stormy tenure, and in 1896 Bulkeley's name was placed in nomination for the vice-presidency of the United States at the Republican national convention. He received 39 votes, not enough to join William McKinley on the national ticket, but it was an honor nonetheless. An even greater honor came his way in 1904, when Bulkeley capped his political career with a six-year term in the United State Senate. All along, he remained as president of Aetna, which under his guidance grew into one of the largest insurance companies in the nation. In 1891, Aetna began selling accident insurance — Bulkeley bought the first policy himself — and the company expanded into the fields of health insurance in 1899 and automobile insurance in 1907. By 1920, Aetna assets had increased more than eightfold under Bulkeley's presidency, and its premium income more than twenty fold.

Morgan Bulkeley was an interesting contrast of personal generosity and political arch-conservatism. He donated his mayoral salary to the city's poor fund, and concerned himself with child labor and relief for widows and orphans. At the same time, he stood in the way of real reform in Connecticut state government. The state still used an outmoded system of representation in the state legislature, in which each town, regardless of population, sent two representatives to the General Assembly. New Haven, with more than 100,000 people, had the same number of representatives as any town of a few hundred people. This left state politics in the hands of the rural and small-town Republican minority, and Bulkeley fought tooth and nail to retain his party's advantage.

When the General Assembly bowed to pressure and convened a constitutional convention in 1902, Bulkeley and his fellow Republican reactionaries gained control of the convention and submitted to the voters a new system of representation that had no chance of passage. The reform movement failed, and Connecticut's system of selecting delegates to the General Assembly survived until the 1960s, when the United States Supreme Court struck it down as a violation of the "one man, one vote" doctrine.

During his term in the United States Senate, Bulkeley distinguished himself by his support of an African-American battalion of the 24th Infantry Division. In 1906, members of the division, stationed at Brownsville, Texas, were accused of rioting and disorderly conduct in the town. Only the 167 African-American members of the division were arrested for the disturbance, and though some of them may have been involved, none of the soldiers would testify against their guilty comrades. President Theodore Roosevelt dismissed the entire battalion from the Army with dishonorable discharges, while the conservative Bulkeley was one of the few senators to oppose the President publicly on the issue. In 1972, 66 years after the incident, the Army reviewed the case and cleared the soldiers involved, changing their dishonorable discharges to honorable ones and vindicating Bulkeley's stance.

Bulkeley retained an interest in sports after leaving the National League, serving as president of the National Trotting Association for more than 30 years. He never returned to baseball, but he did have one more connection with the sport. In 1905 Albert G. Spalding, the former Chicago White Stockings pitcher who became a wealthy sporting-goods magnate, assembled a commission to examine the origins of the national game. Spalding enlisted six men of sterling reputation to comprise the panel. These men were former players Al Reach and George Wright, former National League presidents Abraham G. Mills and Nicholas Young, and two politicians, United States senators Morgan Bulkeley of Connecticut and Arthur Gorman of Maryland. Spalding named Mills, who succeeded William Hulbert as National League president in 1882, as president of the panel, which became known as the Mills Commission.

Spalding's motives were no more altruistic than William Hulbert's had been during the formation of the National League. Spalding pined for political office, and he wanted to use the Mills Commission as a public platform from which to demonstrate his patriotism. Specifically, Spalding expected the commission to conclude that the game of baseball was completely American in character, and not the descendant of English bat-and-ball games such as rounders. Spalding had expressed displeasure at the widely held view that baseball evolved from games played by youngsters in the British Isles. He wanted to certify baseball as a purely American invention, and he recruited Morgan Bulkeley and several other prominent figures to help him accomplish that goal.

Opposing Spalding and his commission was Henry Chadwick, the respected baseball writer who edited the annual *Spalding Guide* at the time. Chadwick disagreed with his friend and boss Spalding, believing that the game of baseball stemmed from the English game of rounders, which the

English-born Chadwick had played himself as a boy. Though Chadwick declared that the game's British origin did not "detract one iota from the merit of its now being unquestionably a thoroughly American field sport, and a game too, which is fully adapted to the American character,"[10] Spalding plowed ahead with his campaign to prove the American genesis of the game.

Bulkeley and the other committee members met several times in the next two years, but it was not until 1907 that they finally found the evidence they needed. An aged mining engineer named Abner Graves wrote a letter to the commission in June of that year, claiming that he had watched one Abner Doubleday invent the game in Graves' home town of Cooperstown, New York, in or about the spring of 1839. Doubleday, claimed Graves, outlined the shape of the diamond with a stick, set the four bases in their present positions, and also invented the name "base ball" to describe the new game. Graves' account excited Spalding's patriotic impulses because Doubleday, who was 20 years old in 1839, became a decorated soldier and attained the rank of general during the Civil War, in which he commanded a battalion at the Battle of Gettysburg. "It certainly appeals to an American's pride," declared Spalding, "to have had the great national game of Baseball created and named by a Major-General in the United States Army."[11]

Spalding, Bulkeley, and the rest of the committee immediately seized on this piece of information and, without much investigation of Graves' claims, proudly presented General Abner Doubleday to the public as baseball's inventor and the village of Cooperstown as its birthplace. The committee's final report, issued on December 30, 1907, stated unequivocally "the first scheme for playing baseball, according to the best evidence obtainable to date, was devised by Abner Doubleday at Cooperstown, N.Y. in 1839." This conclusion was ridiculous, since Doubleday was a student at West Point from 1838 to 1842 and certainly never set foot in Cooperstown in those years, but Spalding, with Bulkeley's assistance, accomplished his objective in proclaiming baseball as a purely American game.

Spalding may have assembled the Mills Commission to advance his own political ambitions, but the strategy did not work, for he lost a race for the United States Senate in 1910. In that same year, Morgan Bulkeley ran for a second term in the Senate but failed to gain the nomination of his party, so he retired from political life and resumed his post as president of Aetna. He and his wife Fannie also spent a large amount of their time in philanthropic pursuits. Fannie Bulkeley served as chairwoman of Hartford's Liberty Loan bond drive during World War One, while Morgan took an active role in saving Hartford's aged City Hall, the former state capitol building, from destruction in 1915. He personally supervised the raising of $100,000 to renovate the building, and today the Old State Capitol is one of Hartford's significant historic landmarks. He also came to the rescue when the drive to build a new Hartford YMCA building came in $11,000 shy of its goal. Bulkeley authorized one-year raises for his employees, who turned their extra money over to the fund and covered the shortfall.

On February 4, 1916, the National League held a banquet at the Waldorf-Astoria Hotel in New York to commemorate its 40th anniversary. William Hulbert was long dead, but the league's first president, Morgan Bulkeley, attended the dinner as a guest of honor. Former President William Howard Taft was the featured speaker of the evening, but Bulkeley pleased the assembled throng with an eloquent toast in honor of his friend Albert G. Spalding, who had died in the previous year.

Bulkeley remained active in charity work and as president of Aetna until the end of his life. When he died at age 84 on November 6, 1922, he was honored for his contributions to the state of Connecticut as a businessman, politician, and civic leader. Shortly after his death, city leaders in Hartford named one of the city's three high schools after Bulkeley, and also designated an impressive stone-arch highway bridge over the Connecticut River as the Morgan Bulkeley Memorial Bridge. Both the high school and the bridge carry Bulkeley's name to the present day.

Morgan Gardner Bulkeley was an impressive man in every way, but does he belong in the Baseball Hall of Fame? Most observers of the present day believe that he does not, and their argument usually goes something like this:

> John Heydler served as president of the National League for 16 years. He's not in the Hall of Fame.
> Nicholas Young, who became the first secretary of the National League in 1876, later served as league president for 17 years. He's not in the Hall of Fame, either.
> Morgan Bulkeley held the office of National League president for 10 months, during which time he made no important decisions and entrusted the management of the league to his eventual successor, William Hulbert.
> Morgan Bulkeley is in the Hall of Fame.
> Go figure.

In this case, it appears that Bulkeley's selection by the Centennial Commission was a well-intentioned mistake, made not because he was the greatest of National League presidents, but solely because he happened to be the first. There are many people who made greater contributions to the development of the sport without gaining a plaque on the wall in Cooperstown. William Hulbert, the guiding force behind the National League and the true creator of the structure of modern professional baseball, was not present in the Hall of Fame until the Veterans Committee elected him in 1995. His selection rectified one of the Hall's most glaring omissions, but did nothing to correct the erroneous enshrinement of Bulkeley some 58 years before.

This is not to say that Bulkeley made no contribution to the sport. He lent dignity and prestige to the infant National League at a time when the circuit needed it most, and for that he received, and deserved, the gratitude of his fellow owners and praise from the nation's sportswriters. If there were a type of secondary honor given by the Hall of Fame — say, a form of recognition for people who made a valuable or useful contribution to the game — then Morgan Bulkeley would be a deserving recipient. Failing that, Bulkeley remains as perhaps the most uninspired selection ever made in the history of the Hall of Fame.

2

◆ CANDY CUMMINGS ◆

I get a great deal of pleasure now in my old age out of going to games and watching the curves, thinking that it was through my blind efforts that all this was made possible. — William Arthur (Candy) Cummings, 1908[1]

Commissioner Kenesaw M. Landis created a Centennial Commission in 1937 to elect worthy 19th century players, managers, and executives to the Hall of Fame. This six-member committee selected five men (Ban Johnson, Morgan Bulkeley, George Wright, Connie Mack, and John McGraw) in December 1937 and two more (Henry Chadwick and Alexander Cartwright) in September 1938. These seven selections barely made a dent in the list of candidates, and following the 1938 election Landis expressed the belief that more old-time stars deserved induction at the first Hall of Fame ceremony, which was scheduled for June of 1939. One glaring omission from the list of those already honored was the late Cap Anson, the greatest player and manager of the 19th century and (perhaps not incidentally) a good friend of Landis.

After the 1938 meeting of the Centennial Commission, Landis whittled the panel down to three members. The new board was called the Old-Timers Committee and consisted of Landis himself, National League president John Heydler and American League president Will Harridge. These three men met in May of 1939, only four weeks before the ceremony, and named six 19th century baseball figures to the Hall of Fame. Those six were Anson, catcher Buck Ewing, pitchers Candy Cummings and Charlie (Old Hoss) Radbourn, and players-turned-executives Charles Comiskey and Albert Spalding. All six of these men were deceased.

Candy Cummings, at first glance, appears to be one of the more

Candy Cummings in the *New York Clipper*, July 9, 1871. (National Baseball Hall of Fame Library, Cooperstown, New York)

unusual choices for Cooperstown immortality. His major league won-lost record is usually listed as 21–22, because most career records count games played beginning with the formation of the National League in 1876. Cummings' pitching career was almost finished by 1876, but he had been perhaps the nation's greatest pitcher in the years immediately following the Civil War, when amateur teams ruled the baseball landscape before players became openly professional.

However, there were other fine pitchers of the pre–1876 era, men like Jim Creighton and Asa Brainard and Alphonse Martin, who were not singled out for enshrinement in the Hall. Candy Cummings was chosen because he is generally accepted to be the inventor of the curveball. His Hall of Fame plaque makes that clear. It reads,

W.A. "Candy" Cummings
Pitched first curve ball in baseball
history. Invented curve as amateur
ace of Brooklyn Stars in 1867. Ended
long career as Hartford pitcher in
National League's first year 1876.

Cummings' status as curveball originator is one of baseball's enduring controversies, and there were many other claimants to the honor. However, most influential baseball figures of the late 19th and early 20th centuries, including Henry Chadwick, Albert Spalding, and many others, credited Cummings as the first pitcher to make a ball curve in flight and also as the first to use the pitch successfully under competitive conditions. The three members of the Old-Timers Committee believed that this was enough to recognize Candy Cummings with a plaque on the wall in Cooperstown. On June 12, 1939, Cummings was honored as one of the 25 charter members of the Hall of Fame.

William Arthur Cummings, called Arthur by his family and friends, was born in Ware, Massachusetts, on October 17, 1848. He was the second child and first son of William and Mary Cummings, who moved to Brooklyn, New York when Arthur was two years old. The family grew to include 12 children and appears to have been well off, because Arthur's parents sent him to a boarding school in Fulton, New York, in his teenage years.

Arthur grew up playing some of the older forms of bat-and-ball games, precursors to modern baseball such as town ball and one-old-cat. Town ball, also called the Massachusetts Game, was played with a ball that the participants usually made themselves out of discarded yarn, wrapped as tightly as they could wind it. In those games a fielder retired a runner by hitting him with the ball before the runner could get to the base. They called it "soaking" the runner, and only when tagging replaced soaking did the ball become harder and easier to hit farther. Instead of bases, there were four corners marked with stakes four feet high, and games lasted until one team scored 100 tallies, or runs.

Young men in New England and New York played town ball under the Massachusetts rules into the 20th century. As late as 1896, noted writer Daniel Carter Beard was able to write of town ball, "Any number of boys may play in one game, and since all the really necessary properties consist of a ball and a bat, both homemade, it makes a game much better suited to boys than base-ball, with all its array of expensive balls, bats, bases, home plate, armor, wire masks, sliding gauntlets, and gloves. As far as skill is concerned, no good town-ball player need hang his head in the presence of the best of base-ball players."[2]

In town ball the pitcher was called the "giver," and his task was merely to put the ball into play and begin the action. Though Arthur Cummings was small for his age, he liked to be in the middle of things, so he usually took the position as the giver. He threw overhand in town ball, but when he played baseball he pitched underhanded with his arm perpendicular to the ground, as stipulated by the rules of the time.

In the summer of 1863, when Arthur was 14 years old, he and some friends amused themselves at a Brooklyn beach by throwing clamshells into the ocean. The flat, circular shells could be easily made to curve in the air, and the boys managed to create wide arcs of flight before the shells splashed into the water. "We became interested in the mechanics of it and experimented for an hour or more," recalled Arthur Cummings in his later years.

The gracefully sailing disks gave Arthur an idea. "All of a sudden," Cummings once wrote, "it came to me that it would be a good joke on the boys if I could make a baseball curve the same way."[3] This seemingly passing thought started Arthur Cummings on a quest that took much of his time and energy for the next four years.

Arthur played a lot of town ball and baseball at the boarding school in Fulton, which he entered in 1864, but he was so intent on making a baseball curve that he later recalled, "I feared that some of [his classmates] thought it was so preposterous that it was no joke, and that I should be carefully watched over."[4] For months, Arthur experimented with different ways to throw the ball. At first he thought that his stance affected the flight of the ball, so he tried all manner of odd poses and angles. After a while he turned his attention to the gripping of the ball, holding it every which way in his hands before release. Sometimes he thought he saw results, but then he could not repeat whatever made the ball bend, and he was back to square one once again.

In the meantime, Arthur Cummings became an outstanding young pitcher in spite of his physical limitations. He grew to be about five feet nine inches tall as an adult, but he never weighed more than 120 pounds at any time in his life. Even in that era, nearly a century and a half ago, he was small for an athlete. He also had small hands, usually a severe handicap for a pitcher. Arthur excelled on the mound anyway, perhaps due to the practice he gained from his almost fanatical pursuit of the elusive curveball.

In 1865, Arthur Cummings graduated from the Fulton school and joined a team called the Carrolls because they played their games at Carroll Park in Brooklyn. He attracted notice for his fine pitching, and in the spring of 1866 Arthur, still only 17 years old, became the featured pitcher for the Star Junior amateur team. This was the junior varsity nine of the famous Stars of Brooklyn, one of the leading amateur teams in the Northeast. The Star Juniors played 39 games, and Arthur pitched them all with an incredible 37–2 record. Later that year he was invited to join the Brooklyn Excelsior Club, one of the best amateur teams in the New York area.

He pitched his first game for the Excelsiors in late 1866 when the team's regular hurler, Asa Brainard, failed to show up. The opponents, a strong nine called the Eurekas of Newark, New Jersey, may have expected an easy contest with the 117-pound teenager on the mound, but Cummings pitched the Excelsiors to a 24–12 victory. Soon Arthur replaced Brainard as the team's leading pitcher, and he was so dominant that people started calling him "Candy," a Civil War-era superlative meaning the best of anything. President Andrew Johnson saw Cummings pitch at a game between the Excelsiors and the Washington Nationals in the nation's capital in early 1867. The National squad, made up of young government officials and clerks, was one of the strongest teams in the nation, but "Candy" Cummings saddled the Nationals with a rare loss.

All the while, Cummings pursued the secret of the curveball, and in April 1867 he found success for the first time. He discovered that he could make the ball curve in the air when he released it by rolling it off the second finger of his hand, accompanied by a violent twisting of the wrist. We now know that the ball curves because the quick spinning motion of the pitch causes the raised seams of the baseball to act against the currents in the air. A ball would not curve in a vacuum, nor would it curve if it were perfectly smooth like a billiard ball. Though it appears that Jim Creighton, a famous New York amateur pitcher, threw a ball with a quick jerk of the wrist in 1861 and 1862, Cummings was the one who combined it with the rolling motion from the fingers to maximize the amount of spin imparted on the ball.

Early in the 1867 season, the Excelsiors traveled to the Boston area to play such strong regional teams as the Lowells, the Tri-Mountains, and the nine from Harvard University in Cambridge. While pitching against Harvard, Cummings finally found the secret of the curveball. "It was during the Harvard game that I became convinced that I had succeeded in doing what all these years I had been striving to do," wrote the older Cummings. "...I began to watch the flight of the ball through the air and distinctly saw it curve. A surge of joy flooded over me that I shall never forget. I felt like shouting out that I had made a ball curve. I wanted to tell everybody; it was too good to keep to myself."[5]

All day long, Harvard batters flailed helplessly at the new pitch as Cummings tried to keep his excitement in check. "I said not a word, and saw many a batter at that game throw down his stick in disgust. Every time I was successful I could hardly keep from dancing with pure joy. The secret was mine."[6] It didn't stay a secret for long, because the Harvard players and fans prevailed upon Cummings to demonstrate his invention after the game. He showed the throng how he threw the pitch, but for several years afterward Cummings was the only pitcher in the nation to claim mastery over the curveball.

The 120-pound Cummings became the most dominant pitcher in the country, and it may not be an exaggeration to say that when the curveball was working for him, Cummings was the most dominant pitcher of all time. He threw a pitch that none of the batters had ever seen or practiced against, and only when other pitchers learned to throw the curveball would batters learn how to hit it. All the other pitchers who sought to copy Arthur Cummings would need months, if not years, of steady practice of the type that Cummings had already accumulated. This gave Arthur Cummings a gigantic head start upon his competitors and made for an advantage that perhaps no other pitcher has ever enjoyed in the history of the game.

Pitching was much more restricted in Cummings' day. The pitcher stood 45 feet from the plate and had to keep both feet on the ground until after he had released the ball. He was further required to throw with an underhanded swinging motion, keeping his arm perpendicular to the ground. "This was a hard strain [with the curveball delivery] as the wrist and second finger had to do all the work. I snapped the ball away from me like a whip, and this caused my wrist bone to get out of place quite often."[7] Cummings wore a wrist support on the field for most of his pitching career.

Cummings was the first to discover that the elements played a part in the flight of the ball. "I found that the wind had a whole lot to do with the ball curving," he said. "With the wind against me I could get all kinds of a curve, but the trouble lay in the fact that the ball was apt not to break until it was past the batter. This was a sore trouble, but I learned not to try and curve the ball very much when the wind was unfavorable."[8] He also found that the homemade balls used at that time varied greatly in size and weight, further affecting his success in throwing the curve. Cummings did not always succeed in getting the ball to bend, but when he did, he had the batters at his mercy.

Arthur had played for the junior team of the Stars of Brooklyn, but in 1868 the Stars invited him to become the featured pitcher for the varsity nine. The Stars billed themselves as the "championship team of the United States and Canada," and with Candy Cummings on the mound they were able to make good on that boast for the next four seasons. The Stars shared a rivalry with the New York Mutuals, and the two ballclubs vied for the title of the best team in the nation. Several Mutual players received money for their efforts, though we do not know if Cummings or the Stars were paid at this time. Baseball was still considered to be a gentleman's game, and most teams in the immediate post–Civil War period still kept up the façade of amateurism. Still, despite the professional status of some of the Mutual players, Cummings and the Stars defeated them by a 24–12 score in 1869 and staked their claim as the best team in the Northeast.

Cummings did not win every game, because the wind was not always favorable for curveball pitching, and also because the art of fielding had not yet caught up with batting and pitching. Many teams, including the Stars, allowed more baserunners on errors than on hits in those days of barehanded fielding. However, one source states that from 1869 to 1871, Cummings posted records of 16–6, 17–9, and 17–13 in top-level amateur play, and won many more in exhibitions against other outstanding ballclubs. In 1871 Henry Chadwick, the first and most influential baseball writer in the nation, named Candy Cummings as the outstanding baseball player in the United States, the closest thing at that time to a Most Valuable Player award.

It is entirely possible that Cummings also invented the reverse curve or "fadeaway." In July of 1871 the *New York Clipper*, one of the nation's main sources of baseball news in that era, said of Cummings, "He pitches with great speed for his size and weight, has full command of the ball, and exhibits great skill and judgment to a strategic point of view. His great skill, however, is his power to send the ball on a curved line to the right or the left, thus puzzling the best batsmen."[9] One year earlier, the *Brooklyn Union*, reporting a victory by Cummings and the Stars over the New York Mutuals, said that Arthur owned "a peculiar power of giving a curve to the line of the ball to the right or the left."[10]

The National Association, precursor to the National League, began play in 1871 as the nation's first professional circuit. Cummings turned down a number of professional offers and remained with the amateur Brooklyn Stars for one more season, though the New York Mutuals joined the new league. The Mutuals fortified their roster with Joe Start, one of the hardest hitting first basemen of the era, and shortstop Dickey Pearce, who in 1856 invented the bunt. Still, in mid–1871 Cummings and the Stars dealt the Mutuals an embarrassing blow by defeating them 14–3 in an exhibition. It was almost unheard of in those days for a pitcher to hold any team, especially a strong professional one, to only three runs.

The rules in 1871 still stated that the pitching delivery must be made with the arm perpendicular to the ground, and the Mutuals complained loud and long that day that Cummings was throwing illegal sidearm pitches. The umpire in charge disallowed the Mutuals' protest and allowed Candy to pitch unimpeded, but it does appear that Cummings was beginning to throw with more of a sidearm style that season. In 1872 the professional and top amateur leagues changed their pitching rules and allowed pitchers to bend their elbows or snap their wrists, so long as the hand remained below the waist at the point of release. This rule change improved Candy's curveball, but also allowed other pitchers to impart more spin on the ball as well. Opposing pitchers noticed Cummings' success and redoubled their efforts in perfecting their own curveballs.

The New York Mutuals took fifth place in the league's first season. They were dissatisfied with the pitching of fastballer Rynie Wolters, so in early 1872 the Mutuals offered Candy Cummings a spot as their pitcher. Cummings' skills were so in demand that he signed contracts with three different National Association ballclubs before the season started, but in mid–February 1872 the Association awarded Cummings to the Mutuals and made the pitcher a professional for the first time. Cummings pitched

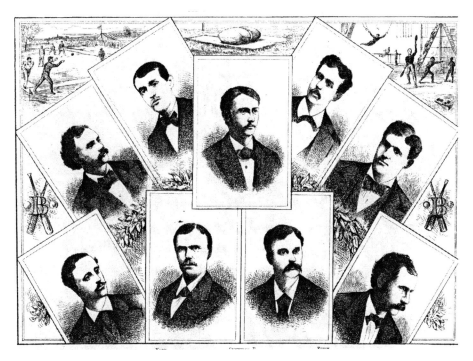

Cummings (top center) with the Lord Baltimores, 1873. (Author's collection)

every inning in all of the Mutuals' 55 games, posting a 33–20 record and helping the New York team to a fourth-place finish. He led the Association in games, complete games, and innings pitched. Candy struck out only 14 men all year, but strikeouts were exceedingly rare then, and he led the league in that category as well.

For the next several years Candy Cummings, who had married Mary Augusta Roberts in June of 1870, pursued increasingly generous financial offers with different teams in the National Association. In 1873 he left the Mutuals and signed with Maryland's entry in the National Association, the Lord Baltimores, while Baltimore starter Bobby Mathews took Cummings' place on the Mutuals. This time, Cummings shared the pitching chores with Asa Brainard, the former pitching star of the Cincinnati Red Stockings, though Cummings pitched in nearly three-fourths of the games that year. Candy posted a 28–14 record as the Lord Baltimores, called the Canaries for their bright yellow stockings, finished a strong third. The 1874 campaign found the 25-year-old veteran in Philadelphia playing for the Pearls, a new club established as a rival to the Athletics, and once again pitching every inning of every game. He posted a 28–26 record with a mediocre ballclub that year, but made national headlines on June 15, 1874, when he struck out six Chicago White Stockings in a row.

By the 1874 season other pitchers began to make up ground on Candy Cummings by developing curveballs of their own. Mathews was the second professional to master the curveball, or so Cummings stated in later life. "The first man to get the curve after myself," wrote Cummings in 1898, "was Bobby Mathews of Baltimore, and as long as he lived he never claimed to have invented the curve, but always told all who asked that he learned it off me."[11] Alphonse Martin of the Troy Haymakers also threw a curve at about this time; some put his first curveball in 1872, his first season in Troy, though Martin himself later claimed that he threw it in amateur play in 1866, a year before Cummings. The controversy over the origin of the tricky pitch had already begun, with several rivals challenging Candy Cummings' claim to preeminence in newspaper articles across the nation. Cummings, proud of his discovery, was keenly protective of his status as the inventor of the curveball, and for the rest of his life he zealously defended his claim from all doubters.

In 1875 Cummings landed on his fifth team in five years, the Hartford Dark Blues, where he went 35–16 and almost single-handedly elevated the new team into third place. He threw seven shutouts in an era when shutouts were almost as rare as no-hitters are in the present day. The 1875 season was longer than previous campaigns, and the Hartford club played 86 games that year after most teams played 55 to 60 games in 1873 and 1874. Therefore, the Hartford club divided the pitching load between Cummings and 19-year-old Tommy Bond, who played right field for the first eight weeks of the campaign while learning the curveball from Cummings. Bond mastered the pitch by mid-season, and by July he and Cummings provided an effective one-two punch for the Dark Blues. Hartford finished in second place as Cummings completed 46 of his 47 starts. Bond posted a 19–16 log and batted .273 as an outfielder.

The National Association fell apart in February 1876 when the strongest teams in the circuit, including Hartford, formed the new National League. Cummings, for the first time in six years, stayed with his previous team and returned to the Dark Blues, but at the age of 26 he began to slow down. The strong-armed Tommy Bond pitched so well early in the season that he became Hartford's main starting pitcher, pushing one of baseball's most celebrated stars to the sidelines. Bond pitched most of Hartford's games until late in the 1876 campaign, when he publicly accused manager Bob Ferguson of throwing games. Hartford management sided with Ferguson and suspended Bond, a move that reinstated Cummings as the team's main pitcher for the rest of the season. In all, Candy pitched 24 games in

1876 with a 16–8 record, while Bond went 31–13 in 45 games as Hartford finished third in the new league. On September 9, 1876, in the first scheduled doubleheader in National League history, Cummings pitched two complete-game victories over Cincinnati.

No evidence exists that links manager Ferguson to gambling or throwing games, but the specter of dishonesty hovered over baseball at the time, and every now and then erupted into full-fledged scandal. The New York Mutuals banned four of their players for life in 1865 for "hippodroming," as it was called then, and other men had come under suspicion in the Association years. Cummings himself had been named in a scandal in 1874 in which his Philadelphia teammate, John Radcliff, was suspended for the rest of the season for offering a bribe to an umpire. Radcliff claimed that Cummings was involved in the bribe attempt, but no evidence of the pitcher's complicity ever surfaced.

From newspaper reports of the time, it appears that few took the charges of the disgraced Philadelphia player seriously. Cummings was well known as a foe of dishonest play, and he did not hesitate to make his suspicions known whenever appropriate. He was a stubborn individual who was widely admired, but made some enemies with his outspoken comments. "Cummings was not over-popular … with a certain class of ballplayers who were mixed up in rather doubtful diamond transactions," wrote New York columnist Sam Crane. "He himself was as honest a player who ever lived, and he never hesitated in telling any player he was suspicious of just what he thought of him, and he invariably hit the nail on the head — the truth hurt."[12]

The club owners controlled the National League, while the power in the Association had been centered in the players themselves, and Candy Cummings missed the freedom that had allowed him to bounce from team to team each year. He declined to sign a National League contract in the winter months of 1876-77, instead joining the Live Oaks of Lynn, Massachusetts, in the new International Association. That winter, Cummings attended the convention that created the new player-controlled league, and the other delegates elected him as the first president of the circuit.

Predictably, the International Association was as weakly governed as the old National Association had been, and Cummings did not stay long with the Live Oaks. He left the team in late June and signed with the Cincinnati Red Stockings of the National League, though he remained president of the International Association for the balance of the season. In Cincinnati, with a worn-out arm and a weak team behind him, Cummings won only five of the 19 games he pitched and quickly fell out of favor with the Queen City fans. One Cincinnati paper complained about the aging star's pitching by stating, "This thing of examining scores of the games ... and seeing from 18 to 25 hits each game piled up against Cummings' record, is getting sickening. His presence on the team is demoralizing. Unless the evil is remedied, the club on its return will not attract 100 people to the games. No change could be for the worse."[13]

At the age of 29, Candy Cummings came to the end of the line as a pitcher, and he did not complete the 1877 season with the Red Stockings. Other pitchers, bigger and stronger than the diminutive Cummings, had learned to throw the curveball, and by 1877 batters had figured out how to hit it. Cummings, with his slender frame and small hands, no longer threw a curve well enough to fool the batters, and his arm was sore from ten years of top-level amateur and professional play. He pitched briefly in the International Association in 1878, but soon dropped back to the amateur and semipro ranks. Later that year he returned to his hometown of Ware, Massachusetts, where he learned the painting and wallpapering trade with an eye toward starting his own business. He continued to play ball sporadically until 1884, when he moved to the town of Athol, Massachusetts and opened his own paint and wallpaper company, which he operated for more than 30 years. In the meantime, he and his wife Mary raised five children.

Athol is a tiny town in the north central portion of Massachusetts, about 50 miles from the metropolis of Boston, and from there Arthur (Candy) Cummings conducted a one-man public relations campaign for more than three decades. Cummings watched the papers closely, especially *Sporting Life*, *The New York Times*, and the Boston dailies, for stories about the invention of the curveball. If any writer credited anyone other than Cummings with its discovery, he would be sure to get a letter from Cummings in the next week's mail.

The chief opposition to Cummings' claim of inventing the curve came in the form of a teenaged pitcher. On August 16, 1870, a 14-year-old named Fred Goldsmith gave a public exhibition of curve pitching at the Capitoline Grounds in Brooklyn. He succeeded in making the ball bend around three parallel stakes in front of a large crowd. The first baseball writer, Henry Chadwick, was present and stated in the paper the next day, "That which had up to this point been considered an optical illusion and against all rules of philosophy was now an established fact."[14] Many people who had never seen Candy Cummings in action naturally assumed that Goldsmith had invented the tricky pitch, but Chadwick later gave credit to Cummings, who began throwing it with great success three years earlier.

Goldsmith insisted that he had never heard of Candy Cummings when he gave his demonstration in 1870, and that he had developed the curve as a boy in New Haven, Connecticut, and showed it to the Yale baseball team in 1866 or so.[15] Goldsmith joined an independent club in Ontario, the Tecumsehs, in 1876 and posted a 31–5 record with his curveball. He played in the International Association in 1877, when Cummings was its president, and landed in the National League in 1879 as the second-line pitcher for Cap Anson's Chicago White Stockings. By 1885 Goldsmith's major league career was over, and he retired to a farm in Michigan and, like Cummings, pursued his claim of authorship of the curve for the rest of his life. He was every bit as tenacious as Cummings, and some reports say that Goldsmith grew to despise Cummings personally and believed that Cummings owed his support to his friendships in the baseball world and the sporting press, not to the weight of the evidence. Goldsmith never wavered in his belief that he, not Cummings, was the true inventor of the curveball.

For many years Cummings and Goldsmith waged war in the pages of the nation's newspapers and magazines. Goldsmith wrote an article for *Sporting Life* in July 1898, detailing his claims and stating that Yale pitching star Ham Avery threw the pitch before Cummings. One week later the magazine printed a letter from Cummings refuting the younger man's assertions. "Enclosed you will find [a] copy of a clipping from the Brooklyn 'Union,' July 9, 1870, which I think will answer Goldsmith's article on the curve ball in your issue of July 16," wrote Cummings to the editors.[16] The clipping described Cummings' use of the curveball a full month before Goldsmith gave his famous demonstration in Brooklyn. Cummings, in his letter, also noted that he was the man who taught Ham Avery how to throw the curve.

Two years earlier, Tim Murnane, the influential *Boston Globe* columnist who played against Cummings in the National Association, came down strongly on the side of Cummings. Murnane listed several famous baseball personages who supported Cummings, such as Cap Anson and Albert G. Spalding, and remarked, "The above names should be a guarantee that Mr. Cummings' claim is a just one, and should put forever the credit of first curving a ball where it belongs."[17] Bobby Matthews, the old Baltimore pitcher who received credit for the curve in some circles, also weighed in, telling *The New York Times* in 1883 that Cummings indeed threw the curve before him or anyone else.[18]

In spite of this controversy, Candy Cummings operated his business and raised his family in Athol. He stopped playing semipro ball in the early 1880s, and made only one more appearance as a pitcher when he journeyed to Boston for Harry Wright Day on April 13, 1896. The event was a benefit for the family of Wright, the former Cincinnati and Boston manager who had died the previous year. Cummings, who told the press that he had not touched a baseball in more than a decade, delighted the fans by showing them how he threw his underhand curve. This event brought Cummings back into the public eye and may have aided his battle for recognition, for in early 1897 the annual *Reach Guide* anointed Cummings as the father of the curve.

For the rest of his life, Candy Cummings freely gave interviews to any writer who requested one, and also wrote articles about his invention. In 1908 he penned the definitive piece on the subject, called "How I Pitched the First Curve," which appeared in *Baseball Magazine* in August of that year. This article introduced Cummings to a new generation of fans who had never heard of the diminutive curveball specialist, and solidified his claim to preeminence among curveball pitchers. By 1911, when Albert G. Spalding supported Cummings in his influential work *Base Ball: America's National Game*, few baseball men still endorsed Fred Goldsmith as the first curveball pitcher. However, one can find books and articles even today that credit Goldsmith, not Cummings, with the breakthrough.[19]

One day in the early 1920s a reporter asked how Cummings would pitch to Babe Ruth, who at the time was revolutionizing baseball with his free-swinging power hitting. Cummings, who had played his last National League game more than 40 years before, confidently laid out a plan to retire the game's greatest slugger. The aging ex-pitcher remarked that he would start Ruth out with a "rise curve" close to his hands, followed by a high "out curve" and then a ball that would start two feet outside and bend in at the knees for strike three.

"I would change the program every time he faced me," stated Cummings. "I'd change the speed of each ball. A free swinger like Ruth goes after a ball that looks good, but you won't fool him often on the same ball. I'd start the ball the same way every time, but make it go another way."[20] The old pitcher compared the players of the 1920s with those of his era, who did not wear gloves in the field. "I think the baseball player of today has quite an easy time compared with the player of my time," said Cummings. "...Just as much speed was used [in the 1870s] as at the present day, and the players' hands, especially the catchers', were covered with calluses and knocked joints."[21]

Cummings retired from his paint and wallpaper business in the late 1910s, and in 1920 the widowed 72-year-old Cummings sold his home in Athol and moved to Toledo, Ohio, to live with his son Arthur. His health deteriorated slowly, and he no longer spoke much to reporters about the curveball, but he was secure in the knowledge that he was the generally recognized inventor of the pitch that changed the game forever. William

Arthur Cummings died in Toledo on May 16, 1924, and three days later he was buried in the Aspen Grove Cemetery in Ware, Massachusetts. In March of 1939 Fred Goldsmith died at age 82, and some say that he was fatally stricken while clutching a newspaper article that supported his claim in the curveball controversy. Six weeks later, the Old-Timers Committee elected Cummings, not Goldsmith, to the Hall of Fame.

Candy Cummings may be the most controversial selection ever made by the Hall of Fame, and there are many who say that Cummings is the least qualified player in the Cooperstown museum. He spent most of his career playing for amateur teams in baseball's infancy, before the game itself had progressed much beyond its town ball origins. Cummings played professional ball for only six seasons before his arm gave out, and none of his National Association or National League teams ever won a pennant. Some have wondered how good a pitcher Cummings could possibly have been, given his small size. At 120 pounds, Candy Cummings was the lightest man, at any position, to play top-level baseball in the long history of the game.

However, one could also make the argument that Cummings stands alongside Babe Ruth as a player who dramatically changed the way baseball is played. Before Cummings' time, the pitcher was merely a necessary component of the action, because someone on the field had to put the ball in play. The pitcher threw the ball to the batter with no more cunning or strategy than the kicker who starts a football game with a kickoff to the other team. The development of the curveball radically changed all that, and if Candy Cummings was the true inventor of the pitch, then he was the man who made the pitcher the most important player on the field.

The entire truth of the curveball controversy may never be known, but, like many great inventions, it was probably developed by several people working independently of each other. Whether he invented the pitch or not, Cummings was certainly the first man to throw it successfully on the highest level of competition, as Jack Chesbro hurled the spitter and Christy Mathewson threw the screwball. As the player who introduced the pitch that is now an indispensable part of virtually every pitcher's repertoire, William Arthur Cummings left a bigger mark on the game than almost any other man who ever played. For that reason alone, he earned his membership in the Hall of Fame.

3

◆ ROGER BRESNAHAN ◆

Bresnahan had a memory almost as good as Mathewson or McGinnity. He never had to be told twice. Once we had discovered a weak spot in the opposition and had discussed a plan for attacking it I could depend absolutely on Bresnahan to carry it out. He did not forget. His whole mind was concentrated on winning that particular game and it was rarely that he overlooked anything.—John McGraw, 1923[1]

Throughout the long history of Hall of Fame balloting, there have been several instances in which either the Baseball Writers Association or the several incarnations of the Veterans Committee have selected players for the Cooperstown shrine in the weeks or months immediately following their deaths. It appears that in some identifiable cases, such as the elections of George Wright in 1937 and Rabbit Maranville in 1954, a player's recent demise vaulted him back into the spotlight and focused attention on him, perhaps providing that player with the momentum needed to win the required votes of the Hall electors. Several executives, too (Warren Giles, Will Harridge, and Branch Rickey, among others) have entered the Hall of Fame shortly after death, courtesy of the Veterans Committee.

Roger Bresnahan, catcher for the New York Giants during the first decade of the 20th century, was one of the first such men to be elected to the Hall. He compiled vote totals in the first few Hall of Fame elections that were merely solid, not spectacular. He received 47 votes from the 226 participating electors in the first election held in 1936, then received between 43 and 67 votes in the next four ballots, held from 1937 to 1942. Bresnahan failed to crack the top ten in any of the first five elections, with his best showing being an 11th place finish in 1942.

When Bresnahan died suddenly one month before the 1945 election, all that changed. His total jumped to 133 votes, good for fifth place in the balloting. It wasn't quite enough to give Roger a plaque in Cooperstown, but the newly appointed Permanent Committee noticed his sudden surge at the ballot box. On April 23, 1945, with the memory of the recently deceased catcher still fresh, the Permanent (later Veterans) Committee elected Bresnahan and nine others to the Baseball Hall of Fame.

Roger Philip Bresnahan was an Irishman through and through. A small, pugnacious man, he stood about five feet and nine inches tall, solid like a football tailback, and possessed a keen intelligence and quick temper. He spoke in a lilting Irish brogue learned from his parents, Michael and Mary Bresnahan, immigrants from the town of Tralee in County Kerry. So proud of his Irish heritage was Bresnahan that he was fond of telling people that he was born there. The sportswriters believed this and called him the "Duke of Tralee." Not until 1943, when Roger was 64 years old, did the writers investigate his birth certificate and find that he was actually born in Toledo, Ohio, on June 11, 1879.

Like so many sons of immigrants of that era, Bresnahan played ball on the sandlots whenever he found the opportunity. He attended school in Toledo, though he was an indifferent student, and by his teenage years he stopped going to classes altogether. Playing ball was more interesting to Roger than sitting in a classroom, and he quickly gained recognition as the best sandlot player in Toledo. Before long, professional teams took notice of the teenage sensation. At 16 Bresnahan began his professional career on the Lima nine in the Ohio State League, where he excelled on the mound and spent his off days in the outfield. He played the 1895 and 1896 seasons in Lima, after which the Washington Senators, a second-division ballclub in the twelve-team National League, bought the services of the 18-year-old righthanded pitcher.

Bresnahan reported to the Senators in late August 1897, and Washington manager Tom Brown opted to break the youngster in slowly. Brown gave the rookie pitcher a starting assignment against the St. Louis Browns, one of the few National League teams that was even worse than the Senators. Bresnahan responded with a six-hit shutout, striking out three and walking two. He showed an impressive array of pitches, including what the papers called "a speedy shoot, an outcurve, an inshoot, and a drop ball." Deacon Jim McGuire, the veteran catcher, told the papers that Roger "comes of the right stuff; good, old gamey Irish blood in that lad."[2]

He pitched in seven contests for Washington in 1897, ending the season with an impressive 4–0 record and a .333 batting average. His record might have been 5–0 if the Cleveland Spiders hadn't ended a game against the Senators by pulling their team off the field. On September 8, 1897, Roger was beating the Spiders and Cy Young by a 6–2 score when he hit Cleveland's Ed McKean with a pitch. The umpire refused to let the batter take first base, believing that McKean deliberately got in the way of the ball. The Spiders argued and then refused to continue the game, leaving the Senators with a 9–0 forfeit victory, but costing Roger the win.

The Washington ballclub soon discovered that the feisty Irishman was never shy about estimating his value. The team offered Bresnahan a $2,000 contract for 1898, a good salary at the time for a teenager with only seven major league games under his belt, but Bresnahan demanded $2,400. Bresnahan stuck to his guns, and the frugal Senators released him rather than pay the extra $400. In May of 1898 Bresnahan returned home to Toledo and signed with the Mud Hens of the Interstate League.

For the next two seasons, he bounced around the high minor leagues, and probably played for semipro teams as well. He pitched in only four games for Toledo in 1898, then appeared in three contests for the Minneapolis Millers of the Western League in 1899, where he caught for the first time. Drafted by the Chicago Orphans (now called the Cubs), Bresnahan reappeared in the major leagues in 1900, where he caught one game and went hitless. When the new American League began its first major league season in 1901, the 21-year-old left Chicago and joined John McGraw's Baltimore Orioles.

In McGraw, Bresnahan found a role model and a friend for life. Bresnahan's win-at-all-costs spirit and enthusiastic umpire baiting made him one of McGraw's favorite players. After one game on the mound, McGraw sent the Toledo native to the catching position, in relief of the oft-injured Wilbert Robinson. In 1902, Bresnahan batted leadoff and filled in wherever he was needed, spending time at third base and in the outfield as well as behind the plate. He was fast, as shown on May 30, 1902, when he belted two inside-the-park homers in a game, a feat he repeated two years later. When McGraw bolted the Orioles and jumped back to the National League in mid-1902, he took the cream of the Baltimore players with him. The valuable Roger Bresnahan was one of the key men who accompanied McGraw to the New York Giants.

McGraw already owned two good catchers in Frank Bowerman and Jack Warner, so he put the speedy Bresnahan in center field in 1903. Bresnahan responded with a .350 average, the highest of his career and only five points less than batting champ Honus Wagner. On July 16 of that year, Bresnahan started a rare triple play from the outfield against the Pirates. He caught a fly ball and threw home, holding the runner at third, but two other Pirates strayed off their bases and were tagged out in a series of rundowns. Bresnahan's average fell to .284 in 1904, but the Giants won the first of 10 pennants under McGraw. Bresnahan, McGraw's jack of all trades, played 96 games in the outfield, 10 at first, four at shortstop, and one each at second and third.

Off the field, Roger and his wife Gertrude, whom he married in his early Giant days, resided at the Washington Inn hotel at 155th and Amsterdam in Manhattan, mere blocks from the Polo Grounds, during the baseball campaign. It was the same hotel where McGraw and his wife Blanche lived. When the baseball season ended each year, Bresnahan returned to his native Toledo and worked as a hotel detective. His teammates called him "Gumshoe," though Roger had more ambitious goals in mind than remaining as a mere hotel employee. Within the next few years, Bresnahan became a co-owner of that Toledo hotel, the Boody House, one of the finest in the city.

Bresnahan with the Giants in the early 1900s. (National Baseball Hall of Fame Library, Cooperstown, New York)

By 1905, Bowerman was slowing down and Warner was gone, so Bresnahan moved back behind the plate. Christy Mathewson, the Giants' star pitcher, felt more comfortable throwing his "fadeaway" pitch (a reverse curve, now called a screwball) to Roger, and Mathewson responded to the move with one of his greatest seasons. Mathewson won 31 games, including a no-hitter against the Cubs on June 23 (though Bowerman caught Mathewson's deliveries in that contest). Led by Mathewson's pitching, the Giants rolled to their second consecutive pennant, and Bresnahan received a great deal of the credit from the writers.

In the World Series that year, Bresnahan caught all five games, three of which were shutouts pitched by Mathewson. "They never came close to beating [Mathewson]," said Roger to a reporter in 1943. "Just pop-up, pop-up all day. You know 90 percent of the hitters in those days were choke hitters. They didn't swing from the end of the bat like nowadays. If Matty were pitching today he'd break their backs."[3] Joe McGinnity also pitched a shutout for the Giants, with Bresnahan catching, as the Giants defeated the Philadelphia A's in the second World Series. The "Duke of Tralee" led all Giant batters with a .313 average in the five games.

To say that Roger was "fiery" is an understatement. Baseball historian Bill James succinctly described the Duke's personality when he wrote that Bresnahan "was one of those guys that if you were on his team and played hard he was as nice to you as could be, but if you got on his bad side you'd think he was the Breath of Hell."[4] Following McGraw's lead, Bresnahan became one of baseball's leading umpire baiters, regularly being ejected or suspended for on-field incidents. There were many instances in which police were called to escort Bresnahan and McGraw from the field.

Once, during a spring training game in Nashville, McGraw and Bresnahan rode umpire Tony Mullane mercilessly, stopping just short of physically assaulting the arbiter on the field. Mullane was an old Baltimore teammate of McGraw, but all umpires were fair game for the Giants in those days. In a 1907 spring game against the Athletics in New Orleans, Bresnahan's demand for a balk call on Philadelphia's Eddie Plank escalated until the umpire called to police to remove Bresnahan from the field. The game resulted in a forfeit, followed by an ugly name-calling incident in a hotel lobby between McGraw and the Athletics team president, and a cancelled series of games that required the National Commission to pay the New Orleans promoters for the lost gate receipts. All this for a meaningless spring exhibition game.

McGraw, with a genius for offending his competitors, ordered new uniforms for his Giants after their 1905 Series win. The new flannels carried the title "World's Champions" across the front, further antagonizing the players and fans of the other fifteen major league teams. The arrogance of the Giants did not sit well in other cities, where mobs threw rocks at the carriages hauling the Giants to and from the ballparks. Bresnahan and teammate Mike Donlin often loaded up their vehicles with missiles of their own, and returned fire at the angry crowds. One day in Philadelphia, Roger failed to reach the carriage after the game before the mob descended. Roger fled down the street and took refuge in the back room of a store until the local police could rescue him.

Of all the positions he played on the field, Bresnahan enjoyed catching most. "Roger had a catcher's personality," said New York sportswriter Fred Lieb. "Not only did he have to be out there every day, but he had very strong leadership instincts. He enjoyed the responsibilities that a catcher has; in fact, I think he thrived on them."[5] He was the master of razzing the opposing batters, getting them off stride with insults and putdowns. Roger also learned the fine art of working the umpires from McGraw. Some could be intimidated, while others needed to be flattered. Most umpires, or so Bresnahan believed, could be frightened or bullied into giving special treatment to the powerful Giants.

In that 1905 season, Bresnahan stood alone as the best catcher in the game, but his preeminence did not last long. Johnny Kling of the Cubs, who owned a stronger throwing arm, surpassed Bresnahan as king of catchers by 1906 and held the title for the next five years or so. McGraw, however, still regarded Bresnahan as the best. "I never thought [Kling] as valuable to a ball club as Bresnahan," said McGraw in 1923. "He could not hit as well as Roger and there were other things that he could not do as well. Nobody, though, could throw better than Kling."[6]

"Watch him while he is catching," said one newspaper article about Bresnahan in the early 1900s. "Watch him throw to bases. Absolute, unerring decision is his. Never a moment of hesitation, a second of doubt. He heaves the ball to second or to third, or to first as the lightning chance may demand, with a sort of cold, infallible ferocity. And he possesses that alacrity of taking a chance which differentiates soldiers of genius from the prudent plodder."[7]

Bresnahan was bothered by the knowledge that catchers suffered more injuries than other players. In those days, few catchers managed to stay healthy enough to play in more than half of their team's games. Bresnahan couldn't stand sitting on the bench, away from the action, but he and other catchers kept getting hurt with errant throws, foul tips, and spikings by baserunners. Injuries were considered to be a part of the job description for a catcher, and a poem from the early 1900s captured the prevailing attitude about the rigors of catching:

> We wore no glove upon our hand,
> No mask upon our face;
> We stood right up and caught the ball
> With courage and with grace.

Unlike other catchers, who accepted their lot, the Irishman did something about the problem. On April 11, 1907, Bresnahan appeared on the field at the Polo Grounds on opening day wearing a pair of oversized leg guards. Cricket players had been wearing such protection for years, so Bresnahan bought a pair, worked out with them during spring training, and unveiled them that day. The New York crowd, long accustomed to seeing catchers absorb their punishment without complaint, hooted at Bresnahan, calling him "sissy" and worse, but the Duke of Tralee ignored them. The crowd hooted even louder in the fifth inning, when a foul tip make a loud booming noise when it bounded off one of Bresnahan's pads.

The game, played in bitter cold, ended ignominiously when the Giant fans began throwing snowballs at umpire Bill Klem, who forfeited the game to the visiting Phillies. However, Bresnahan caused a sensation with his adaptation of cricket equipment to baseball, and other major league catchers soon followed his lead. Bresnahan caught a career-high 139 games in 1908, mostly because his leg protection kept him free from injury. Pittsburgh manager Fred Clarke filed a protest with the league after Roger wore the shinguards against the Pirates, but the league denied the protest and approved of Roger's new equipment.

The press did not approve of the Irishman's innovation. "The latest protection for catchers looks rather clumsy, besides delaying a game while the guards are strapped above the knee and around the ankle, and it is doubtful that the fad will ever become popular," harrumphed the *New York Sun*. The stately *New York Times* also expressed disapproval. "Roger Bresnahan," said the *Times* in September 1908, "makes an entrance, accompanied by a dresser, who does him and undoes him in his natty mattress and knee pads."[8] Despite the razzing, shin guards became standard catching equipment.

Bresnahan is usually credited with inventing the shin guards, though he never claimed that distinction for himself. "I didn't invent anything," said Roger to a reporter in 1926. "I simply got a pair of shin guards, such as the ones cricket players wore, and I strapped them outside my stockings. I was sick and tired of wild pitches, foul balls, thrown bats, and flying spikes bruising and cutting my legs."[9] Other players had experimented previously with similar equipment, but Bresnahan was the man who made it work in the face of disapproval. Another Bresnahan innovation was the padded facemask, which softened the blow of a foul tip against a catcher's head. It, too, became standard equipment for catchers, and remains so to this day.

He also experimented with a primitive batting helmet, but almost waited too long to do so. On June 18, 1907, Roger was hit in the head by a fastball thrown by Cincinnati pitcher Andy Coakley, a veteran righthander who pitched for the A's in the 1905 World Series. The pitch knocked Bresnahan unconscious, and a priest gave him the last rites of the Catholic Church as he lay motionless on the ground near home plate. Bresnahan recovered after a 10-day stay in a hospital, and drew plans for a plastic helmet during his convalescence. This particular idea did not gain acceptance, and although Roger had a prototype made and wore it a few times, major league teams did not begin using helmets on a regular basis until after the Second World War. Bresnahan, tough Irishman that he was, returned to the lineup 24 days after the beaning and belted two hits off Coakley in a 3–2 Giant win.

By 1907, age began to catch up to the Giants, and the Chicago Cubs ascended to the top of the league. The Giants challenged for the flag in 1908, losing the pennant to the Cubs on the infamous "Merkle boner," but McGraw recognized that his ballclub needed a major overhaul. Pitchers Dummy Taylor and Joe McGinnity were at the end of the line, and the Giants had no team speed. Bresnahan had once been fast enough to bat leadoff, but in 1908 he batted second or third in the lineup while first sacker Fred Tenney, a 13-year veteran, batted first. McGraw set out to make the Giants into a younger, faster team.

Roger Bresnahan, at 29, caught all but 15 of the 154 games on the New York schedule in 1908, and by the end of the season he began to slow down in the field. Roger, still a good hitter, batted .283 and led the league in walks, but McGraw had John (Chief) Meyers, a Cahuilla Indian from California, ready to take over behind the plate. Some of the newspapers speculated that Bresnahan would soon succeed McGraw as manager of the Giants. Such speculation was premature, since McGraw was in the middle of a long-term contract at the time, but other teams began to regard Roger as a potential manager.

When the St. Louis Cardinals, then the worst team in the National League, approached McGraw about trading for Bresnahan, McGraw drove a tough bargain. He got the Cardinals to give him the two best players on the St. Louis team, pitcher Bugs Raymond and outfielder Red Murray, in addition to catcher George (Admiral) Schlei, for Roger. The Cardinals eagerly accepted, and in December 1908 the two teams consummated the deal. Bresnahan went to St. Louis to manage a team that finished in last place in 1908 and traded its best position player and its best pitcher to acquire him.

The Cardinals had won 49 games and lost 105 in 1908, and Bresnahan knew that the team presented a major challenge. Progress was slow, but Bresnahan began winning small victories. On May 24, 1909, the Cardinals defeated Christy Mathewson for the first time in more than four years. Mathewson had beaten the Cardinals 24 straight times in that span.

Bresnahan nudged the team up to 54 wins in 1909 and 63 wins in 1910,

BRESNAHAN
Catcher, St. Louis N. L.

Roger Bresnahan as St. Louis Cardinals manager, 1909. (Library of Congress)

good for seventh place both years, while his hustling style of baseball put fans back into the park. The moribund St. Louis franchise drew only 205,000 fans in 1908, but improved to 299,000 in 1909 and 355,000 in 1910. On June 5, 1909, a group of St. Louis fans showed their appreciation for Bresnahan's efforts. They stopped the game against the Giants and presented Roger with an expensive diamond ring at home plate.

Roger, predictably, became a carbon copy of McGraw as a manager. In April 1911, National League president Thomas Lynch ordered his umpires to stop catchers from verbally abusing batters and goading them into fights. The directive mentioned Bresnahan, and no one else, by name. In June of that same year, an argument in Cincinnati between Roger and umpire Bill Klem ended when Klem took off his padded facemask and whacked Bresnahan in the head with it. Klem paid a fine of only $50, no doubt thinking the money was well spent in belting Bresnahan with his own invention. Roger also became involved in a nasty public feud with Chicago Cubs president Charles H. Murphy, in which the two men shouted threats and accusations against each other in a hotel lobby at the 1910 winter baseball meetings.

Bresnahan's term in St. Louis came to an ugly end in 1912. Team owner Stanley Robison died in 1911 and left the team to his niece, Mrs. Schuyler Britton. Before he died, Robison, grateful for the club's marked improvement in the standings and at the gate, rewarded Roger with a five-year contract at $10,000 per year, plus a cut of the team's operating profit. However, the Cardinals fell to sixth place in 1912 and Mrs. Britton began criticizing her manager to the press. Roger answered the owner with some stinging verbal salvos, using the same language that served him so well on the ball field. Mrs. Britton, deeply offended, then fired Roger and hired Miller Huggins as her new manager.

Roger still had four years left on his contract, and when Mrs. Britton refused to pay, Bresnahan took her to court. Mrs. Britton tried to release Bresnahan, but Roger did not clear waivers; apparently other National League teams still considered him a potentially valuable property. In June 1913, after a long public sniping match in the St. Louis dailies, the Cardinals sold Bresnahan to the Chicago Cubs, where Roger played as a second-string catcher in 1913 while battling his former boss in a series of lawsuits.

Roger was involved in another unpleasant public squabble in late 1912, though for once the trouble was not of his own making. After Roger's old team, the Giants, breezed to the pennant in 1912, Philadelphia Phillies owner Horace Fogel publicly accused Bresnahan and other ex–New Yorkers of rigging the pennant race for the Giants to win. The charge was ludicrous, since the Giants won the flag by 10 games, and Roger's Cardinals managed to beat the Giants more often that the Phillies did that season.

Bresnahan in 1915. (Library of Congress)

Fogel, whose wild accusations publicly embarrassed the National League, was banned for life by the circuit and forced to sell his ballclub.

After more than two years of legal wrangling, Roger received half of his money from Mrs. Britton. The two sides settled on a $20,000 payout, completing Bresnahan's ferocious legal battle with the Cardinals. On November 18, 1914, he signed a three-year contract to manage the Cubs.

Bresnahan brought the Cubs home in fourth place in 1915 with a 73–80 record, and he batted .204 while sharing the catching duties with Jimmy Archer. Unfortunately for Roger, the rival Federal League collapsed in the fall of 1915, and he lost his job in the fallout. The major leagues allowed Charles Weeghman, owner of the pennant-winning Chicago Whales of the Federal League, to buy the Cubs and move the team to Weeghman Park, now known as Wrigley Field. Weeghman fired Roger (after paying off the remainder of his contract) and hired Joe Tinker, manager of the

Whales, to run the Cubs for 1916. For the first time since 1900, Roger Bresnahan was out of major league baseball.

In early 1916, an opportunity arose for Roger to own and manage his hometown team. Charles Somers, owner of the Cleveland Indians, had moved his American Association club from Toledo to Cleveland two years before, having the former Mud Hens play in town when the Indians were on the road. Both ballclubs floundered in the standings and lost large amounts of money, forcing Somers into near-bankruptcy after the disastrous 1915 campaign. Somers sold off his assets, and in March 1916 Roger bought the Cleveland minor-league club and moved it back to Toledo.

After an absence of two years, a Toledo team would once again play ball at Swayne Field on Monroe Street, just north of the downtown area, with Roger as manager, owner, and part-time player. The local daily newspaper, the *Blade*, ran a contest to name the team; entries included the Rajahs and the Bresna-Hens, reflecting Roger's popularity in his hometown. The name Mud Hens won the contest, but barely, and a significant number of fans appeared to favor a name change. Roger then announced that the team would be known as the Iron Men.

Bresnahan's biggest contribution to Toledo came in re-establishing baseball in the city. His eight-year tenure as owner was not, for the most part, a successful one. With Roger managing and catching part-time, the Iron Men finished sixth out of eight teams in 1916 and last in 1917. They occupied last place on June 23, 1918, when the league closed operations due to the military draft of World War One. Roger reinstated the Mud Hens name in 1919 and hired Rollie Zeider as manager, but Bresnahan retook the reins late in the season as the Hens finished seventh.

The Hens bounced up to third place in 1920, but fell back to seventh in the following year and dropped to last again in 1922. Bresnahan's primary accomplishments in those years centered on developing players for John McGraw's New York Giants. Bill Terry, a lefthanded pitcher from Memphis, went 9–9 on the mound for the Hens in 1922 and served as captain of the team. Switched to first base at McGraw's direction, Terry batted .377 in 1923 and also managed the Hens for the last few weeks of the season. Terry was ready for the major leagues, and took over first base in New York in 1924. In a few short years, Terry was on his way to stardom, a successful managerial career, and, eventually, the Hall of Fame. Another future Hall member, Fred Lindstrom, arrived in Toledo as a 16-year-old infielder in 1922. After two years of tutoring by Bresnahan, Lindstrom went to the Giants and became a standout third baseman for the next decade.

The Toledo operation lost money steadily, and after a 54–114 season in 1923, Roger sold the club. He spent 1924 out of baseball, then coached for McGraw and the Giants for the next four years, where he tutored a lefthanded screwball pitcher named Carl Hubbell. Roger was a personable, popular figure with the New York sportswriters, which no doubt assisted his future Hall of Fame chances, and he was one of McGraw's most trusted assistants. His experience as a hotel detective made him invaluable in enforcing McGraw's strict curfew rules. Roger also managed the team for six weeks in 1928 while McGraw recuperated from injuries received in a traffic accident. After the 1928 season, Roger announced his retirement from baseball and returned home to Toledo.

Bresnahan expected to spend his remaining years in comfort, but the Great Depression interfered. Most of Roger's money was tied up in the stock market, and the crash of 1929 wiped out his life savings and forced him to sell his Toledo home. He, his wife Gertrude, and his daughter Marian moved into a smaller house, and Bresnahan was obliged to go back to work. He coached for the Detroit Tigers under manager Bucky Harris in 1930 and 1931, but the Tigers let him go in a cost-cutting move. He held several jobs in the next few years, including a stint as a turnkey at the Lucas County workhouse, a few miles west of Toledo. Bresnahan never complained, and contributed his time and efforts to local charity organizations whenever possible. Though he suffered from a weak heart, the old Giant also enjoyed teaching baseball to young players.

Like most old ballplayers, Roger told the sportswriters that players were much better and tougher in his day. He picked an all-time All-Star team for United Press in 1936, and put only one latter-day player, second baseman Charlie Gehringer (whom Roger had coached in Detroit) on the team. "Modern baseball lacks strategy," complained the old Giant. "Inside baseball, as practiced by the old-timers, is missing from the game today. In the old days, ball teams were always trying to out-guess and out-smart the opponents.... Today, most teams are just so many individual ballplayers."[10]

One day in 1938, a young outfielder for the Minneapolis Millers spotted the 59-year-old Bresnahan walking down Superior Street in downtown Toledo, where the Millers were playing a series against the Mud Hens. "You're Roger Bresnahan, aren't you?" asked the young man politely. "Well, I'm Ted Williams, and I'm playing ball with Minneapolis. I'd like to have you give me some advice on how to play baseball." Bresnahan talked with Williams for two hours, impressing on the young slugger the need to hustle and play hard all the time, as he had learned the game from John McGraw many years earlier.[11]

In 1943, elder statesman Bresnahan appeared on the playing field for the last time, catching the deliveries of Walter Johnson at a war bond exhibition game at the Polo Grounds in New York. Babe Ruth, the 48-year-old Yankee legend, batted, while Johnson pitched and Bresnahan caught. Johnson, who ended his major league career 16 years before, could still throw the ball hard. "He must have been quite a pitcher," remarked the Duke of Tralee, "because he's still fast. His ball sails."[12] Ruth thrilled the crowd when he belted a homer into the right field seats, and Roger, at age 64, caught Johnson's best fastballs without apparent difficulty.

At this time, Bresnahan was employed as a salesman for the Buckeye Brewing Company in his hometown, and he retained his popularity with the people of Toledo. In 1944 the local Democratic Party asked him to run for a seat on the Lucas County commission. Bresnahan, much to his own surprise, won the party nomination in the May 1944 primary election. "I've had a lot of thrills," said Roger to the newspapers, "and I've been in and come out of many a tough spot, but winning the nomination is to me the greatest thrill of all."[13] He lost the general election in November by only a few hundred votes out of more than 140,000 cast.

The popular local athlete might have run for office again, but his chronic heart problem began acting up shortly after Election Day. His doctor ordered him to bed in late November 1944, and his condition deteriorated rapidly. On the morning of December 4, 1944, Bresnahan died of a heart attack at his home in Toledo. He was buried in Calvary Cemetery, fondly remembered as Toledo's greatest contribution to major league baseball. Five months later, the Veterans Committee named Roger to the Hall of Fame. He was the second catcher, and the first 20th-century catcher, to gain induction.

Roger Bresnahan's presence in the Cooperstown pantheon remains as one of baseball's greatest controversies, and many lists of underqualified Hall of Famers begin with the Duke of Tralee. In 1986, Bill James wrote that Bresnahan was no better than several catchers who are not in the Hall, "yet neither was he the absolute bottom of the Hall of Fame barrel."[14] Fifteen years later, James turned his opinion around, stating that Roger "wandered into the Hall of Fame on a series of miscalculations" and that, in Bresnahan, "the Hall of Fame had, for the first time, selected a player who clearly had no damn business being there."[15]

Statistically speaking, Bresnahan suffers by comparison to later Hall of Fame catchers. Bill Dickey, Yogi Berra, Mickey Cochrane, Gabby Hartnett, and Johnny Bench all hit for more power, lasted longer, and (except for Bench) compiled higher career batting averages. All five of the men listed above played in multiple World Series, while Roger played in only one.

	Games	Hits	HR	RBI	Average	World Series
Johnny Bench	2,158	2,048	389	1,376	.267	5
Bill Dickey	1,789	1,969	202	1,209	.313	8
Yogi Berra	2,120	2,150	358	1,430	.285	14
Mickey Cochrane	1,482	1,652	119	832	.320	5
Gabby Hartnett	1,990	1,912	236	1,179	.297	4
Roger Bresnahan	1,410	1,251	26	530	.279	1

Roger's statistical totals are closer to those of Rick Ferrell and Ray Schalk, two other catchers whose selections to the Hall of Fame have been frequently criticized:

	Games	Hits	HR	RBI	Average	World Series
Roger Bresnahan	1,410	1,251	26	530	.279	1
Rick Ferrell	1,884	1,692	28	734	.281	0
Ray Schalk	1,760	1,345	12	596	.253	2

Bresnahan's batting statistics are generally unimpressive, but Roger played in the middle of the dead ball era, and his batting averages were usually well above the league average. He finished in the top six in the league in on-base percentage seven times due to his ability to draw walks, and he stole 212 bases, a large number for a catcher. He made an important offensive contribution to John McGraw's championship teams.

In addition, Bresnahan was one of the central characters in many of baseball's most storied incidents during the first decade of the 20th century. He was one of many players who jumped from the National League to the American in 1901; in 1902, he returned and helped McGraw turn the failing New York Giants into champions. Roger earned, and deserved, much credit for handling pitchers like Christy Mathewson, Joe McGinnity, Red Ames, Dummy Taylor, and others on the pennant-winning New York pitching staff of 1904-05. Bresnahan caught all three of Christy Mathewson's shutouts in the 1905 World Series, directing perhaps the greatest Series pitching performance of all time. Roger also played an important role in the wild 1908 pennant race, though the playoff game against the Cubs was his last in a Giant uniform.

He redefined the catching position, making important innovations in equipment that allowed catchers to stay in the lineup longer, and it is not much of an exaggeration to say that Roger was the first modern baseball catcher. Before Bresnahan came along, almost all catchers were big, lumbering men with no speed. Roger, who was fast enough to bat leadoff early in his career, changed the requirements of the catching position, and set the mold for many future catching stars like Berra, Cochrane, and Dickey.

Perhaps Bill James was correct the first time. This feisty Irishman is not the most qualified catcher in the Hall of Fame, but neither is he the least.

4

◆ JACK CHESBRO ◆

Chesbro had great faith in the spitball when he was at the height of his career and predicted that it would be the delivery of the future. His success with it gave him his faith in it, but he was completely wrong in his estimate of its value to baseball. Its effectiveness has never been disputed; its uncleanliness has never been denied.—The Sporting News, 1931[1]

In early 1936, 226 members of the Baseball Writers Association of America cast ballots for the first inductees into the new Baseball Hall of Fame. The results of the voting were announced on February 2 of that year. Ty Cobb led the balloting with 222 votes, while Babe Ruth and Honus Wagner tied for second place with 215 each. In all, more than 70 players, some of whom were still active in 1936, received votes. Even the disgraced slugger Shoeless Joe Jackson, banned from the game for life in the Black Sox Scandal of 1919, received two votes from the writers.

Jack Chesbro, a spitball pitcher who won 198 games in a career that ended in 1909, received no votes at all in that first election. He appeared on one ballot in 1937, two in 1938, and six in 1939, after which the Baseball Writers Association decided to conduct a vote every three years instead of every year. In the 1942 and 1945 elections, Chesbro's vote total reverted to zero.

Chesbro was well known for several reasons. He was the first major league pitcher to make his living throwing the spitball, and his success ignited a rage for the wet pitch that lasted for nearly two decades. He also set the 20th century major league record with 41 wins in the 1904 season, a mark that will probably never be surpassed. On the negative side, he threw one of the most famous wild pitches in history, one which cost the

New York Highlanders the 1904 American League pennant. He pitched in only 11 seasons, and won fewer than 200 major league games. After the sixth Hall of Fame election was completed in 1945, there were several pitchers with many more wins than Chesbro who had not yet received a plaque in Cooperstown.

Many of the baseball writers who participated in the annual Hall elections did not know much about the ballplayers of previous generations, so in the mid–1940s Commissioner Kenesaw M. Landis formed the Permanent Committee and charged it with the task of identifying and selecting the outstanding players of the pre–1910 period. When the committee members met in New York on April 23, 1946, they surprised many fans and sportswriters when they elected Jack Chesbro and ten others to the Hall of Fame.

The future Hall of Fame pitcher was born John Dwight Chesebrough on June 5, 1874, in North Adams, Massachusetts, a small town near the Vermont border in the northwest corner of the state. John's ancestor, William Chesebrough, came to America from eastern England in 1630, only ten years after the Pilgrims landed on Plymouth Rock. John's father Chad was a Union Army veteran who served with the 22nd Massachusetts Regiment; at the end of the Civil War, he married and established his own farm near North Adams with his wife Martha, though it appears that he also worked in a shoe-repair business.[2] The family members pronounced their last name "Cheese-bro."

John Chesebrough, whom everyone called Jack, was the most athletic of the five Chesebrough children. He played sandlot baseball in Houghtonville and other small western Massachusetts towns in the early 1890s. Jack, a stocky right-handed pitcher who stood five feet nine inches tall and weighed about 175 pounds, began his career in semi-professional baseball in the spring of 1894, when he was not quite 20 years old. Jack earned a spot on a baseball team sponsored by a mental hospital in Middletown, New York, and worked there as an attendant in addition to his pitching duties for the Middletown Asylums. The inmates liked the friendly young ballplayer. They called him "Happy Jack," a nickname that followed the pitcher into the major leagues.

From Middletown, Jack Chesebrough made his way to the professional ranks. He played for Albany of the New York State League in 1895; when the Albany team folded, he moved to the Johnstown club and pitched there until early July, when the entire league suspended operations.

Jack won only seven of his 19 decisions for Albany and Johnstown, but someone must have seen a spark of talent in the young pitcher, for he signed a contract with the Springfield team of the higher-level Eastern League. He finished the 1895 season with a 3–0 record in seven games for Springfield, which lost the pennant to Erie that year by only one game.

In 1896, Jack signed with Roanoke of the Virginia League, a circuit that proved nearly as unstable as the New York State League. The Roanoke Magicians scuttled along in last place for most of the season, and Jack posted a 7–11 won–lost mark before the team disbanded on August 20 of that year. However, he began experimenting with the pitch that would bring him success in the major leagues. Somewhere along the line, someone taught Jack Chesebrough the secret of the spitball.

When the bosses of baseball moved the mound ten feet farther away from the plate (to its present distance of 60 feet, six inches) after the 1892 season, many pitchers found it difficult to adjust to the new, longer pitching distance. Batting averages skyrocketed all over baseball in the next few seasons, and the pitchers frantically searched for ways to catch up to the hitters. As a result, trick pitches came into vogue in the 1890s. Tim Keefe of the New York Giants introduced the "slow ball," a pitch that did not rotate on its way to the plate and almost certainly was the first instance of what is now called a knuckleball. Some minor league pitchers tried to snap off a curveball with a reverse motion of the wrist, in an attempt to create a pitch with a reverse curve on it, but this "fadeaway," now called the screwball, was too difficult for most pitchers to master. Many hurlers tried to throw the fadeaway, but Christy Mathewson, the star pitcher of the Giants from 1900 to 1916, was the first man to employ the pitch successfully.

Jack Chesbro in 1904, the year he set a 20th century record with 41 wins. (Author's collection)

Jack Chesebrough, however, learned a different trick. By wetting his fingers with saliva before throwing the baseball, he could send the ball hurtling toward the plate with a minimum of rotation. This caused the ball to drop suddenly before it reached the batter like an exceptionally sharp-breaking curveball. It was an unusually difficult pitch to control —

one pitcher compared throwing the wet ball to shooting a slippery watermelon seed with his fingers—but it gave the batters fits. The spitball became a useful new weapon for pitchers to employ against the hitters.

Big, hard-throwing pitchers like Cy Young and Amos Rusie did not need to devise trick pitches, but Jack Chesebrough was not such a physically imposing specimen. He was a rugged-looking individual—people called him "Algernon," an 1890s term for a sissy, for the same reason that a large man is nicknamed "Tiny"—but he was not a big man. Jack was a comparatively small hurler with a good, but not exceptional, fastball and curve, and he relied on his control like most smaller pitchers. Even in the 1890s, many major league pitchers stood six feet tall or more, and Jack realized that the spitball might help him overcome the handicap of his average stature.

When the Roanoke team disbanded, Jack made his way to Cooperstown, New York, where he spent the rest of the 1896 campaign pitching for a local team, the Athletics. He threw his fastball, curveball, and the occasional spitball, with mixed results. "'Ches' was either steady or wild as a hawk; no middle ground with Chesbrough," said a Cooperstown newspaper in the summer of 1896, "but he always had some trick up his sleeve.... He fed the visitors on tender little 'dew drops' [spitters] with slight curves, but awful drops."[3]

He also acquired a new last name along with the new pitch. The Cooperstown paper dropped the second "e" from his name that summer in its accounts of the games, but "Chesbrough" was still too long to fit into the box scores. It didn't take long for the last three letters of Jack's last name to disappear as well. The young pitcher became Jack Chesbro, a name that he kept for the rest of his life.

Jack married a North Adams woman named Mabel Shuttleworth in 1896, and then reported to the Richmond Bluebirds of the Atlantic League the following spring. He threw the spitball occasionally, but he mostly depended on his fastball, his curveball, and his control. He posted a 16–18 mark in 1897, and then improved to 23–15 for the pennant-winning Bluebirds in 1898. He pitched even more successfully for Richmond in 1899. His 17–4 mark in early July was one of the best in organized ball, and earned Jack the attention of major league scouts. The Pittsburgh Pirates offered the Richmond team $1,500 for the 25-year-old right-hander, and in late July 1899 Jack entered major league ball as a member of the Pittsburgh team.

The Pirates were a seventh-place club in the twelve-team National League, and by the time Chesbro joined the club the Pirates were merely playing out the string of a disappointing season. Jack appeared in 19 games with a 6–9 record, but better times for Chesbro and his new team were just around the corner.

The National League divested itself of its four worst teams at the end of the 1899 campaign, one of which was the Louisville Colonels. Louisville was a mediocre ballclub, but many of their players were desirable talents who attracted the attention of the remaining eight teams. Though the members of the other disbanded teams were dispersed around the league, Pittsburgh owner Barney Dreyfuss managed to corral all of the best men from Louisville. In a complicated series of maneuvers, he traded Jack Chesbro and four other Pirates to Louisville in return for fourteen members of the Colonels. A few weeks later, Dreyfuss bought the dormant Louisville franchise and transferred Chesbro and the others back to Pittsburgh.

The combined Louisville-Pittsburgh ballclub immediately became one of the best teams in the National League. Stars like left fielder and manager Fred Clarke, utility man Honus Wagner, and starting pitchers Deacon Phillippe and Rube Waddell filled some of Pittsburgh's most glaring weaknesses and turned the Pirates into an instant contender. While many teams of that era piled most of the pitching load on two or three men, the Pirates now owned five credible starters in Phillippe, Waddell, Chesbro, and holdovers Sam Leever and Jesse Tannehill. In 1900, Phillippe and Tannehill each won 20 games as Chesbro and Leever compiled matching 15–13 logs. For the first time in team history, the Pirates challenged for the pennant, finishing the season three and a half games behind the champion Brooklyn team.

Rube Waddell, 8–13 in 1900, jumped to the new American League in 1901, but the Pirates found another fine starter in lefthander Ed Doheny. No other team could match Pittsburgh's five-man starting corps, and in 1901 the Pirates won their first National League flag. Jack Chesbro, maturing as a pitcher, won 20 games for the first time, leading the league in winning percentage with a .700 mark and in shutouts with six. In the meantime, Jack and his wife Mabel moved from North Adams to a farm near Conway, Massachusetts, a small town about 25 miles to the southeast. There the Chesbros tended chickens, pigs, and horses, and raised a son named Philip. Jack also spent several springs coaching the pitchers at Harvard University.

Chesbro made another leap forward in the next year. Some reports maintain that he began to throw the spitball that season at the suggestion of manager Fred Clarke, though an older Chesbro recalled that the spitter did not become part of his arsenal until later. Backed by the most powerful team of the deadball era, Jack posted a 28–6 record in 1902 and vaulted into the ranks of the National League's elite pitchers. He led the circuit in wins, shutouts, and winning percentage, leading the Pirates to their second title in the most lopsided pennant race in baseball history. Paced by Chesbro, twenty-game winners Jesse Tannehill and Deacon Phillippe, and batting champion Ginger Beaumont, the Pirates won the flag by an astounding 27 and a half games over second-place Brooklyn.

Pittsburgh, the dominant team in the National League, was also the most tempting target for the new American circuit. The American League, founded in 1900, emerged from its early struggles and established itself as a competitor to the National League. The new circuit raided the older one, offering bonuses and higher salaries to star players, and several Pirates received offers to jump to the newer league. In early 1902, the American League secretly hired Pirate first baseman Jack O'Connor to act as a liaison between the new league and any Pirates who could be induced to switch.

Chesbro was one of the most sought-after players, and in August 1902 the new league, through O'Connor, secretly offered Chesbro and five other Pirates $1,000 each if they would make the move. The Pirate owner, Barney Dreyfuss, found out about the scheme when pitcher Jesse Tannehill was injured in a clubhouse scuffle. Tannehill was put under ether to allow a doctor to pop his arm back into its socket, and while under the influence of the medication, Tannehill spilled the details of the offers to Dreyfuss. Shortly thereafter, O'Connor was unceremoniously released by the Pirates and branded by Dreyfuss as a "traitor" and a "spy."

Chesbro finished the season in Pittsburgh, although he had already accepted the $1,000 bonus from the American League. After Chesbro and Tannehill refused to pitch in a post-season series against an all-star team, Dreyfuss released both men from the Pirate squad. Chesbro's career in Pittsburgh was finished, and in January of 1903, just before the two leagues signed a peace agreement, Jack Chesbro and Jesse Tannehill signed on to pitch for the New York Highlanders.

The Highlanders, now known as the Yankees, were created from the wreckage of the Baltimore Orioles, a club that had been decimated when manager John McGraw jumped back to the National League in 1902 and took all of the best Oriole players with him. The Baltimore ballclub teetered on the brink of oblivion after McGraw left, but the league took over the club and kept it going for the remainder of the 1902 season. American League president Ban Johnson, wishing to put a competitive team in the nation's largest city, then sold the franchise to New York interests and convinced the new owners to build a ballpark, called Hilltop Park, in upper Manhattan. Johnson also recruited the respected pitcher and manager Clark Griffith to run the new team, and fortified the roster with National League stars like Chesbro, Tannehill, and three-time batting champion Wee Willie Keeler.

Some of the papers called the new team the Invaders, and for a while it looked like the American League had made a mistake when it invaded Manhattan. An enthusiastic crowd of 16,000 watched the Highlanders in their home opener on April 30 as Jack Chesbro defeated Washington, but as the season wore on the new team sank in the standings and failed to capture the attention of the New York fans. The Giants, playing at the Polo Grounds a short distance away, drew far more interest from the fans and the sportswriters, while the Highlanders finished seventh among the eight American League teams in attendance. The ballclub fared better in the second half of the season, finishing in fourth place with a 72–62 record, but they still occupied second place in the nation's largest city. *The New York Times* called the Giants the "New Yorks," while dismissing the Highlanders as the "Greater New Yorks" as if they came from the outer boroughs.

The Highlanders depended on three starting pitchers, not five, so manager Clark Griffith increased Jack Chesbro's workload. Jack had never pitched more than 289 innings in a season for the Pirates, but in 1903 he threw 325 innings, with 33 complete games in 36 starts. Chesbro led the team with a 21–15 record, while Jesse Tannehill went 15–15 and manager Griffith posted a 14–10 log.

Chesbro's performance convinced Griffith that the pitcher could handle even more work, so Griffith made a series of moves before the 1904 season. The manager traded Tannehill to the Red Sox for righthander Long Tom Hughes, and sent Harry Howell to St. Louis for another workhorse, Jack Powell. Griffith figured to cut back his own pitching assignments in 1904, leaving Chesbro, Hughes, and Powell to carry most of the burden.

Jack decided to unveil his secret weapon that season. "I became a spitball pitcher in the spring of 1904," said Chesbro many years later, "but I did not tell any of the other Yankee pitchers. Prior to that time I had been a fastball pitcher, but I saw Elmer Stricklett, the inventor of the damp delivery, at work, and I decided to practice that."[4] Chesbro had worked with the spitter before, but Stricklett, a journeyman pitcher with several teams in the era, showed Jack how to control the difficult pitch.

The eventful 1904 season began on a chilly April 14 at Hilltop Park, where Jack Chesbro pitched and batted the Highlanders to an 8–2 win over their Boston rivals. Jack scattered six hits and pounded a homer and a single in his own support. In an early season game against Cleveland, Jack threw fastballs and curves and allowed two runs in the first inning. As Griffith later remembered it, Chesbro came back to the bench and said, "Griff, I haven't got my natural stuff today. I'm going to give 'em the spitter the next inning, if it's all right with you."[5] Chesbro threw mostly spitballs for the rest of the game, striking out eight men and pitching eight shutout innings. He defeated Cleveland by a 3–2 score, and from that day forward Jack threw the spitball on a regular basis.

Hughes stumbled, winning only seven of his 18 starts, and was traded to Washington before the season was two months old, leaving the Highlanders with only two credible starters. Accordingly, manager Griffith gave both Chesbro and Powell more starts than either had ever pitched before in their careers. Chesbro took the mound every third, and sometimes every second, day. Right-hander Al Orth arrived from Washington in the Hughes trade and won 11 games, but for most of the season Jack Chesbro and Jack Powell shouldered almost the entire Highlander pitching burden. The result was one of the most extraordinary pitching performances in the history of the American League.

Chesbro thrived under the new work regimen. Since the Highlanders had little in the way of a reliable bullpen, Chesbro was required to complete almost all of his starts. For the first four months of the season he did exactly that. Chesbro completed all of his first 30 starting assignments; not until August 10, in a loss to the White Sox, did any team manage to knock Chesbro out of a game. By early August he sported an amazing 25–7 record, including 14 wins in a row from May 14 to July 4. Powell pitched steadily, and Willie Keeler challenged for the batting title, but for the most part Chesbro kept the Highlanders in the pennant race almost single-handedly. He won his 30th game of the year in early September, before any other American League pitcher had chalked up 20.

Jack was now the undisputed master of the spitball. "It's the most effective ball that possibly could be used," remarked Jack, and he told the sportswriters that he could make the ball break two inches or two feet if he so chose. He described the pitch further for *The Sporting News* that season. "The spit ball is worked entirely by the thumb," explained Chesbro. "The saliva one puts on the ball does not effect its course in any way. The saliva is put on the ball for the sole purpose of making the fingers slip off the ball first.... By wetting the ball it leaves the fingers first and the thumb last, and the spit ball could be rightly called a thumb ball."[6] Few, if any, opposing batters had ever seen the pitch, and their unfamiliarity with the spitter gave Chesbro a sizable advantage over the rest of the league.

As Chesbro's fame spread, a controversy developed over the origin of the spitball. Elmer Stricklett claimed to have invented the pitch before he showed it to Chesbro in 1904, while another minor league pitcher, future major league umpire George Hildebrand, claimed that he threw the first spitter and taught it to Stricklett in the spring of 1902. Perhaps neither man is correct, because we know from newspaper accounts that Chesbro himself experimented with the pitch as early as 1896. Others said that Bobby Mathews, one of the earliest pitching stars in professional baseball, threw the wet one in the first few years after the Civil War, in 1867 or 1868. No matter its origin, the pitch became a fad in the major and minor league ranks beginning in 1904, mostly due to the successful pitching of Jack Chesbro.

Still, the pitch had its limitations. The Highlanders made more throwing errors with Jack on the mound, due to the slippery ball. Chesbro himself made 15 errors in 1904, mostly of the throwing variety, the highest total ever for a pitcher in the American League.[7] Also, balls were rarely removed from the game back then — even balls hit into the stands were retrieved and put back into play — and since the ball became soggy late in the game, it was harder to hit. If the Highlanders fell behind in the early innings, the wet ball made it harder for them to catch up. On July 16, 1904, Chesbro took matters into his own hands. With the score tied 8–8 in the bottom of the tenth inning, Jack singled, made his way around to third on a fly ball and a groundout, then stole home for the winning run.

Fortunately, the Highlanders usually scored runs and allowed Chesbro to pitch into the late innings of most games with a lead. Happy Jack carried the club on his shoulders, and his pitching boosted the Highlanders to the top of the league in a wild five-team scramble for the pennant. By late September Chicago, Cleveland, and Philadelphia had fallen back, and the pennant race developed into a dogfight between the Highlanders and the defending champion Boston Pilgrims (now called the Red Sox).

The first showdown came in mid–September, when Boston and New York played three doubleheaders in four days. On September 14, the Highlanders scored two runs in the first on a throwing error by Boston catcher Lou Criger. Chesbro pitched shutout ball until the ninth, when he wild-pitched a run home, but made his lead stand up for a 3–1 win. The nightcap ended as a 1–1 tie after five innings, but New York slipped into the league lead by half a game. The Pilgrims won one and tied one the next day to reclaim the lead.

On September 16, more than 23,000 fans, the largest baseball crowd ever in Boston, stormed the Huntington Avenue Grounds to see Chesbro face off against Bill Dinneen. The Highlanders scored six times in the first three innings, and Chesbro held on for a 6–4 win, his seventh in a row and 35th of the season against only eight losses. The Pilgrims reclaimed first place in the second game, when Cy Young topped recently-acquired starter Ned Garvin by a 4–2 count. The league lead changed hands four times in the six game series, but the Pilgrims left town with their half-game lead intact. Little changed in the next few weeks; the White Sox knocked Chesbro out of the box in a 4–0 loss on September 30, but the Highlanders clung to a half-game lead over Boston as the teams entered the last ten days of the season.

Happy Jack came back the next day and defeated the White Sox, 7–2, on eight hits, then took two days off as the Highlanders won two of their next three. Boston, however, kept winning and moved a half-game ahead. On October 4, Chesbro shut out St. Louis for his 40th win of the season, becoming the first major league pitcher to win 40 since Chicago's Bill Hutchison in 1891, but the Pilgrims kept pace with a victory over Chicago. The next day, Jack Powell defeated the Browns, while Boston's Cy Young shut out the White Sox, leaving the Pilgrims half a game ahead of the Highlanders.

The Highlanders closed the 1904 season with a five-game series against Boston. The first game was played on Friday, October 7, and the exhausted Chesbro shut down the Pilgrims on four hits, winning his 41st game of the season by a 3–2 score and restoring New York to a half-game lead once again. The season came down to two doubleheaders, scheduled for Saturday and Monday, since there was no baseball on Sunday in the Eastern cities.

The two twin bills were originally scheduled for Hilltop Park in Manhattan, but the Columbia University football team played there on Saturdays, so the first doubleheader was moved to the Huntington Avenue grounds in Boston. Clark Griffith, fully aware that the Highlanders needed to win two of the four games, decided to save Chesbro for Monday's games in New York. He ordered Chesbro to remain in New York and rest, but the spitballer showed up at Grand Central Station that Saturday morning, determined to travel with the rest of the team to Boston and pitch. "You want to win the pennant, don't you?" Chesbro demanded, so Griffith took Chesbro to Boston and started him in the first game. One newspaper writer quoted Boston shortstop Fred Parent as saying, when he saw Chesbro warming up before the game, "That fellow again. Don't he ever have enough?"[8]

Happy Jack did not have enough in his 50th start of the season. In front of 30,000 Boston fans, Chesbro gave up six runs in four innings and failed to complete a game for only the third time in the 1904 campaign. The Highlanders lost the first contest by a 13–2 score, then lost the second to Cy Young, 1–0, in a game halted by darkness after seven innings. Now the Highlanders were a game and a half behind, and would need to sweep the Monday games to win the pennant.

On October 10, for the third time in four days, Jack Chesbro took the mound for New York as Clark Griffith sent Chesbro to face the Pilgrims' Bill Dinneen. More than 28,000 people, including hundreds of rooters from Boston toting megaphones and noisemakers, packed Hilltop Park to see the finale of the American League's first great pennant race.

The game started well for the Highlanders. Chesbro mowed down the Pilgrims for the first several innings, and when Happy Jack came to bat in the third inning, a delegation of friends from North Adams stopped the game and presented Chesbro with a fur coat. Jack showed his appreciation for the gift by belting a triple, although his teammates could not get him across the plate. The Highlanders scored the first two runs of the game in the fifth inning on three singles (one by Chesbro, a liner off Dinneen's chest) and two walks, but Dinneen kept them off the board after that. In the seventh, Boston tied the game when two runs scored on an error by New York second baseman Jimmy Williams, who made a wild throw with the wet baseball. The two teams entered the last inning tied at 2–2.

Boston catcher Lou Criger opened the ninth with a single off Chesbro, then made his way around to third on a sacrifice and a groundout. With two outs, Jack, exhausted from his pitching load and from running around the bases all day, faced Pilgrim shortstop Fred Parent. With an 0–2 count on Parent, disaster struck. Jack uncorked a spitball that sailed far out of the reach of his catcher, Red Kleinow, and rolled to the backstop as Criger scampered home. Chesbro then retired Parent, but the Pilgrims carried a 3–2 lead into the bottom of the ninth. The New Yorkers rallied, putting two men on base, but Dinneen struck out Patsy Dougherty for the final out, clinching the second pennant in a row for the Boston team. The Highlanders won the anticlimactic second game of the doubleheader, but the 1904 campaign ended with the Highlanders in second place, one and a half games behind the Pilgrims.

Jack Chesbro's wild pitch on October 10, 1904, remains as one of the most famous on-field incidents in the history of the game. Thirty-seven years later, a New York newspaper offered the opinion that the errant toss was a passed ball, not a wild pitch. Kid Elberfeld, who played shortstop for the Highlanders in 1904, refuted that notion. Said Elberfeld to writer Fred Lieb, "That ball rode so far over Kleinow's head that he couldn't have caught it standing on a stepladder."[9] Chesbro himself, in later years, weighed in with his opinion. "They said it was a wild pitch, and I'll let it go at that," said Jack. "But I think the ball might have been caught."[10]

Jack, despite his record-setting season, became the first "goat" of an American League pennant race, and the lost pennant haunted Chesbro for the rest of his life. Though the Highlanders probably would not have finished

Chesbro in a Highlanders uniform around 1905. (Author's collection)

in the first division without Jack's 41–12 record, the sportswriters never let Jack forget that errant spitball. Seventeen years elapsed before New York's American League entry finally won its first pennant in 1921 as the Yankees.

Despite the disastrous end to the American League's first great pennant race, Jack Chesbro compiled one of the greatest pitching seasons ever seen in the game. Jack's totals of 41 wins, 51 starts, and 48 complete games set major league records for the 20th century, and his total of 454 innings pitched still stands as a record for the New York Highlanders/Yankees franchise. His 239 strikeouts remained a team record until Ron Guidry broke it in 1978, and his standard of 14 consecutive wins lasted until Roger Clemens won 16 in a row in 2001.

After his incredible 1904 season, Jack's pitching statistics returned to earth. He spent nearly four weeks on the sidelines in early 1905 with a sore arm, and ended the season with a 19–15 log as the Highlanders sank into sixth place. On August 30 of that year, Jack pitched against the Tigers in Detroit as an 18-year-old rookie, Ty Cobb, made his major league debut. Cobb belted one of Chesbro's spitballs into the gap in right field for a double, the first of Cobb's 4,191 major league hits. Jack went 23–17 in 1906 as the Highlanders jumped back into second place, but in 1907 a sore arm and an ankle injury curtailed Jack's pitching. Jack publicly blamed the spitter for his arm woes and announced that he would lessen his reliance on the wet pitch, but he stumbled to a 10–10 mark in 1907 and a 14–20 record in 1908. After 1904, Jack did not complete nearly as many games; after completing 48 of 51 starts in 1904, the overworked Chesbro finished only 24 of his 38 starts the next year, and his percentage of completed starts never again approached his 1904 standard.

Jack grew a bit peevish as his career wound down. After the 1906 season he complained to the papers that umpires misjudge the spitter more than any other pitch. "I tell you," said Jack, "that a man who tries to deliver the spit ball has his troubles with the umpires. Even the best of them don't seem to understand that delivery.... They seem to jump to the conclusion that every spit ball that is started low is going to cross the plate below the knee of the batsman, and it seems the fashion of [the umpires] to yell 'Ball' at every one of them."[11] In August 1908, the fading pitcher criticized the baseballs themselves, and publicly charged that a ball he used in a loss at Detroit was not up to standard. The A. J. Reach Company, manufacturer of American League baseballs, obtained the ball in question and examined it thoroughly. Company president Benjamin Shibe rejected Chesbro's assertion that the ball was inferior and pronounced it "a regulation ball" in every way.[12]

While Jack Chesbro battled the effects of injury and overwork, the spitball that he popularized revolutionized the game. After Jack's phenomenal success in 1904, many other hurlers experimented with the new pitch, and before long nearly every major league team employed one or more spitball artists. Offense fell to unprecedented lows, and the American League batting average fell from .255 in 1903 to .247 in 1907 and .239 in 1908, mostly due to the spitball rage sweeping the majors at the time. Ed Walsh of the White Sox, who (it is said) learned the pitch from Chesbro, nearly matched Jack's record when he won 40 games in 1908 and broke Chesbro's league standard for innings pitched in so doing.

Walsh, like Chesbro, suffered from the effects of overuse, and within a few years both Walsh and Chesbro struggled with sore arms. In 1909, Chesbro managed to pitch in only nine games for the Highlanders, winning none and losing four, and by the last month of the season it was clear that the career of the 35-year-old hurler was effectively over. On September 11, 1909, the Highlanders released Jack to the Boston Red Sox for the waiver price. Chesbro appeared in only one game for Boston, a loss on the last day of the season in which he gave up seven hits and four walks in six innings, and at the end of the 1909 season the Red Sox sent Chesbro back to the Highlanders. When 1910 rolled around, Jack's arm was still aching, and he did not report to spring training.

Happy Jack was nothing if not stubborn. The sore-armed spitballer was convinced that he could still pitch, and he tried to line up a minor league pitching job for the 1910 season. Failing that, he pitched in semipro games for a mill team in Whitinsville, Massachusetts, waiting for his speed to return.

Despite his sore arm and advancing age, Jack was not yet ready to end his career in organized baseball. He coached at Amherst College in the 1911 season, but Jack, 37 years old, still wanted to pitch. He made the rounds of the semipro teams of his native Massachusetts, even pitching for a brief time at Houghtonville, where he got his start nearly twenty years before. However, Jack's ailing arm could no longer control the spitball properly, and he did not throw the ball fast enough to get it by people, not even sand-lotters. He made a failed attempt at a comeback with the Highlanders in 1912, then returned to Massachusetts and tried out for minor league and town teams, looking for a place to play. In the summer of 1912 a story appeared in the national sporting press that Jack's local town team in Conway had released the man who was once the winningest pitcher in the major leagues. The 38-year-old righthander could not even make the grade in the lowest levels of semipro ball.

Taking the hint, Jack finally retired from professional ball and occupied himself with farming and business. He still pitched for semipro teams whenever he found the opportunity, though the papers said that the sand-lotters found Jack's pitches easy to hit. He operated a lumberyard and saw-mill near North Adams for a while, raised horses, and managed his chicken farm. Some reports say that his lumber business was so successful that the government took it over during World War One, deeming it essential to the war effort.

Chesbro's greatest baseball legacy, the spitball, flourished for almost twenty years before the leagues clamped down on it. F. C. Lane, writing for *Baseball Magazine* in June of 1919, called the spitter "the villain of the diamond," and made Chesbro Exhibit A in the controversy over its use. "Chesbro, using the spitball, toiled like a giant to win [the] pennant," wrote Lane. "And yet by the irony of fate it was a single wild pitch, and that a spitter by this same twirler which decided the race and lost the flag.

"For a time, Chesbro was almost unbeatable, then he went the way of spitball pitchers, the route to sudden and lasting obscurity. The spitter had used up his arm. He was through."[13]

Many observers called for the banishment of the spitball for sanitary and competitive reasons, and in February 1920, 16 years after Chesbro introduced it to the major leagues, the pitch was severely restricted. Each team designated two pitchers who would be allowed to throw it in the 1920 campaign. This restriction met with widespread approval, and in 1921 the major leagues named only 17 pitchers who would be allowed to continue throwing the pitch for the remainder of their careers. By 1935 there were no more legal spitball hurlers in the majors. It is no coincidence that offense, especially home runs, took a sharp turn upward all over baseball after the spitter was legislated out of existence.

Jack Chesbro had little contact with major league baseball until 1924, when his old New York manager, Clark Griffith, hired him as pitching coach of the Washington Senators. Unfortunately, though the Senators would win their first and only World Series title that fall, Griffith's tight budget dictated personnel cutbacks early in the season, and Chesbro was released from his coaching duties at the end of May. He never again worked in organized ball; instead, Jack returned to Conway and resumed the operation of his chicken farm. He did, however, surprise many when he surfaced at the 25th anniversary celebration of the Pittsburgh Pirates' 1901 pennant-winning team in 1926. With the rancor of his long-ago abandonment of the Pirates apparently forgotten, Jack mingled with old teammates Fred Clarke, Honus Wagner, Tommy Leach, and many others.

After that brief return to the spotlight, Jack continued to manage his farm as his health began to fail. On November 6, 1931, Jack Chesbro suffered a heart attack at his home. Within minutes, he was dead at the age of 57. In *The New York Times* the next morning, a sub-headline in his obituary identified the old pitcher as a "Veteran, whose wild throw once cost New York Americans [the] pennant..." Chesbro was buried in the cemetery in Conway, where his grave (and that of his wife Mabel, who died in 1940) is marked with a metal nameplate affixed to a large rock. Mabel Chesbro gave several

Jack Chesbro throwing his spitball. (Author's collection)

newspaper interviews in the nine years of her widowhood, repeatedly expressing the opinion that the wild pitch charged to her husband in the penultimate game of the 1904 campaign should be changed to a passed ball in the official records.

Chesbro's election to the Hall of Fame in 1946 is, by all appearances, a direct result of the selection of Charley (Old Hoss) Radbourn seven years earlier. Radbourn gained election on the strength of his remarkable 1884 season, in which he won a record 60 games for the pennant-winning Providence team and set the National League standard for wins in a season. The Permanent Committee, apparently, believed that since the National League record-holder was already in the Hall, the American League leader should be there as well. It is difficult to find any other rationale for Chesbro's election. The committee chose Chesbro, who won 198 major league games, and bypassed 300-game winners Tim Keefe, Mickey Welch, Pud Galvin, John Clarkson, and Kid Nichols, all of whom were far better candidates for the Hall than Chesbro.

Perhaps the committee discounted the records of those men who pitched before 1893, when the mound was set at its present distance from home plate. Still, the selection of Chesbro over Nichols is especially mystifying. Nichols, whose career overlapped Chesbro's from 1899 to 1906, won 162 more games and threw 13 more shutouts than did Chesbro. Chesbro won 25 games or more in a season only twice, while Nichols did so nine years in a row from 1890 to 1898, and won 30 or more seven times in that span. What's more, Chesbro had been dead for 15 years at the time of his election in 1946, while Nichols was still living.

It is apparent that Chesbro is not uniquely qualified for the Hall of Fame based on his statistical record. Chesbro's career numbers are remarkably similar to those of the other three members of the Pittsburgh starting rotation at the turn of the century:

Pitcher	Won–Lost	Percent	ERA	Shutouts
Jack Chesbro	198–132 (+68)	.600	2.64	35
Deacon Phillippe	189–109 (+80)	.634	2.59	27
Sam Leever	194–100 (+94)	.660	2.47	39
Jesse Tannehill	197–116 (+81)	.629	2.79	34

Chesbro leads this group in career wins (by one), but also lost more games and compiled a lower winning percentage than any of the other three. Bill James, in his book *The Politics of Glory*, suggested that Chesbro might be the least qualified Hall of Fame candidate of the four men listed above. Nevertheless, none of those other three men has yet gained election to the Hall.

It seems obvious, then, that in the mid–1940s the Permanent Committee was more impressed by single-season accomplishments than career records in making their selections for the Hall of Fame. They also bypassed Kid Nichols in favor of Rube Waddell and Ed Walsh:

Pitcher	Won–Lost	Percent	ERA	Shutouts
Kid Nichols	360–205 (+155)	.637	2.95	48
Rube Waddell	193–143 (+50)	.574	2.16	50
Ed Walsh	195–126 (+69)	.607	1.82	57

Waddell's career won–lost log was not even as good as Chesbro's, but he was one of the fastest pitchers of his era, and set a record of 349 strikeouts in a season for the Philadelphia Athletics in 1904. Walsh, like Chesbro a spitball artist, was rewarded for his sensational 40–15 mark for the Chicago White Sox in 1908. He was a highly popular figure with fans and sportswriters, and was the last major leaguer to win 40 games in a single season. Happily, Kid Nichols was still alive in 1949 when the Permanent Committee rectified its oversight and elected the aged pitcher to the Hall of Fame, four years before his death.

Jack Chesbro was a fine pitcher, better than most, but (outside of the 1904 season) could never be considered as the best in the major leagues by any stretch of the imagination. He was probably not even the best starter in the Pittsburgh Pirates rotation in the 1899–1902 period. His presence in the Hall rests on that record-setting 1904 season.

Though many other pitchers won more games in their careers, Chesbro set the post–1900 major league record for wins in a season with 41, and will probably hold that distinction forever. "Chesbro's record will never be broken," said baseball writer George Vass in 1970, "unless the game goes to a 200-game, eight-month season."[14] Starting pitchers today, whose teams are zealously protective of their valuable arms, appear in far fewer games than did Chesbro and his contemporaries. No pitcher has started as many as 41 games in a season since 1979, and starters now appear only 30 to 35 times per year. Chesbro's record appears safe, and his remarkable performance in the 1904 campaign gave Jack Chesbro a plaque on the wall in Cooperstown.

5

◆ JESSE BURKETT ◆

In the days before the foul strike rule came in [Burkett] was one of the most feared men in the game because he could stand up and foul them off until pitchers would fairly gnash their teeth in frenzy. In short, Burkett was one of the few men who have been able to make batting a science.—Baseball Magazine, 1911[1]

Jesse Burkett was a diminutive left fielder and leadoff man for the Cleveland Spiders in the 1890s, and his phenomenal bat control made him the premier high-average hitter in the National League. He compiled amazing statistics, hitting .423 and .410 in consecutive seasons in 1895 and 1896 and winning three National League batting titles. When he retired from the major leagues in 1905, he stood second on the all-time list in hits and third in runs scored. However, by the time the Hall of Fame held its first election more than 30 years later, Burkett was one of the many forgotten stars of baseball's receding past. Despite his .342 lifetime batting average and his status as perhaps the greatest bunter in the history of the game, Burkett drew only one vote in the 1936 Hall election and one in 1937.

Burkett's low vote tally illustrated a problem with the election process. By the mid–1930s few sportswriters remained who had witnessed Burkett and other stars of the 1890s play. Those long-forgotten greats received scant attention from Hall electors, and many qualified ballplayers were being ignored in the balloting. In May of 1939 Commissioner Kenesaw Mountain Landis moved to remedy this problem when he and the two league presidents selected six nineteenth-century players and executives to the Hall in time for the first induction ceremony, which was held in June of that year. Shortly afterward, Commissioner Landis appointed a new four-man board, the Old-Timers Committee, charged with identifying and electing old-time players and contributors. This board consisted of Philadelphia Athletics manager and president Connie Mack, executives Ed Barrow and Bob Quinn, and veteran writer Sid Mercer.

For some unknown reason, this committee did not manage to meet as a body until 1944. In the meantime, the Baseball Writers Association decided to hold a Hall of Fame vote every three years instead of every year, and no elections were held in 1940 or 1941. In 1942, with the backlog of qualified candidates for the Hall of Fame growing by the year, the writers managed to elect only one man, Rogers Hornsby, as Jesse Burkett received only four votes from the 198 electors. The writers did not vote in 1943 or 1944, and such old-time stars as 360-game winner Kid Nichols, sluggers Dan Brouthers and Hugh Duffy, and bunter extraordinaire Jesse Burkett remained outside the walls of the Cooperstown museum.

In 1944, after the Hall had inducted only one new member in the previous five years, Landis made significant changes to the dormant Old-Timers Committee. He added two more members, Boston writer Mel Webb and Hall of Fame president Stephen C. Clark. Landis also gave the committee the power to act as trustees of the institution, allowing them to set policy concerning the selection process for Hall of Fame honorees. When Landis died in November 1944, this committee, which became known as the Permanent Committee, met for the first time and named the late commissioner to the Hall.

The Permanent Committee exercised its power for the first time in 1945. In January of that year, the Baseball Writers Association held its first vote since 1942. Because of the large number of outstanding candidates, voting was widely split among many deserving players, and no one man managed to gain the required number of votes for election to the Hall. In response, the Permanent Committee met on April 25, 1945, and unilaterally elected what Bill James once called "a bargeload of 19th-century guys" to the Hall of Fame. In one stroke, ten new Hall of Famers entered the doors of Cooperstown. The committee tapped such deserving old-time stars as Duffy, Brouthers, and King Kelly, but these selections made only a small dent in the burgeoning pool of candidates.

Many more players awaited the call to Cooperstown, so on April 23, 1946, the Permanent Committee met again and named 11 more old-time players to the Hall of Fame. This time, the panel selected the man who won three National League batting titles and retired in 1905 with a career average of .342. Jesse Burkett, who in 1946 was living in retirement with his wife Nellie in Worcester, Massachusetts, was one of only five of the 11 new inductees still alive.

Burkett was known during his baseball career as an irascible individual. His teammates and opponents called him "The Crab" due to his prickly personality, though he mellowed a bit with age. His reaction to his Hall of Fame election was pure Crab. "It took them a long time," remarked the 77-year-old Burkett. "I thought they weren't going to, because everybody had forgotten me."[2]

Jesse Cail Burkett was born in Wheeling, West Virginia. Some sources list his date of birth as December 4, 1868, while others state that he was born on February 13, 1870. Jesse did not own a birth certificate, and he was never really sure of his age or his birth date.[3] He was the eldest child of Granville and Ellen Burkett, an Irish Catholic couple who lived on South Wabash Street in that gritty industrial town. Granville Burkett was a laborer and painter who held down several jobs while his son played ball for hours on end during the summer months. "All I was thinking about was baseball, baseball," said Jesse many years later. "They couldn't get me in for supper. I played till dark."[4]

The family home stood only a few blocks from the Ohio River, where young Jesse became a strong swimmer. It was there, in the water, that one of the most searing memories of Jesse's life occurred. When Jesse was about 12 years old, he saw a rowboat capsize in the river, and watched as a young girl fell into the water. No one else reacted, so Jesse swam over and frantically began looking for the child in the muddy water. "I crawled about the bottom," he said many years later, "but I couldn't see anything. Finally one of my hands touched her and I brought her to the surface. Her heart was still beating but they couldn't bring her to."[5] The girl died within minutes, and Jesse Burkett was haunted for the rest of his long life by his failure to save her.

As a teenager Jesse worked as a gatherer in a glass factory, but he was not interested in a career in the steel mills and glass plants of Wheeling. Jesse wanted to follow his cousin, Jack Glasscock, into major league baseball. Glasscock, who was about ten years older than Jesse, reached the National League in 1879 as an infielder for the Cleveland team. Glasscock was a small man, only five feet and eight inches tall, but he lasted in the majors for 17 seasons. Jesse was the same height, but recognized that he was a better athlete than his older cousin. Burkett knew that he could succeed in the big leagues as well.

The lefthanded Jesse pitched on local teams in Wheeling in the mid-1880s, making a name for himself in the tough industrial leagues. By 1887 he was the premier player in the city, and his cousin Glasscock introduced him to Sam Crane, manager of a Central League team in Scranton, Pennsylvania. Crane signed the lefthander to a contract in early 1888 for $85 a month. Records are sketchy from this era of minor league ball, but one source credits the 19-year-old Burkett with a 27–6 pitching record. At any rate, Jesse performed well enough to earn a promotion to Worcester, Massachusetts, of the Atlantic Association, where he played for $125 a month. He pitched and also played left field and second base, hit .280, won more than 30 games, and led Worcester to the league title. Jesse also met his future wife in Worcester. She was Ellen (Nellie) McGrath, like Jesse a strong Irish Catholic, and the two married in 1890. They had three children, a son and two daughters, and the Burketts made their home in a three-story house on Grove Street in Worcester, only one block away from the local ballpark.

Jack Glasscock became the manager of the National League's Indianapolis Hoosiers in mid–1889, and he noticed Jesse's success at Worcester. At season's end Glasscock offered his younger relative a contract to play for the Hoosiers in 1890, but when the New York Giants bought out the Indianapolis franchise that winter, both Burkett and Glasscock landed in New York. The Giants, desperate for talent after the defections of most of their stars to the new Players League, signed Burkett as a pitcher for the 1890 season. Jesse hit well in New York, batting .309, but his pitching was a disaster. He posted a won–lost record of 1–11, completing only six of his 21 games and walking more men than he struck out. He played the outfield on days that he didn't pitch, but his fielding left much to be desired. He committed 28 errors for a ghastly .824 fielding percentage.

One fielding miscue, in a game against Boston in September 1890, caused great embarrassment for the young ballplayer. He dove for a ground ball in deep right field, missed it, and tore the foul flag (which marked the boundary between fair and foul territory) out of the ground in so doing. He could not locate the ball, so he assumed that the ball rolled into the hole where he had torn the flag out of the ground. An unidentified newspaper clip from the Baseball Hall of Fame described the aftermath with the headline "Jesse Burkett's Brief Engagement as a Star Comedian":

"Burkett wheeled around several times with the flag in his hands, as if he were hunting for a place to plant it. Then he threw it down and began to dig up dirt in great handsful. A Scotch terrier in the quest of a chipmunk could not have made the dust fly more furiously. All at once it dawned upon the spectators that Jesse was digging for the ball and a roar of laughter went up all around, the players on both sides joining in. Jesse, however, dug the harder and only ceased after Whistler had recovered the ball and Hines and Hardie had both got home.

"The crowd had a great deal of sport with Burkett after this little incident. Next time he started to the field some one yelled 'Here's a shovel,

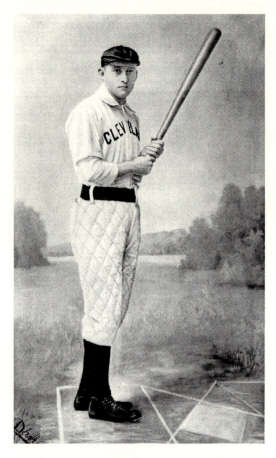

Burkett in his early Cleveland years. Note the diamond-shaped home plate, which did not assume its present five-sided shape until 1900. (National Baseball Hall of Fame Library, Cooperstown, New York)

Jesse.' When he went to bat he was advised to knock it into the hole where he had dug out the other. Still another was unkind enough to yell 'Rats!' and 'Sic 'em Towser.'"[6] For the rest of the season, Jesse was known as "Rabbit" Burkett, a nickname that, fortunately, did not stick.

He also took a great deal of ribbing for his uncanny physical resemblance to his cousin and teammate Jack Glasscock. Some opposing players suggested, unkindly, that the cousins were actually father and son, an accusation that always made Jesse eager to throw a few punches. A gentler young man might have been demoralized by the constant hooting and derision, but Jesse Burkett wasn't fazed. He learned his baseball in the rough and tumble Wheeling industrial league, and he was tough enough to handle the inevitable volleys of insults and challenges offered by more experienced players. "You got to be a battler," he once explained. "If you don't they'll walk all over you. After you lick three or four of them they don't show up any more looking for a fight."[7]

The Giants had no room for Burkett after the Players League defectors returned to the team, so they sent Jesse to Lincoln, Nebraska, for seasoning in 1891. Playing exclusively in the outfield, Burkett batted .349 in 93 games before he was sold to the Cleveland Spiders late in that season. Jesse joined the Spiders in August 1891, batting .271 in 40 games and playing well enough to earn a roster spot for 1892.

In Cleveland, Jesse Burkett became the regular left fielder and leadoff batter for Patsy Tebeau's team. He scored 117 runs and hit .278 in 1892 as the Spiders won the second half of the split-season format, though the Cleveland nine lost the postseason series to Boston in five games. Burkett was well on his way to stardom and in 1893, after the bosses of baseball moved the pitching mound back ten feet, Jesse's average zoomed to .373. His career as a pitcher was over; he pitched only once for Cleveland, as a mop-up man in a 22–7 blowout in July of 1894.

Though he committed a league-leading 42 errors in the outfield that season, he worked diligently on his fielding. "I couldn't catch a medicine ball with a net," admitted Burkett a few years later, "but I went to school with Jim McAleer [the Spider center fielder]. He would coach me during a game when a ball came my way ... and the schooling with Jim soon took the awkward edges off my fielding."[8] Burkett was never a great outfielder, but by the mid–1890s he could handle most of his outfield chances successfully.

Burkett, a small man who used a large, heavy bat, became adept at dropping bunts. More players practiced the art of bunting after 1892, when the pitching mound was moved ten feet farther away from the plate. This reconfiguration of the infield allowed more room for bunts to fall safely. Before long, Burkett became the premier bunter in the National League, and many baseball historians consider Jesse to be the greatest bunter of all time. Jesse often claimed that he could hit .300 merely by bunting. He had phenomenal bat control, and an 1896 newspaper clipping describes his batting in a contest against the Louisville Colonels:

"The first time up he smashed a pretty hit in between the second baseman and first baseman. When he went to bat in the second inning the fielders moved over to the right to play for him. Burkett grinned and planted one directly over the second base bag, where neither the second baseman nor the shortstop could reach it. Then the Louisville fielders were miserable and moved back towards left. In the fourth inning Burkett varied things by making as pretty a bunt as ever was seen and easily reached first. This time the Louisville fielders thought they had him and played close in on him for another bunt. But instead of bunting the great hitter waited until he got a ball to his liking and then he sent it just over the heads of the infielders. He certainly is a great one."[9]

Burkett took advantage of the pre–1903 rule that did not count foul balls as strikes. With his excellent bat control, he could foul balls off one after another without penalty until he found a pitch he liked. He gained many of his hits on bunts, and others with sharp line drives, often after forcing the pitcher to throw a dozen pitches or more. Jesse proclaimed that he went to the plate with "the old confeedience," as he put it, in his batting skill.

The feisty Burkett fit in well with Patsy Tebeau's ballclub. Tebeau was a hard-drinking, quick-fighting manager, and he cast the Spiders in his own image. Some called the Spiders the dirtiest team in the National League, even worse than the notorious Baltimore Orioles, winners of three straight pennants from 1894 to 1896. Tebeau's Spiders tried their best to emulate the Orioles, and player brawls and fan rioting became common-place occurrences wherever the Spiders played. "Show me a team of fighters," said Tebeau to the newspapers, "and I'll show you a team that has a chance."[10]

Jesse was not much of a drinker ("Oh, I'd take a glass of beer now and then," he once said), and never smoked tobacco in his life, but he was as hard-nosed as any member of the Spiders. Despite his small stature — he stood only five feet and eight inches tall and weighed about 160 pounds— Jesse participated in his share of battles with opposing players, umpires, and fans. On June 22, 1896, he and several of his teammates attacked umpire Stump Weidman after a hard-fought game in Louisville. Jesse and four other Spiders were arrested by Louisville police, hauled before a judge, and ordered to pay fines and court costs. In the first game of a doubleheader against Louisville on August 4, 1897, Jesse called umpire Jimmy Wolf a vile name and was ordered out of the game. He refused to leave and Tebeau refused to replace him, so the umpire declared the game forfeited to Louisville by a score of 9–0. In the second game, Burkett once again cursed Wolf, who ordered Jesse removed from the game by force. It took six Louisville policemen to drag the protesting Burkett from the field.

He had no use for sportswriters, because he felt that they did not understand the "scientific baseball" that he espoused. "You could hit the _____ out of the ball and no newspaperman would say a word about it," complained Jesse during the 1896 season. "They're all alike."[11] Burkett traded insults, and sometimes punches, with sportswriters off the field, though he saved his most stinging barbs for umpires and opposing play-ers. "Jesse is one of the most constant and one of the rankest kidders in the business," said The Sporting News in 1903. "That would be alright if he could take a kid himself, but the moment that somebody comes back at him with a few facts stated in sarcastic words he goes wild and wants to fight."[12]

Jesse could always be counted on to give rough treatment to the rook-ies. When Mike Donlin became Jesse's teammate in the spring of 1899, the veteran Burkett wasted no time in pushing the younger man around. "Bur-kett sized me up as a fresh Bush Leaguer and made life miserable for me," said Donlin years later. "One day he bawled me for keeps. I determined to jump the club that night and go back to California." Donlin might have quit if Bobby Wallace had not advised him to stand up to Burkett's bullying, which he did shortly afterward. "As soon as the game was over, I climbed into the same carriage with Burkett and jostled him as hard as I knew how." Patsy Tebeau broke up a potential brawl, induced the two to shake hands, and from that day forward Donlin remained on friendly terms with Burkett. "I was only joshing," claimed Jesse.[13]

By 1895, only Baltimore's Willie Keeler posed a challenge to Jesse Burkett's status as the premier high-average hitter in the National League. After his .357 campaign of 1894, Jesse blistered National League pitching in 1895 for an incredible .423 average. He belted a league-leading 235 hits and scored 149 runs in only 132 games. The Spiders challenged the Baltimore Orioles for the pennant, eventually finishing three games behind but earning the right to face the hated Orioles in the post-season Temple Cup series. After a particularly contentious series, marred by indifferent play by the Orioles and rioting by the Baltimore fans, the Spiders won four out of five to claim the Temple Cup championship.

The next season, 1896, was an even better one for Burkett, as Jesse won his second batting title with a .410 average and led the league in hits (240), runs (159) and also in games played and times at bat. Jesse's play sparked the Spiders to another second place finish behind the Baltimore Orioles and another berth in the Temple Cup series, though this time the Orioles won four games to none. His 240 base hits set a new major league record that stood until 1911, when Ty Cobb broke it.[14] The Cleveland fans appreciated their two-time batting titlist, and presented him with a bicycle inscribed to the "Champion Hitter of the World."

During the off-season, Jesse lived in Worcester and helped his Cleveland teammate, third baseman Chippy McGarr, coach the baseball nine at a nearby Roman Catholic institution, the College of the Holy Cross. In early 1896 Burkett offered batting tips to a phenomenal Indian athlete, Louis Sockalexis, who quickly became one of college baseball's greatest stars. Sockalexis, with Burkett's coaching, batted .444 for Holy Cross in 1896 and drew the attention of several National League teams. Burkett recommended that Patsy Tebeau sign Sockalexis to a Spiders contract, which the manager did, and Sockalexis joined the Cleveland team in the spring of 1897.

Sockalexis quickly captured the interest of the Cleveland fans and sportswriters. Within days of Sockalexis' arrival at the Cleveland spring training camp, the writers started referring to the Cleveland team as "Tebeau's Indians" or merely the "Indians." Jesse basked in the glow of his star pupil for a while, but as the new man garnered the lion's share of press and fan attention, the jealous side of Jesse's personality won out. Burkett started the season in an uncharacteristic slump, and when a rival player teased Jesse about the Indian, Burkett exploded. "Don't tell me about that bead peddler!" shouted Jesse in full hearing of the other players. "He's a Jonah [a jinx]. I haven't batted over .100 since he joined the team! ...Wait till I strike my gait and I will make him go back to the woods and look for a few scalps."[15] Soon the Cleveland papers reported that Jesse and Sockalexis were "on the frosts," though Sockalexis denied that a rift existed and praised Burkett for his coaching at Holy Cross.

Jesse batted .383 after his slow start, but the Cleveland ballclub fell to fifth place in 1897. Sockalexis suffered an off-the-field ankle injury in July when he jumped or fell from a second-story window, and soon it became apparent that Cleveland's newest star had a serious drinking problem, one that he never overcame. The club could not find a viable replacement for Sockalexis in the outfield, and Patsy Tebeau had to use pitchers in right field for much of the campaign. Burkett missed two weeks of action when Fred Klobedanz beaned him on May 17 in a 21–3 loss to Boston. Burkett was knocked unconscious and suffered dizziness and headaches for days afterward, but returned to the lineup on May 31 with two hits against Brooklyn.

The Cleveland team suffered off the field as well that year. Attendance at League Park fell dramatically as a dispute between the team ownership and the city's ministers over Sunday baseball turned increasingly venomous. On May 16, 1897, the Cleveland team defied the local clergy and played a Sunday contest against the Senators, but the police stopped the game in the first inning and arrested all the players on the field, including Jesse. Only one player, rookie pitcher Jack Powell, was required to stand trial, but the incident further poisoned the relationship between the team and the local authorities and made it impossible for the club to turn a profit. The team owner, Frank Robison, then publicly threatened to move the club to Detroit, Milwaukee, or elsewhere.

As the ballclub's pennant chances slipped away, Jesse's mood turned sour. On July 5, in the second game of a doubleheader at Pittsburgh, Jesse misplayed a line drive that went through his legs and rolled behind him. The bases were loaded with Pirates at the time, but Burkett, thoroughly disgusted, refused to retrieve the baseball. Shortstop Ed McKean ran all the way from the infield to the left field fence to corral the ball, but the batter and all three Pittsburgh baserunners scored. A few weeks later, manager Patsy Tebeau complained about Jesse's hustle, or lack thereof, to the newspapers. "I know that Jesse Burkett loafed on a hit to left field the other day," lamented Tebeau, "but what are you going to do? It's almost a clock that we can finish no higher than fifth notch, and we are certain to remain in that position."[16] The Spiders ended the season in fifth place, and needed a 12-game winning streak in September to finish that high.

The 1898 campaign proved even more difficult for the Cleveland club. Frank Robison again tried to schedule a game on a Sunday, though he did so outside of the Cleveland city limits. He set up a temporary ballpark at an amusement park in Collinwood, nine miles from Cleveland, and arranged for Sunday contests at that locale. The Spiders and Pittsburgh Pirates played there on Sunday, June 12, without incident, but one week later the police invaded the field in the eighth inning of another game against Pittsburgh and arrested Burkett and the rest of the players on both teams. After this humiliation, Robison moved almost all of Cleveland's home games to other cities, and the Spiders played 76 of their last 80 games on the road that season.

Jesse Burkett led the league in hits in 1898 for the third time, but his average dipped to .345, and the statistics of most of the other Spiders suffered during the never-ending road trip. "We haven't gotten a close call [from the umpires] in months," complained Jesse to the newspapers. "I never was as tired of a baseball season as I am of this one. Most of the time we have been without a home. Without morning practice, and with the umpires against you, what chance have you? I hope I'll never have to go through another season like this one."[17] He and his wife Nellie also suffered a tragedy when their eldest child, a seven-year-old daughter, died of a fever on April 17 of that year.

Jesse and the other Spiders went to spring training in 1899 with no idea where they would play that season. Rumors abounded that Frank Robison would buy the moribund St. Louis Browns franchise, and in March the rumors became fact. Robison took control of the Browns, soon renamed the Perfectos, and moved Cy Young, Jesse Burkett, Patsy Tebeau, and the rest of the Cleveland stars to St. Louis.

Most people believed that the Perfectos would run away with the league pennant in 1899, but the team played disappointing ball in St. Louis and finished in sixth place. Jesse did not win the batting title, but he batted .402 and became the first man in baseball history to clear the magic .400 mark for the third time. In the 20th century, only Ty Cobb and Rogers Hornsby have matched Burkett's feat.[18]

When the National League dropped its four least profitable teams in 1900, the Perfectos (who changed their team nickname to Cardinals that year) bought the contracts of John McGraw and Wilbert Robinson from the defunct Baltimore Orioles. This move put the ex–Spiders and ex–Orioles on the same team, and created friction between the former enemies that lasted all season. Tebeau appointed McGraw as field captain of the

Cardinals, which angered Burkett and others who wanted former Spider Jack O'Connor to have the job. McGraw, who did not like playing in St. Louis, was already plotting to jump to the new American League the next year, and got himself intentionally thrown out of games so that he and Robinson could spend the afternoon at a local race track. In August 1900, Patsy Tebeau, tired of the constant fighting, resigned as manager, and the Cardinals stumbled to a sixth-place finish.

After McGraw and Robinson bolted for the new league in 1901, the Cardinals returned to a semblance of normality as Jesse Burkett put together one of his finest seasons. He batted .382 in 1901 and won the National League batting title for the third time. He also led the circuit in games played, times at bat, runs, and hits as the Cardinals bounced up to fourth place. His performance made Jesse a desirable property for the American League, which moved its Milwaukee franchise to St. Louis in the fall of 1901. The new St. Louis Browns ballclub, managed by Jesse's old Cleveland teammate Jimmy McAleer, then made offers to several of the Cardinal stars. On October 20, 1901, Jesse, Bobby Wallace, and five other Cardinal players signed contracts with the Browns.

The Cardinals went to court to prevent the seven players from making the move, but in May 1902 the circuit court ruled against the Cardinals, who fell to the bottom of the league without their seven best players.

JESSE C. BURKETT
Manager Worcester Club

Jesse Burkett as playing manager of Worcester, 1909. (Library of Congress)

Jesse became the starting left fielder for the Browns, who finished in second place in their first American League season. He still scuffled with opposing players—he earned a suspension when he punched Washington Senators manager Tom Loftus on the field in 1903—but he was now a respected veteran, and became something of an elder statesman on the Browns. Jesse mentored younger players like Bobby Wallace and Emmett Heidrick and served as a sort of chaperone to young men making their way around the league for the first time.

Jesse's $5,300 annual salary made him one of the highest-paid players in the game, but his batting average fell sharply in the new league. He batted .306 in 1902, a drop of more than 70 points from his 1901 performance, and he never batted .300 again in the major leagues. The American League counted foul balls as strikes for the first time in 1903, robbing Jesse of one of his most important weapons and bringing his average down to .296 in 1903 and .273 in 1904. He also began to lose his speed as he passed his 30th birthday, and his stolen base totals and outfield range decreased with each passing year. By 1904 Jesse, while still a solid contributor, was no longer one of the league's most feared batsmen.

In January 1905 the Browns traded Jesse to the Boston Pilgrims (now called the Red Sox) for $2,500 and outfielder George Stone, who won the batting title for the Browns a year later. Jesse enjoyed playing close to his Worcester home, but age began to adversely affect his performance. Burkett's speed was gone, and he batted only .257 and committed 22 outfield errors as the Pilgrims fell to fourth place after winning two consecutive pennants. Jesse proclaimed to the newspapers that he was "disgusted" with his showing, and at the end of the season he retired from the major leagues. He left a lifetime batting average of .342, which still stands as the ninth-best mark of all the players in the Hall of Fame, and his 2,872 hits placed him second on the all-time list behind Cap Anson.

Jesse decided that he wanted to continue playing in the minor leagues, and took the unusual step of purchasing his own release from the Boston club. In early 1906 Jesse bought the Worcester Busters of the Class B New England League, two steps below the majors, and served as manager, outfielder, and team president for the next ten years. Unlike most former star players, Burkett became a successful manager and team executive, and his Worcester club never finished lower than fourth place under Burkett's management. He won pennants in his first four seasons at Worcester, and won the league batting title in 1906 with a .344 mark. In 1911, when Jesse was well past his 40th birthday, he batted .342. He enjoyed playing and managing in his adopted hometown, where the ballpark stood only a block away from his Grove Street house.

He was still a prickly individual. One day a rookie apologized for his poor play by telling manager Burkett, "Gosh, I'm sorry. I just couldn't get going out there today." Jesse responded, "Don't worry, son, you'll get going tonight. Here's your ticket for home." Jesse also never gave up feuding with the umpires. He put himself in as a pinch-hitter one day and refused to tell the umpire for whom he was batting. The umpire turned to the stands and intoned, "Burkett batting for exercise."[19]

All of the high minor leagues suffered during the Federal League war of 1914–1915, and Jesse decided to sell out after an unprofitable 1915 campaign. He sold the ballclub to local investors and managed at Lawrence,

Hartford, and Lowell in 1916. In 1917 he began a four year stint as the head baseball coach at the College of the Holy Cross in Worcester, where he helped develop Joe Dugan, Jigger Statz, and Rosy Ryan, all of whom later enjoyed successful careers in the major leagues. Burkett left Holy Cross after the 1920 season to take a job as a coach for the New York Giants under the direction of his old Baltimore Oriole nemesis, John McGraw.

McGraw's Giants were a rowdy bunch, and the manager needed a sober professional like Jesse Burkett to keep watch over his crew of hard-living young ballplayers. The players, quite naturally, did not appreciate Jesse's barbed comments about their nighttime activities, and when the Giants won the World Series that year the players refused to give Jesse a share of the Series money. McGraw paid Jesse a full Series share out of his own pocket. In 1922 Jesse was not officially a coach, but McGraw enlisted Burkett as a "keeper" for Phil Douglas, a talented but alcoholic pitcher. Jesse was assigned to follow Douglas, 24 hours a day if necessary, and keep him out of trouble. This arrangement worked for a while, but Douglas soon tired of Burkett's company and fell spectacularly off the wagon. One weekend Douglas shook himself free from Jesse and went on a bender. While intoxicated, Douglas foolishly wrote a letter to a friend of his on the Cardinals, offering to quit the Giants for an unspecified amount of money, and found himself banned from baseball for life by Commissioner Landis.

Burkett managed several New England League and Northeastern League teams for the next few years and also performed some scouting work for the Giants, though not all of his judgments proved correct. In 1921 a catcher named Charles "Gabby" Hartnett played for the Worcester team, and McGraw sent Burkett to check Hartnett out. Burkett reported that Hartnett's hands were too small for a major league catcher, so McGraw passed on the opportunity to sign him. The Cubs eventually obtained Hartnett, who played in the majors for 19 seasons and helped the Cubs win four pennants. In 1955 the baseball writers elected Gabby Hartnett to the Hall of Fame. Jesse also arranged a Giants tryout for his son Howard Burkett, a shortstop, who never reached the majors but played minor league ball for more than a decade in the International and Pacific Coast circuits.

After the mid–1920s, Burkett stayed closer to home. In 1928, and again in 1931 and 1932, Burkett coached at another Catholic institution in Worcester, Assumption College, where former Giants pitcher Rube Marquard served as his assistant for the last two seasons. He was as acid-tongued as ever, but Burkett worked well with younger players, and in his later years he gained a reputation as a successful teacher. He gave up active participation in organized ball in 1933, when he was in his mid–60s, and returned to live at the same house in Worcester where he and his wife Nellie set up housekeeping in 1890.

He mellowed in his old age, attending reunions of old-time ballplayers and maintaining friendships with fellow baseball legends such as Connie Mack and Ty Cobb. Burkett was too ill to attend his Hall of Fame induction, though he was honored at a dinner in Worcester to celebrate the occasion. Burkett used the opportunity, not to praise his own accomplishments, but to promote the Hall candidacy of his recently deceased friend and fellow Worcester resident Billy Hamilton, the old Boston center fielder and base-stealing king.[20] Nellie Burkett died in 1950, but Jesse acquired a housekeeper and continued to live at the Grove Street address.

Jesse never visited the Cooperstown museum, because he suffered from hardening of the arteries and was bedridden for the last several years of his life. He lived out his days in an upstairs room where a steady stream of relatives, friends, and reporters visited the elderly ballplayer. Burkett enjoyed talking to reporters, though he had not gotten along well with newspapermen during his playing days. When he was past his 80th birthday, he modestly suggested to a local sportswriter that "there were better players than me," and that Ty Cobb was the greatest player of all time. "Cobb could do anything around the plate — hit, bunt, drag the ball. He could field and throw, do everything. He'd fight at the drop of a hat. He was just breaking in [the big leagues], when I was going out."[21] Cobb played his first major league game in August 1905, about one month before Jesse retired from the Boston Pilgrims.

The only somber note in his reminiscences came when he recalled the girl whom he failed to save from drowning in the Ohio River some 70 years before. The thought of that unsuccessful rescue attempt brought tears to the old man's eyes, and he would quickly change the subject to a happier topic. The newspapermen remarked in their columns how Jesse, despite his physical ailments, still owned a pair of sparkling, penetrating eyes. Jesse never used glasses, not even to read, during his lifetime.

In 1952 Jesse received perhaps his greatest honor. The city of Worcester organized a Little League and decided to name it after the city's most famous contribution to major league baseball. When a local newspaperman informed Jesse that the organization would be called the Jesse Burkett Little League, the feisty old ballplayer cried. "I am not a forgotten man after all," said Burkett, "thanks to fellows like you." Jesse Burkett was 84 years old when he died of a heart attack on May 27, 1953.

Burkett's name reappeared in the nation's newspapers in 2001, when the Jesse Burkett All-Stars represented Worcester in the Little League World Series and advanced to the final game before losing to the eventual national champions from Louisville. Until then, Worcester's greatest ballplayer was a virtually forgotten man, and it is a safe bet that many, if not most, of the city's Little League players and fans had no idea who Jesse Burkett was.

Though he won three batting titles and batted .400 a record three times, Jesse Burkett is rarely mentioned in the ranks of the game's greatest batters. Perhaps his feats, like those of most 19th century stars, have been discounted because most reference books accept the year 1900 as the beginning of the "modern era" of major league baseball, and most of Burkett's greatest seasons came before that year. The diminutive Jesse may also have been ignored because he was not a power hitter. He never hit more than 10 homers in a season and swatted only 75 in his career, most of them of the inside-the-park variety. Barry Bonds, like Jesse a left fielder, belted only two fewer homers in 2001 than Burkett hit in his entire career.

Despite all that, Jesse Burkett earned his place on the wall in Cooperstown. Some of the 21 selections made by the Permanent Committee in its 1945 and 1946 meetings may be questionable in retrospect, but the committee made a good choice in Burkett, whose statistics closely resemble those of his contemporary Willie Keeler:

	Games	Runs	Hits	Homers	Average
Keeler, 1892–1910	2,124	1,720	2,955	33	.345
Burkett, 1890–1905	2,062	1,708	2,872	75	.342

The Baseball Writers Association elected Keeler to the Hall in 1939, but the same organization never gave Burkett more than seven votes in any election. The Permanent Committee rectified this oversight when it recognized Jesse Burkett's outstanding, if long forgotten, career and honored the prickly outfielder as one of the game's all-time greats.

6

◆ KID NICHOLS ◆

I take pride in two things. My election to baseball's Hall of Fame and the fact I never was removed from a game for a relief hurler. — Charles (Kid) Nichols[1]

When the Hall of Fame was created in the mid–1930s, the institution wrestled with the issue of electing early players, executives, and other deserving contributors. A separate election for 19th century stars was held in 1936, but the voting process was not well planned, and no one gained the required number of votes for selection. In response, Commissioner Kenesaw M. Landis created a committee to select 19th-century players and pioneers for induction. This committee went through several changes and emerged in 1944 as the Permanent Committee, charged with electing men whose careers ended before 1910.

Perhaps it was inevitable that some deserving candidates would fall through the cracks and escape the committee's attention. One such player was Charles "Kid" Nichols, who pitched in the National League from 1890 to 1906 and won 360 games, the fourth-highest total in league history. He also led the Boston Beaneaters to five pennants in the Gay Nineties. Nichols, who in the early 1940s was alive and well and managing a bowling alley in Kansas City, had been retired from baseball for nearly four decades. Since no major league team at the time played further west than St. Louis, Nichols had remained outside of baseball's orbit for all those years. "I went back out West when I quit baseball," said the Kid. " … People just forgot about me. I guess they thought I was beyond the frontier or something."[2]

In the four earliest Hall of Fame elections conducted by the BBWAA in the 1930s, Nichols had never gained more than seven votes from more than 200 participating voters. In 1945, the Permanent Committee, later known as the Veterans Committee, selected ten old-time players to the Hall. The committee members chose three of Kid's Boston teammates (Jimmy Collins, Mike "King" Kelly and Hugh Duffy), but bypassed Nichols. Many writers and fans, those who remembered the long-retired Kid, thought it strange that a pitcher who won 30 or more games in a season a record seven times had not yet been honored with a plaque in the Cooperstown museum.

Ty Cobb, Cy Young, Clark Griffith, and other old-time stars lobbied both publicly and privately for Nichols' election, but in 1946 the Permanent Committee threw another curveball. The committee selected pitchers Rube Waddell (193 wins), Jack Chesbro (198 wins) and Ed Walsh (195 wins) and bypassed the 360-game winner, Nichols, once again. "I'd like to be in there [in Cooperstown]," said Nichols in 1941, "but they forget about us old codgers in a hurry."[3]

The committee, stung by the public criticism of its 1946 selections, went into hibernation for three years, but on May 7, 1949, the Permanent Committee met again and named the 79-year-old Kid Nichols to the Hall of Fame. "I was never so pleased in my life as when I was selected," said the old pitcher. "It's a fine thing for my four great-grandchildren."[4] He attended the induction ceremony that summer, traveling by car from Kansas City to Cooperstown with a side trip to Buffalo, where he attended the annual convention of SPEBSQSA, the national association of barbershop-quartet enthusiasts. At the Cooperstown ceremony, held on June 13, 1949, principal speaker Branch Rickey praised Nichols as "one of the great pitchers of the olden days."

Charles Augustus Nichols, the son of a butcher and a housewife, was born on September 14, 1869, in Madison, Wisconsin. He was the seventh child of Robert and Christina Nichols, who began their married life in New York state and moved to Madison about ten years before Charles was born. Not much is known about the future ballplayer's early life, except that the family moved West once again, this time to Kansas City, Missouri, when Charles was 11 years old.

His older brothers worked for their father in the family butcher shop, but from an early age Charles Nichols set his sights on a baseball career. Charles, though not a big or muscular boy, was nonetheless a fine athlete. He played ball on vacant lots in his new hometown, and soon graduated to pitching for local amateur teams. Charles weighed no more than 135 pounds as a young teenager, but he displayed a surprisingly good fastball and fine control.

In 1886, when Charles was 16, he secured a tryout with the major league Kansas City Cowboys of the American Association. He didn't make the team, but in 1887, after the Cowboys dropped out of the Association and entered the lower-level Western League, Charles Nichols tried out again. Once more the Cowboys turned him down, but by June the injury-riddled club was short on pitchers. They signed Charles to a contract on June 10 of that year. The older players on the club were surprised by the presence of this baby-faced teenager; they first addressed him as "Batboy," then as "Kid," a name that stuck and became the young man's nickname for the rest of his life.

The newly-christened Kid pitched well for a 17-year-old, posting an 18–13 record while batting .298 in 33 games for the Cowboys. Nichols was not yet a finished pitcher — he struck out only 65 men in 285 innings and allowed 386 hits — and the Cowboys released him after the season. In 1888 Kid joined Memphis of the Southern League and went 10–9 before the league collapsed in mid-season. Kansas City re-signed him in July of 1888, and Nichols rewarded the Cowboys with 16 wins in 18 games and a microscopic 1.14 earned run average.

Kid Nichols, now 18 years old, began to mature as a pitcher. As he grew bigger and stronger with age, his fastball improved until it was one of the best in the Western League. Kid threw four shutouts among his 16 wins and, for the first time, allowed less than one hit per inning.

The Cowboys re-entered the American Association for the 1889 season and decided not to take their teenaged pitcher with them, so Kid Nichols signed with Kansas City's Western League rival, Omaha. Managed by future Hall of Fame member Frank Selee, Omaha won the pennant as Nichols turned in one of the most remarkable pitching performances of the 19th century. He compiled a won–lost record of 39–8, striking out 368 men in 438 innings. In September 1889, William Conant, one of the three principal owners of the National League's Boston Beaneaters, paid the Omaha club $3,000 for Nichols' release and signed the 20-year-old pitcher to a contract for 1890.

Nichols was a levelheaded young man, and he responded well to the managing style of Frank Selee. Selee, who once remarked "if I make things pleasant for the players, they reciprocate," was a good judge of talent and gained a reputation for working well with young players. Kid Nichols and other youngsters blossomed under Selee's tutelage, and Omaha's 1889 pennant brought Selee to the attention of William Conant, who hired him as manager of the Beaneaters for the 1890 campaign.

The Boston club was decimated by Players League defections, and Selee inherited a desperate situation in the early months of 1890. The team

Kid Nichols with Omaha in 1889. (National Baseball Hall of Fame Library, Cooperstown, New York)

managed to keep its star pitcher, John Clarkson, away from the new league, but the rest of the team was full of holes. Selee moved to fill those holes with players from the Western League, including his star pitcher from Omaha. "John," said Conant to Clarkson in late 1889, "I have a good man to help you. This Nichols is a strapping fellow and looks very much as Buffinton did when he first came to Boston."[5] Nichols paid immediate dividends when he won his first game, defeating Brooklyn by a 5–2 score on April 23, 1890. Kid also belted three hits in four trips to the plate that day.

Most major league teams, up until 1890, used only two main starting pitchers, and some still piled the lion's share of the pitching load upon one hurler. In 1889, John Clarkson pitched in 72 games for Boston, completing 68 and working in 620 innings. Selee recognized that too many managers destroyed their star pitchers from overwork, and resolved to spread out the load among three starters. He pitched Clarkson, Nichols, and veteran Charlie Getzien in an evenly divided three-man rotation, one of the first in baseball history. Each man made between 40 and 47 starts in 1890; Nichols, the rookie, posted a mark of 27–19, with Clarkson at 26–18 and Getzien at 23–14 as the Beaneaters finished in fifth place. Kid, who turned 21 a few weeks before the 1890 season ended, led the National League with seven shutouts.

One of Nichols' losses came in one of the most famous pitching duels in baseball history. On May 12, 1890, the Beaneaters played the Giants at the old Polo Grounds in New York, with Nichols facing Amos Rusie. The New York Players League club was playing at the same time in their stadium, which abutted the Giants' park, and as Nichols and Rusie dueled through one scoreless inning after another, fans in both parks cheered the action. After twelve innings, the game remained scoreless, and Rusie set down the

Beaneaters in the thirteenth. In the bottom of the inning, Nichols finally faltered. Giants outfielder Mike Tiernan belted a Nichols fastball over the center field fence for a 1–0 win, which set off wild celebrations in both New York ballparks.

The Players League collapsed after the 1890 campaign, and manager Selee signed four of the league's former stars—second baseman Joe Quinn, catcher Mike "King" Kelly, pitcher Harry Staley, and third baseman Billy Nash—to Boston contracts for the 1891 season. These players provided the spark that the Beaneaters needed. The Boston club trailed Cap Anson's Chicago Colts by six and a half games with less than three weeks left in the season, but Kid and the Beaneaters closed the campaign with 18 wins in a row to edge the Colts by three and a half games. Nichols went 7–0 in that span while Clarkson won all six of his decisions, and Boston won the pennant as both Clarkson (34–18) and Nichols (30–16) crossed the 30-win mark, Nichols for the first time and Clarkson for the last. Nichols, who was sometimes used in relief when other pitchers could not complete their games, also led the National League in saves that year with three.

Boston's winning streak was marred by controversy. The Beaneaters swept five games in a row (with two wins by Nichols) from the New York Giants, who played without star pitcher Amos Rusie and cleanup hitter Roger Connor, and Cap Anson later insisted that "a conspiracy was entered into whereby New York lost enough games to Boston to give the Beaneaters the pennant." Anson was unpopular for his loyalty to the National League during the Players League revolt of 1890, and some say that the Giants and other teams let Boston win without a fight. The fact that the Boston team management owned stock in the Giants at the time played a part in the controversy as well. At any rate, Boston won its first pennant in eight years, but the possibly tainted 18-game winning streak is ignored in many baseball record books.

After the season, the American Association collapsed as well, leaving the National League as the only major league, and Selee gained the services of outfielders Hugh Duffy and Tommy McCarthy and pitcher Jack Stivetts from defunct AA teams. By early 1892 Kid had displaced John Clarkson as the team's number one starter, and when Clarkson suffered a sore arm in May of that year, Selee released the veteran sidearmer and replaced him with Stivetts. The Boston club didn't miss a beat, as both Nichols and Stivetts posted 35–16 records and led the Beaneaters to another National League flag.

The 1892 season was the only time in baseball history (except for the strike-interrupted 1981 campaign) that the major leagues tried a split-season format. The National League held two pennant races, with the winners of each half-season meeting in a post-season playoff for the championship. Boston won the first half and the Cleveland Spiders (who signed Clarkson in July of that year) took the second. In the best-of-nine series that began in Cleveland on October 17, Jack Stivetts and Cy Young battled to a 0–0 tie in a game halted after 11 innings by darkness. The Beaneaters swept the next five games, with Nichols winning the fourth game with a shutout and closing the series with an 8–3 win over Young on October 24 at Boston. Kid drove in the tying and winning runs with a single in the fourth inning of the deciding game.

Kid Nichols, who stood five feet ten inches tall and weighed 175 pounds as an adult, was not the biggest pitcher in the game by any means, but he displayed an excellent fastball from his first day in the major leagues. Some said that he threw as hard, if not harder, than almost every other pitcher in the major leagues at the time. Only the powerfully built Amos Rusie, the 19-year-old sensation of the New York Giants, hurled a better fastball than the 20-year-old Nichols. Kid threw with a straight overhand motion, unlike teammate John Clarkson and other older pitchers who still relied on the sidearm deliveries that were required by baseball rules until the mid–1880s. Kid was not big or muscular, but his fluid, easy delivery made the ball dash across the plate.

Unlike most pitchers, Nichols rarely threw a curveball, and many contemporary accounts insist that Nichols did not throw the curve at all. He relied on his fastball and the occasional change of pace, while concentrating on location and control of his pitches. Despite his speed, Kid was never a strikeout artist. Nichols learned to allow the batter to put the ball in play, relying on the excellent defense that manager Selee built for the Boston team. Rusie, the Giant flamethrower, struck out far more men than Nichols, but walked many and lost more games than his Boston rival. "I have yet to learn that Nichols has any wonderful, elusive curves and quick-breaking shoots," said Pittsburgh's Pat Donovan, "but he has one thing that makes an effective pitcher, and that is command of the ball and speed to back it up."[6]

Kid may have been the least fancy pitcher of his era. Most pitchers then used elaborate windmill-type windups, but Kid believed in simply throwing the ball with a minimum of fuss. "Many a pitcher uses an elaborate swing," he wrote in a newspaper article in 1901, "and I have been asked repeatedly to adopt one, but [I] have persistently refused. I don't approve of it because it interferes with the control of the ball, and the one using it has to master two deliveries, since a swing is out of the question when one of the bases is occupied." He threw his pitches with a straight overhand motion. "The most common fault of amateur pitchers is that they deliver the ball from the side," wrote Nichols. "It should always come straight over the shoulder."[7]

He was a good hitter, too. A switch-hitter, he batted .226 and belted 16 home runs in his career, and in 1894 he batted .294 and drove in 39 runs for the Beaneaters. Kid was a fast runner, with 24 career triples, and a good fielder who pitched the entire 1896 season without committing an error. Team rosters were much smaller back then, so Kid filled in at first base and in the outfield several times a year whenever necessary.

During the winter months, Nichols kept himself in shape by working out in an indoor gym. He disliked spring training, because the constant traveling and the rainy spring weather caused many interruptions in his training regimen. Kid was perfectly happy to run and throw indoors for six weeks prior to the baseball season, gradually building himself up to peak condition by the time the season began in April each year. He and the other Boston pitchers kept their arms in shape during the season by throwing every day, under Selee's direction, and many opponents were surprised when they saw Kid throwing on a side lot next to the Boston ballpark while a game was in progress. The regimen must have worked, because Nichols pitched over 400 innings per season each year from 1890 to 1894, and threw over 300 innings in 12 of the first 13 seasons of his career.

Though he played in Boston, Kid Nichols continued to live in Kansas City, where he remained all of his adult life. In 1890 he married a Kansas City girl named Jane Curtis, who shared Kid's enthusiasm for sports. Kid helped organize Kansas City's first bowling league in the winter of 1892; a few years later, Jane Nichols assembled the city's first bowling league for women. The couple raised one daughter, Alice, and in the mid–1890s Kid and Jane opened a laundry business in Kansas City. The business proved so successful that they soon opened a second laundry in town. Kid also operated a bowling alley, one of the first in the state of Missouri, before the 1890s ended.

Personally, Kid was every inch the dedicated, clean-living type of professional that Frank Selee wanted on the Boston team. Mal Kittridge, one of Kid's Boston catchers, called Nichols "the most perfect husband and father I have ever met."[8] In 1898 *Sporting Life* wrote in admiration that "Kid Nichols is a monument. He's other things too. But he's a living, breathing, effective argument to all ball players of what they might be if they took proper care of themselves."[9]

The Beaneaters, paced by Kid's 33 wins, won their third pennant in a row in 1893, but discord and tragedy ended the team's successful run the following year. In January of 1894, Boston catcher Charlie Bennett fell under a train in Wellsville, Kansas and lost both legs, ending his career.

Hugh Duffy and Tommy McCarthy, the popular "Heavenly Twins" of the Boston outfield, held out for more money and did not report to the team until Opening Day. On May 16, a hotly contested game against the Orioles ended when someone set the Boston ballpark on fire; the blaze destroyed the Beaneaters' stadium and more than 170 other houses and buildings in Boston's South End. Though Nichols passed the 30-win mark again and Duffy paced the league's batters with a .438 average and 18 home runs, the Baltimore Orioles grabbed the league lead and held it to the end of the season.

The Beaneaters fell all the way to sixth place in 1895, and manager Frank Selee decided to rebuild the team. He released centerfielder Tommy McCarthy after McCarthy and pitcher Jack Stivetts fought in a St. Louis hotel room, and the manager filled the centerfield slot with Billy Hamilton, acquired in a trade from Philadelphia. Selee then brought in youngsters Fred Tenney, Jimmy Collins, and Chick Stahl to replace aging stars Tommy Tucker, Billy Nash, and Jimmy Bannon respectively. The manager kept Nichols (who went 27–16 in 1895) as the anchor of his rotation, and added lefthander Fred Klobedanz and righthander Ted Lewis to the staff. By 1897 the transformation was complete, and the Beaneaters were ready to challenge the Orioles for National League supremacy once again.

Boston and Baltimore battled all season long, and the 1897 pennant race came down to a three-game series in Baltimore in late September with the two teams in a virtual tie for the league lead. On Friday, September 24, Nichols defeated the Orioles 6–4, but Baltimore's Bill Hoffer bested the Beaneaters the next day. They didn't play ball on Sunday in Baltimore in those days, but on Monday more than 25,000 people jammed the park with an additional 5,000 watching from rooftops to see the deciding game. Frank Selee sent his best pitcher, Kid Nichols, to the mound to face the Orioles in a game that would virtually decide the pennant race.

The Baltimore management put several thousand fans in the outfield behind rope barriers, which made the playing area so small that the two teams were required to play under special ground rules that resulted in 15 doubles that day. Baltimore took a 5–4 lead off Nichols in the first two innings, but the Boston batters pounded four Baltimore pitchers for one run in the third, three in the fourth, and nine more in the seventh before the Kid surrendered another tally. The Beaneaters won the wild affair by a 19–10 score, and clinched the pennant with a win at Brooklyn three days later.

In October the same two teams met in the Temple Cup post-season series, but after the exhausting pennant race the Boston and Baltimore players showed little interest in playing each other again. Kid Nichols started the first game for Boston, but took himself out in the sixth inning and did not pitch again in the series. "My arm grew lame in the second game in Baltimore last week," said Kid to the newspapers, "and I will now let some of the other boys finish the season, as I want to be right next season."[10] The Orioles won the Temple Cup series in five games, mostly because Kid Nichols rested his arm on the sidelines.

The Beaneaters, with rookie pitcher Vic Willis taking Jack Stivetts' place in the rotation, claimed the pennant again in 1898 as Kid passed the 30-win mark for the seventh and last time. The 1898 Boston team won a then-record 102 games and has been called the greatest team of the 19th century. Kid put together perhaps his best season, posting a 31–12 record with a 2.13 earned run average that was more than a run and a half better than the league average that year. However, the pennant excitement turned sour when club management, which claimed that the Spanish-American War held down

Nichols on an 1895 tobacco card from Mayo Cut Plug. (Library of Congress)

attendance in 1898, rewarded each Boston player with a paltry $235 bonus at season's end.

For the first time in his career, Nichols held out for more money from the miserly Boston ownership in the spring of 1899. Kid was earning the National League's maximum salary of $2,400 a year at the time, but Boston was the league's most profitable team, and Nichols believed he deserved better compensation. In late March 1899 the Boston owners reached a compromise with their star hurler. They kept his salary at $2,400, but added a few incentives and bonuses to be paid at the end of the season. Kid reluctantly agreed to the terms and returned to the fold in early April.

Perhaps Nichols tried to rush himself into condition too quickly, for Kid threw his hardest fastballs in a frigid spring training game in Norfolk, Virginia, and complained afterward of a sharp pain in his shoulder. The arm hurt all season long, and Kid fell to a 21–17 record as Vic Willis supplanted Nichols as Boston's number one starter, as Kid had surpassed John Clarkson many years before. Kid suffered from pain in his shoulder and dropped to 13–16 the next season, though he won his 300th major league game on July 7, 1900 against Chicago and became the youngest man ever to reach that plateau. A healthier Kid improved in 1901, but his earned run average rose for the fourth season in a row as the Beaneaters fell to sixth place in the eight-team league.

Kid took the loss in the highest-scoring Opening Day game in National League history. On April 17, 1900, manager Selee selected Willis instead of Nichols as Boston's Opening Day starter, but the Phillies bombed Willis out of the box and took a 17–8 lead into the ninth. The Beaneaters then pulled off one of the most remarkable comebacks in history when they scored nine times in the bottom of the inning to tie the game. Kid came in to pitch the tenth, and the *Herald* reported, "When Charley Nichols walked to the pitcher's box, everybody felt secure that the day would go to Boston after all." The Philles reached Kid for two runs in the tenth and won the game by a 19–17 score. Despite the loss, the *Herald* called it "one of the most remarkable ball games ever played on the South End or any other ground between teams that were the leading exemplars of the beauties of the national game."

The 1901 season represented a changing of the guard among star pitchers in the National League. Kid won his first game that season, a 7–0 shutout against the Phillies, but then suffered through a seven game losing streak that lasted until mid–June. At the same time, the 21-year-old Christy Mathewson began his first full season for the New York Giants, and he defeated Kid twice by 2–1 scores in the first half of the campaign. On July 29 the two hurlers matched up again, with Kid winning a 5–4 decision in 10 innings.

The future star and the fading veteran faced each other three times in seven days. On August 13 the two men threw one scoreless inning after another and completed nine innings in a 0–0 tie before the Beaneaters scored three times in the tenth and gave Kid a 3–0 win. Two days later Mathewson and Nichols battled to an 11-inning 5–5 tie in a game called by darkness, and on August 19 Kid bested his younger competitor by an 11–6 score. Kid finished the season with a 19–16 record, while Mathewson posted a nearly identical 20–17 mark, but it was clear to all that Mathewson's greatest days lay ahead of him. Kid Nichols was only 32 years old at the end of the 1901 campaign, but his stardom was fading quickly.

With Kid's career on the downside, the Boston team owners felt no need to continue paying Nichols' high salary. They made him an offer that included a substantial pay cut for the 1902 season. Nichols responded by accepting a position as manager of the Kansas City Blue Stockings, the Western League entry in his hometown. At age 32, Kid left the major leagues. His last win in 1901, a 7–4 victory over St. Louis, was the 328th of his career and broke John Clarkson's record for wins by a pitcher in National League history. Kid held that record until Christy Mathewson surpassed it 14 years later.

Kid Nichols pitched and managed the Blue Stockings to the pennant in his rookie year as a manager and led the league with 27 wins on the mound as well. After a third-place finish in 1903, Kid tried to buy his way into the ownership of the team, but the owners disbanded the club instead. The American Association had placed a new team, the Cowboys, in Kansas City to compete with Nichols' ballclub, and the Blue Stockings lost the attendance battle despite their on-field success. "They sold the team right out from under me," complained Kid, but he picked himself up and began looking for another position in the major leagues.

In December 1903, St. Louis club owner Frank Robison offered Kid a job as playing manager of the Cardinals. Kid returned to the National League after a two year hiatus and lifted the club to a fifth-place finish in 1904. He posted a 21–13 record, tying for the team lead in wins with Jack Taylor, and threw three shutouts. On August 11, Kid pitched one of his greatest games, defeating the Dodgers 4–3 in a 17-inning, complete-game performance with 15 strikeouts. On September 11 Nichols, in an attempt to give some relief to his exhausted pitching staff, threw complete games in both ends of a doubleheader against the Reds. He won the first game and lost the second.

The Cardinals, who had finished in last place in 1903, were one of the least disciplined teams in the major leagues, and Kid had his hands full in managing them. On July 30, 1904 rumors abounded that gamblers in Pittsburgh had wagered a substantial amount of money on the Pirates to beat the Cardinals that afternoon. During the game, Cardinal pitcher Jack Taylor walked seven men and threw three wild pitches as the Pirates won by a 5–2 score. As it turned out, Taylor had not been bribed; instead, he and first baseman Jake Beckley had spent the previous evening on a public drinking spree, and everyone in town knew of their hung-over condition by game time the next day.

Frank Robison appreciated Nichols' work, but when Robison's health failed in the winter of 1904, his brother Stanley took over the team on an interim basis. Stanley, the vice-president and treasurer of the Cardinals, did not have the same cordial relationship with Nichols that Frank Robison had enjoyed. "Somehow, I always felt Stanley Robison had it in for me," stated Nichols.[11]

The Cardinals got off to a poor start in 1905, and Stanley Robison began to publicly criticize the players and manager Nichols. Kid devoted most of his energies to managing, not pitching, in the first part of the 1905

Kid Nichols as playing manager of the St. Louis Cardinals in 1904. (National Baseball Hall of Fame Library, Cooperstown, New York)

campaign, much to Stanley Robison's displeasure, since the Cardinals were paying Nichols both as a manager and as a player. Nichols made only one start in April, which he won, but the other Cardinal starters failed to carry the burden. On May 3, with the team buried in seventh place, Robison fired Kid as manager (though Nichols was retained as a pitcher) and replaced him with infielder Jimmy Burke. The Cardinals reacted to the change by losing seven of their next eight games.

Nichols, free of the responsibilities of managing, then worked for the next few weeks to bring his arm into shape. In late May he told Burke that he was ready to pitch, but he was now 35 years old and battling an attack of pleurisy, and no longer threw the ball with the speed of old. Weakened by his illness, Kid made only seven starts for the Cardinals in 1905, going 1–5 with a 5.40 earned run average. His last appearance, in the second game of a July 4 doubleheader against the Cubs, ended in an 11–1 loss, the 12th defeat in a 14-game Cardinal losing streak.

The tension between Robison and Nichols erupted in the following week. When the Cardinals traveled to Cincinnati for a series against the Reds, Robison ordered Nichols to watch the gate before the game. In those days, visiting teams assigned a player or two to count the people coming through the turnstiles and make sure that the home team was not under-reporting the attendance. Kid once told a reporter that counting thousands, or sometimes tens of thousands, of fans was more difficult than pitching nine innings. However, younger players and benchwarmers usually received this assignment, and Kid suggested that he had enough to do without the responsibility of counting noses. "I told Robison I wasn't going to watch any gate," recalled Nichols many years later. "I was going over to the Latonia race track."[12] It was the wrong answer. The irate Robison then handed Nichols his outright release.

He signed with the Philadelphia Phillies (managed by Kid's old Boston teammate Hugh Duffy) a week later, and defeated the Cardinals by a 2–1 score in his first game in a Phillies uniform. "That gave me a measure of satisfaction," said Kid afterward, and he proved that he still had some life left in his arm with a 10–6 record in 17 games. Still, Kid's arm did not recover as quickly between starts, and he knew that his days as a star were long past. He returned to Philadelphia in 1906, but pitched in only four games before he called it a career and went home to Kansas City. He retired as the second-winningest pitcher of all time (behind only Cy Young) with 360 wins, and to this day only five major league pitchers have won more games than Kid Nichols.

Nichols never returned to organized baseball, mostly because he was so busy doing other things. He sold insurance, managed a laundry business with his brother, and sold automobiles. In 1913 he received a patent on an electronic scoreboard for sporting events, though the idea never made it into production. Kid also invested in a chain of movie theaters with Chicago Cubs shortstop Joe Tinker. He remained active in the local baseball scene, coaching at Missouri Valley College and volunteering his advice to local youth, amateur, and semipro nines.

The Stengel family lived across the street from Nichols, and one day around 1910 Kid Nichols engaged the teenaged Charles Stengel in a chat about professional ball. Kid told his young neighbor, "I understand you get in a lot of trouble and in a lot of arguments. Now I want to tell you something. Don't be arguing all the time. Listen to your manager. Or, if you have an old player teaching you, listen to him. Never say, 'I won't do that.' Always listen.

"If you're not going to do what he says, don't tell him so. Let it go in one ear, and let it roll around in there for a month, and then if it isn't any good let it roll out the other ear. But if it is good, memorize it and keep it. You do that and you'll learn something, and you'll keep out of a lot of trouble."[13] Charles Stengel broke into the major leagues with the Dodgers in 1912 and remembered Kid's advice all of his life. As "Casey" Stengel, he eventually joined his old neighbor Nichols in the Hall of Fame.

Kid and his wife Jane were enthusiastic bowlers who did much to popularize the sport in the Kansas City area. In later years, Kid became the manager and part owner of a bowling alley and billiards parlor in Kansas City called the Pla-Mor, one of the biggest in town. In 1933, when Kid was 64 years old, he won the bowling championship of Kansas City, sealing his victory with a 299 score in the championship match. He showed as much pride in his bowling trophies as he did in his accomplishments on the baseball field. By the early 1940s, when Kid was past 70, he still worked 15 hours a day at the bowling emporium, overseeing 34 lanes and the billiards room.

Kid enjoyed giving interviews to newspaper reporters, and like most old ballplayers he thought the players of his era were superior to those of the present. "If a pitcher wins fifteen games a year," stated Kid in the early 1950s, "he is considered great. We used to work forty or fifty games a season and pitch every other day. If we got a kink in the arm, we just kept on pitching until we worked it out. Nowadays they rush a pitcher off to the hospital." Nichols, who rarely threw anything but a fastball and a change-up, also criticized modern hurlers for throwing too many pitches. "These young pitchers try too much fancy stuff and ruin their arms. I pitched with a straight overarm motion and never had much trouble."[14]

He started slowing down as he passed the age of 75. He gave up golf and bowling, but turned his energies to singing with barbershop quartets and following the exploits of his children, grandchildren, nephews, and nieces. Jane Nichols died in 1933, and Kid moved in with his daughter Alice, who married a Kansas City doctor. The old pitcher remained active and involved in a wide range of interests. He always answered to the name "Kid," despite his advanced age. "Everybody calls me Kid," he once said. "Probably wouldn't answer if they said Mr. Nichols or Charles."[15]

Nichols lived for four years after his long-awaited induction to the Hall of Fame. His final illness, which began as a neck ailment, struck him in 1952 and confined him to bed for the last year of his life. He died in Kansas City on April 11, 1953, at the age of 83.

Kid Nichols and Cy Young both began their major league careers in 1890, though Young was two years older than Nichols. Both men quickly zoomed to the forefront of National League pitching stars, and they became the two winningest pitchers of the 1890s. Young is baseball's all-time win leader with 511 victories, but Nichols, in the first ten years of their parallel careers, outpaced Young in nearly every category. He won 30 more games than Young, with eight more shutouts and a higher winning percentage:

	Wins–Losses	+/–	Percent	Shutouts	Pennants
Young, 1890–1899	266–151	+115	.639	28	0
Nichols, 1890–1899	296–148	+148	.667	36	5

At the dawn of the 20th century, Kid remained with a failing Boston team, while Young jumped to the American League and posted two more 30-win seasons. From 1900 on, the careers of Nichols and Young diverged sharply:

	Wins–Losses	+/–	Percent	Shutouts	Pennants
Young, 1900–1911	245–164	+81	.599	48	2
Nichols, 1900–1906	64–57	+ 7	.529	12	0

The difference in the two pitchers might be explained by their physical attributes. Nichols, at five feet ten inches and 175 pounds, faded as he passed the age of 30, though his two-year absence from the major leagues in 1902 and 1903 also depressed his final statistics. Cy Young, who stood six feet tall and weighed over 200 pounds, was probably the most durable pitcher of all time. Young was a remarkable physical specimen who won 19 games in 1909 at age 42 and continued pitching until he passed his 44th birthday.

Young arrived in Boston (with the Pilgrims, later called the Red Sox) in 1901, which was also Nichols' last season with the Beaneaters in the same city. As Young's exploits filled the Boston newspapers, it appears that the local sportswriters forgot all about Nichols. As a result, Nichols' legacy suffered in comparison to that of Young, which might explain why the Hall of Fame electors of the 1930s and 1940s paid almost no attention to Nichols. The Kid spent his remaining years in Kansas City, out of the major league spotlight, while many other old players who retired in the eastern half of the country drew more notice in the newspapers.

Still, one wonders how the Permanent Committee, in 1945 and 1946, managed to reject the candidacy of Nichols while selecting several other clearly inferior players. Not only was Kid Nichols one of baseball's premier pitchers, he was also one of the greatest forgotten stars of the 19th century.

7

◆ BOBBY WALLACE ◆

When Bobby Wallace was elected to the Hall of Fame in 1953, a lot of people asked who-in-hell he was. More than thirty-five years later, when fans file past his plaque in Cooperstown, most of them ask the same question. — John Thorn and Pete Palmer, *Total Baseball*[1]

In 1953, the directors of the Baseball Hall of Fame divided the Permanent Committee into two new bodies, the Board of Trustees and the Committee on Veterans. The Board of Trustees was charged with making policy for the Hall, while the task of electing players and executives from past generations became the province of the Committee on Veterans. This committee, which has since been popularly called the Veterans Committee, was formed with 11 members, including sportswriters, executives, and ex-players, along with Hall of Fame treasurer Paul Kerr.

The previous panel had not chosen any new members in four years. It rectified two glaring omissions in 1949 by inducting pitchers Kid Nichols and Mordecai (Three-Finger) Brown, overlooked in the 1945-46 balloting, and the new Veterans Committee also was asked to identify other stars of the past that the Hall had overlooked in the 1940s.

Given this mandate, the Veterans Committee approached the task with enthusiasm. On September 28, 1953, the members met in the New York office of Commissioner Ford Frick. When the meeting adjourned after less than one hour, the panel announced that it had unanimously elected six new Hall of Famers, including (for the first time) two umpires, Bill Klem and Tommy Connolly, one from each league. The Committee also honored Harry Wright, the first baseball manager, and the recently retired manager and executive Ed Barrow. Two players rounded out the list; they were Charles (Chief) Bender, the pitching star of the Philadelphia Athletics from 1903 to 1914, and Bobby Wallace, who played most of his career at shortstop for the St. Louis Browns in the early part of the 20th century.

The committee, faced with a large number of qualified old-time candidates, had taken a poll of its members through the mail in the weeks prior to the meeting. Of the 37 names on the ballot, Chief Bender was the only one to gain more than one first-place vote. He was the top choice of six of the 11 committee members, and the committee quickly moved to elect Bender unanimously to the Hall of Fame.

Discussions on the second old-timer inductee centered on Bobby Wallace and Billy Hamilton, the speedy leadoff man in the 1890s for the Boston Beaneaters. Both men were considered to be qualified, but Hamilton had died in 1940, while Wallace was still living. In addition, Branch Rickey, Wallace's long-ago manager with the St. Louis Browns, was the dominating personality on the new Veterans Committee. Rickey strongly supported Wallace's nomination, and after much discussion the committee took another vote. Wallace's name appeared in first place on 10 of the 11 ballots (with Hamilton gaining the other top vote) and Wallace was, like Bender, elected unanimously to the Hall.

The fact that Wallace was a shortstop may have assisted his candidacy. At the time of his election, there were only four shortstops in the Hall of Fame. Honus Wagner was among the first five men honored in 1936, while George Wright was elected in 1937 and Hugh Jennings and Joe Tinker gained the honor in 1945-46. None of these men earned their stardom in the American League. The committee appears to have decided that, since there was no American League shortstop in the Hall of Fame, someone needed to be elected. Wallace, who held the league record for games played and chances accepted at the position, was the obvious choice.

Commissioner Ford Frick expressed pleasure at the election of Bobby Wallace. "I am sure glad they picked Wallace," said Frick to *The Sporting News*. For a while it looked as if his card was hidden in the old-timers' deck, and I am pleased that the new committee dug it up and gave Bobby the recognition he so deserves."[2] Other baseball men and newspaper writers, many of whom felt that the Permanent Committee had unjustly overlooked Wallace in the 1940s, echoed Frick's sentiments in the next few weeks.

Wallace's election met with public approval because he was still alive and active in baseball as a part-time scout for the Cincinnati Reds in 1953, and also because he was a highly popular figure in St. Louis. Though his batting average topped .300 only three times in his 25-year career, Wallace became the first American League shortstop to enter the Hall. On August 9, 1954, Wallace's plaque was unveiled at the annual ceremony in Cooperstown, though the 80-year-old ex-ballplayer was too ill to attend.

The two greatest shortstops of the early 20th century grew up only a few miles from each other in the Pennsylvania coal country. Honus Wagner was born in Mansfield (now called Carnegie) in 1874, while Roderick John Wallace entered the world in Pittsburgh on November 4, 1873. The future shortstop was the third child of John Wallace, an immigrant from Scotland who worked as a store clerk, and Mary, the daughter of German immigrants from Saxony.

Roderick, called Roddy as a young man, was nicknamed the "Little Highlander" for good reason. As an adult he stood only five feet and eight inches tall, and never weighed more than 170 pounds in all the years that he played baseball. He grew up in the town of Millvale, just outside Pittsburgh, where he worked in his brother-in-law's feed store and played semi-pro ball whenever he could find the opportunity.

Roddy Wallace was a skilled ballplayer, one of those athletes who excelled wherever he played on the field. He played all infield and outfield positions, though he gained the most attention as a pitcher. In 1893 Wallace was offered $25 and carfare to pitch a game for a team in Clarion, Pennsylvania, against their bitter rivals from nearby Franklin. "I believe," said Wallace, "after getting that offer I set an all-time record for the suddenness in which I stopped lifting horse and chicken feed."[3] Roddy performed well, though many years later he could not recall if he won the game or not, and in 1894 the Franklin nine offered him $45 a month to pitch for them on a regular basis. He pitched for Franklin until the team ran out of money to pay its players and folded in mid-season.

Roddy dreamed of playing for his hometown Pittsburgh Pirates, and attended a tryout at the Pittsburgh ballpark in early September 1894. However, the new Pirate manager, Connie Mack, told Wallace that he was too small to pitch in the major leagues. John Stovick, who caught Wallace for the Clarion team, disagreed with Mack's assessment and wrote a letter of recommendation to Cleveland Spiders manager Patsy Tebeau. Tebeau had not scouted Wallace personally, but he trusted Stovick's judgment. The Spiders, in desperate need of pitching help, immediately summoned the 20-year-old Wallace to the National League.

When Wallace reported to Cleveland on September 13, 1894, Tebeau declared that "Roddy" was no name for a ballplayer. From that day on, at Tebeau's insistence, the young Scotsman was known as Bobby Wallace. "Since then," remarked Wallace many years later, "I've always regarded all Fridays the 13th as my lucky days."[4]

Cleveland's new pitcher was canny enough to shave a year off his age when he signed his contract. He told the Spiders that he was born in 1874, not 1873, knowing that he might be able to buy himself an extra year in

Bobby Wallace. (National Baseball Hall of Fame Library, Cooperstown, New York)

which to prove himself, and as a result some reference books still list his year of birth as 1874.[5] He lost his first game to the Boston team by a 7–2 score, giving up 14 hits in six innings, but broke into the win column against the Phillies a week later. Bobby pitched in four games for the Spiders in September of 1894, compiling a 2–1 record and earning an invitation to 1895 spring training.

The Spiders relied on two outstanding pitchers, Cy Young and George (Nig) Cuppy, to carry the lion's share of the pitching load. Bobby, with a fine performance in spring training, earned the third spot in the rotation. His job was to keep his team in the game every third or fourth day, and the Spiders hoped that Wallace would win about half of his starts while saving the heavy lifting for Young and Cuppy. Bobby performed well, going 12–13 on the mound with 21 complete games in 27 starts in 1895. Young posted a 35–10 log, while Cuppy went 25–14 as Cleveland battled the Baltimore Orioles for first place all season long. The Orioles won the pennant by three games, but Cleveland finished in second place and defeated the Orioles in the post-season Temple Cup series.

Wallace enjoyed particular success against the Brooklyn Dodgers. From May 22 to September 4, Bobby pitched against the Dodgers six times and won all six games, including a two-hitter and a three-hitter. The Dodgers finally defeated Bobby on September 6, though the Little Highlander allowed only four hits in a 2–1 loss. Problem was, Bobby could not pitch against Brooklyn every day. He posted a 6–1 mark against the Dodgers and a 6–12 record against the rest of the National League. Though Bobby received a full share of $528.33 from the Temple Cup series, he did not pitch in any of the post-season games.

Bobby held down the end of the rotation, but was hampered by his inability to keep the ball up in the strike zone, which in the 1890s went all the way to the top of the batter's shoulders. Power pitchers like Cy Young and Amos Rusie threw shoulder-high fastballs past a lot of batters, but low-ball hitters found Bobby's deliveries easy to hit. "I had one weakness that cost me many a game," said Bobby a few years later. "I pitched too many low balls, and the more I tried to break myself of the habit the worse I seemed to get. In practice I managed to hoist my low ball to a point opposite the shoulder, but in a game I couldn't elevate the low one even if I had a derrick."[6]

Wallace improved to a 10–7 record in 1896 with two shutouts as the Spiders finished in second place behind the Orioles once more. The two teams battled once again in the Temple Cup, but this time the Orioles swept Cleveland four games to none. Bobby pitched the second game of the series, losing by a 7–2 score. During the 1896 season, Tebeau began to recognize that the Little Highlander's future lay elsewhere on the ball field. Accordingly, Tebeau played Bobby in the outfield and at first base, in addition to his 22 pitching assignments that season.

Cleveland finished second again, but the gap between the Spiders and the Orioles widened to nine games. Third baseman Chippy McGarr was aging, and shortstop Ed McKean had added about 20 pounds to his frame in the previous two years and could no longer cover much ground. Tebeau recognized that his infield needed an infusion of youth and athleticism, so he proposed to play Bobby Wallace at third base. Tebeau had two new pitchers, righthanders Zeke Wilson and Jack Powell, ready to compete for Wallace's spot in the rotation, so before the team's season opener against Louisville Tebeau told Wallace, "You're on third." McKean's range had decreased with each passing season, so Tebeau told his new third baseman, "Get everything you can!"

Bobby heartily endorsed the move. "I'm glad that Tebeau will keep me on third," remarked Wallace to the papers, "as I hated to pitch. When I was an amateur, I played in the infield and pitched. Though I was signed by Tebeau to help out with the pitching, every pitcher who can practice fielding ought to try it."[7] Wallace was an immediate success at third, so much so that by June the Spiders released McGarr. Wallace never pitched in the major leagues again, save for a two-inning stint in the 1902 season, and the Brooklyn papers reported that the Dodger fans rejoiced when Bobby Wallace moved from the pitcher's mound to the infield.

In 1897, most of the spotlight in Cleveland shone on an exciting rookie named Louis Sockalexis. A Penobscot Indian, Sockalexis was one of the nation's leading college athletes at Holy Cross in 1895 and 1896, and the Cleveland team had been following his progress. Tebeau journeyed to Notre Dame, where Sockalexis had enrolled in the winter of 1896-97, and signed the college man to play right field for the Spiders. So popular and impressive was this Native American athlete that the papers started calling the Cleveland team the "Indians" soon after his arrival. Sockalexis batted nearly .350 in the first two months of the 1897 campaign, and though Bobby Wallace belted National League pitching at a .380 clip in the early going, the charismatic Sockalexis garnered most of the headlines.

Cleveland's season collapsed in July 1897, when Sockalexis was suspended for drunkenness, leaving a gaping hole in the outfield and the batting order. Cy Young was inconsistent all year, Nig Cuppy's arm problems returned, and injuries mounted in the heat of the summer. The Spiders-turned-Indians fell to fifth place in the standings, and it took a 12-game winning streak in September for the club to climb that high. However, Bobby Wallace became a full-fledged star in 1897. He batted .339 and led the team in triples with 20 and in home runs with four. No one counted runs batted in at the time, but researchers found, many years after the fact, that Bobby also led the team in RBI with 112. On July 14, he belted a grand slam homer, the only one of his career, during an 18–2 trouncing of Boston.

He also became, almost by default, the second-best third baseman in the National League behind Boston's veteran Jimmy Collins. There was much more bunting in the 1890s than there is today, since small, fast players like Bobby's teammate Jesse Burkett fattened their averages by dropping bunts. Collins perfected the art of dashing in, fielding the ball, and throwing accurately to first all in one motion. Wallace, with his quickness and strong arm, and Collins were the only third basemen in the league skilled enough to perform that play.

Wallace helped Cy Young gain credit for his first no-hitter, which Young threw on September 18, 1897, against the Cincinnati Reds. In the sixth inning, Bobby stopped a hot grounder, but was unable to pick it up and throw the runner out in time. "It looked like a hit off me more than it did an error for Bobby," remarked Young later, "but [Wallace] sent a note to the scorer's box begging to be given an error in order to allow me a no-hit game ... I've never forgiven him for that, but it was only one instance of the good fellowship prevailing in the old Cleveland club."[8]

Bobby was now one of the brightest young stars in the game, but he almost lost that distinction early in the next campaign. On May 7, 1898, a pitch thrown by Chick Fraser of Louisville hit Bobby in the head, knocking him unconscious. He was still unresponsive when his teammates loaded him onto a stretcher and rushed him to a Cleveland hospital, fearing that his skull had been fractured. Fortunately, he recovered and returned to the lineup four days later, swatting a double and a single in three trips to the plate.

He finished the year with a .269 average, but off-the-field concerns caused almost all the Cleveland players to put together worse statistics that they had compiled in 1897. The Spiders were not allowed to play in Cleveland on Sundays, making it virtually impossible for the team to turn a profit at home. Twice — once in 1897 and again in 1898 — all the members of the Spiders, including Bobby Wallace, were arrested when Cleveland team owner Frank Robison attempted to defy the law and play on the Christian Sabbath. After the team's second unsuccessful attempt to play Sunday games, Robison angrily moved almost all the rest of Cleveland's home games to other cities. The Spiders played the last three months of the 1898 season almost exclusively on the road, and the never-ending road trip plunged the Cleveland club, in second place in May, down to a fifth-place finish once again.

As the Spiders reported to Hot Springs, Arkansas, for 1899 spring training, rumors hit the papers that Robison would move his team out of Cleveland. In late March, the rumors became fact. Robison bought the near-bankrupt St. Louis Browns and moved all the best Cleveland players, including Bobby Wallace, Ed McKean, Cy Young, manager Patsy Tebeau, and all the other Cleveland stars, to St. Louis. This move marked the beginning of Wallace's long association with St. Louis baseball.

The new Browns, renamed the Perfectos by the newspapers, finished a disappointing sixth in the twelve-team league, but Wallace's star continued to rise. He batted .302, drove in 108 runs, and finished second in the league in home runs with 12. On June 6, 1899, ex–Spider Ed McKean finally reached the end of the line at shortstop, and Patsy Tebeau moved Bobby over to take McKean's place. "We were in Philadelphia when Manager Pat shifted me from third to short," recalled Wallace, "and right off the bat I knew I had found my dish."[9] In his sixth major league season, Bobby settled into the position that he would play for the rest of his career.

The Perfectos became the Cardinals in 1900, and when the National League disbanded its four least profitable teams (Washington, Cleveland, Baltimore, and Louisville) the Cardinals bought the contracts of former Oriole stars John McGraw and Wilbert Robinson. This made the St. Louis team perhaps the most talented in the league, but infighting between the ex–Spiders and their old enemies from Baltimore poisoned team chemistry and doomed the Cardinals to a sixth place finish, despite Bobby's emergence as one of the brightest young stars in the game. His batting average dipped to .272 in 1900, but his fielding made him the premier shortstop in baseball.[10]

It was inevitable that the new American League would cast its eyes in Wallace's direction, and in the spring of 1901 Bobby signed a contract to play in the new league, accepting a dollar as "consideration." However, Bobby soon found out that many players were receiving more money than he was. "I quickly sent back the contract and the dollar bill to my good friends, omitting my regards,"[11] said Wallace years later. He returned to the Cardinals in 1901 after McGraw and Robinson jumped to the new league and gave the

St. Louis club a more pleasant atmosphere in which to play. The Cardinals jumped two notches to fourth place that year as Bobby put together his best season since his rookie year, batting .322 with 91 runs batted in.

At the end of the 1901 campaign, the American League was ready to offer Wallace the money he thought he deserved, especially after the new league moved its Milwaukee club to St. Louis for the 1902 season. Agents of the new circuit made offers to Bobby and several other Cardinal stars, and on October 20, 1901, Bobby and six other Cardinals signed contracts with the new St. Louis Browns of the American League. The Cardinals challenged the signing in court, but failed to stop the seven players from jumping to the new league. Bobby, who signed a $32,000 five-year deal with a $6,500 advance, became the highest-paid player in the major leagues.

Though Bobby never batted .300 again after 1901, he was widely recognized as the best fielding shortstop in the American League, and if there had been an annual All-Star game then, Bobby would have been the league's starting shortstop for many years. His quickness gave him more range than any other shortstop in the league, and his strong arm enabled him to throw out batters from deep in the hole. The Browns recognized his value, for although Bobby usually hit somewhere between .250 and .270 in those seasons, he was the highest-paid major league player until about 1910, when Detroit's Ty Cobb passed Wallace on the salary list.

His reputation as the premier shortstop in his league was partly due to the fact that he had no real competition for the honor. The only Hall of Famer (besides Bobby) who played as a regular American League shortstop in that period was Chicago's George Davis, who was three years older and on the downside of his career for most of the decade. The pennant-winning teams of the 1903–1910 period featured shortstops such as Boston's Freddy Parent, Philadelphia's Monte Cross and Detroit's Charley O'Leary, all of whom are almost completely forgotten today. Bobby hit as well as any of his shortstop contemporaries and fielded better than all of them.

Bobby was a master of the scoop-and-toss method of fielding a slow ground ball. He played a slow roller much like a third baseman played a bunt. "I noticed the many infield bounders which the runner beat to first by the thinnest fractions of a second," related Wallace after his retirement from the game. "I also noted that the old-time three-phase movement, (1) fielding a ball, (2) coming erect for a toss, and (3) throwing to first wouldn't do on certain hits." Bobby, with the strong arm of an ex-pitcher, combined the three movements into one smooth process. His outstanding range allowed him to field balls in short left field or behind second base with no time to plant and throw; in such cases, said Wallace, "you had to learn to throw from the ankle and off either foot as well."[12]

One of Bobby's best-remembered fielding plays knocked Cleveland out of the 1908 pennant chase. Cleveland and St. Louis were tied in the next-to-last game of the season when the Naps, who needed to win both games against the Browns, rallied in the ninth inning. They put the potential go-ahead run on third with two out when Harry Hinchman belted a sharp grounder past the mound. Bobby caught up to the ball past second base and, still running at top speed toward right field, arched a throw to first to nip the runner and retire the side. The Browns won the game in extra innings and ended Cleveland's pennant chances.

On a personal note, Bobby waited until he was well established in the American League before settling down. On August 9, 1906, the 31-year-old shortstop married June Mann, an 18-year-old from Chicago. Roy Hartzell, who played third base next to Wallace in the St. Louis infield, served as best man. The couple stayed together for 13 years until the marriage ended in divorce, according to a letter on file at the Baseball Hall of Fame. They had no children, and neither Bobby nor June ever married again.

Bobby was popular with the fans and respected by his peers as well. Though he learned the major league ropes with the battling Cleveland Spiders, he was a friendly ballplayer with a kind word for everybody. He even refused to criticize Ty Cobb when the Detroit star slid into Bobby one day with spikes high and cut a gash in the shortstop's forehead. The press asked Bobby, years later, if the play caused hard feelings. "Nonsense," replied Wallace. "Ty had every right to slide as he did. It was up to me to protect myself in the clinches." Wallace was one of Cobb's "warmest admirers," he said. "I won't say, however, that some of the boys, including Jimmy McAleer [his first manager with the Browns] felt the same."[13]

He was also cooperative with the press. Both the Cardinals and the Browns struggled in the standings in the first decade of the 20th century, which made Bobby Wallace the biggest star in a town with two poor teams. As a result, the writers found themselves writing about Bobby more than any other player, and the Little Highlander established lasting friendships with many members of the St. Louis press corps. One of Bobby's biggest boosters, St. Louis sportswriter John B. Sheridan, gave Wallace the title "Sir Rhoderick," adding an extra H to his name for emphasis, and to this day one sees the ballplayer identified as "Rhoderick" or "Rhoddy" Wallace.

Wallace reigned as the American League's "King of Shortstops," though his hitting statistics suffered during the depths of the deadball era. He never hit above .258 in any full season after 1905, and his lifetime batting average fell all the way from its peak of .293 in 1902 to .267 by the end of his career. Still, baseball insiders considered him to be one of the most valuable properties in the game. Barney Dreyfuss, owner of the Pitts-

Browns manager Bobby Wallace (center) with catchers Paul Krichell (left) and Jim Stephens in 1911. (Library of Congress)

burgh Pirates, paid tribute to Wallace in 1911 when he said, "The best player in the American League, the only man I would get if I could, plays on a tail-end team, and few people pay any attention to him. I mean Bobby Wallace of St. Louis. I wish I had him."[14] Wallace had batted only .258 in 1910, but he was still the outstanding shortstop in the circuit.

There was no official annual All-Star game then, but informal aggregations of stars played together for benefit games and on other special occasions, and the organizers of such events invariably put the Little Highlander on the team. In 1908 and again in 1909, the American League champion Detroit Tigers played a team made up of the stars of the league's other seven teams in a tune-up match before the start of the World Series in October. Wallace, despite his advancing age, was the consensus choice at shortstop. When the Cleveland Naps organized a benefit game in 1911 to raise money for the family of pitcher Addie Joss, who died in April of that year, the 37-year-old Bobby Wallace was one of the first players chosen for the All-Star team.

The Browns, managed by Bobby's old Cleveland teammate Jimmy McAleer, bounced up and down the standings in Bobby's first few years in St. Louis. The Browns finished a strong second in 1902, but dropped to sixth in the next two seasons and fell to last place by 1905. They worked their way back up to fourth in 1908, but dipped to seventh again in 1909, after which another ex–Cleveland Spider, Jack O'Connor, replaced McAleer. O'Connor, who grew up in St. Louis, had been Patsy Tebeau's right-hand man with the Cleveland Spiders many years before.

O'Connor failed to ignite the Browns, who not only finished in last place but managed to embarrass the entire league on the last day of the season. Cleveland's Nap Lajoie and Detroit's Ty Cobb were locked in a battle for the batting title, with Lajoie closing the season against the Browns in St. Louis. To keep the hated Cobb from winning the title, O'Connor ordered his third baseman, rookie Red Corriden, to play halfway into the outfield when Lajoie came to bat. Lajoie dropped down seven bunts for hits in the season-ending doubleheader. He also reached base on a throwing error by Bobby Wallace, after which a Browns coach offered the official scorer a new suit of clothes to change his ruling to a hit.

Robert Hedges, owner of the Browns, and American League president Ban Johnson fumed over O'Connor's shenanigans, although the official league statistics eventually gave Cobb the batting title by a tiny margin over Lajoie. After the Lajoie debacle, the Browns fired O'Connor and, on January 14, 1911, appointed Bobby Wallace as new manager of the Browns. "I never had the slightest desire to be a major league manager and all knew it," related Wallace many years later, "but Ban Johnson, Bob Hedges, and Jimmy McAleer, then with Washington, persuaded me that the Browns were in sort of a jam and it was up to me, as an old standby, to do what I could."[15]

Bobby asked the St. Louis fans for patience, telling *Baseball Magazine* that "you must not ask me to work miracles overnight," but his rookie managerial campaign was a disaster. The talent-starved Browns finished in last place, 56 and a half games behind the pennant-winning A's and 18 games behind the seventh-place Senators. When the Browns started 1912 poorly as well, the team management relieved Bobby of command and replaced him with former Cleveland skipper George Stovall, though Wallace remained at shortstop.

Wallace was not a successful manager, but at least he didn't do anything to embarrass the team, unlike both his predecessor and his successor. Stovall, like O'Connor a fiery sort, expectorated himself out of his job in 1913 when he spit tobacco juice in the face of umpire George Ferguson. The entire league recoiled in disgust at Stovall's outburst, so the Browns fired Stovall and appointed third baseman Jimmy Austin as manager. Through all the turmoil of the early 1910s, the Browns finished regularly in the second division, drawing fewer fans than the cross-town Cardinals of the National League.

After 1912, Bobby was a part-time player. He turned 40 in November 1913, and although he batted only .211 in 1913, his fielding and popularity with the fans kept him on the ballclub. He missed part of the 1912 season with a broken hand, playing in 99 games that year and 52 in 1913. Branch Rickey, the new manager of the Browns, expected Wallace to come back strong in 1914 —"Wallace has got a great deal of good baseball still in his

Wallace on a felt collectible issued by a consortium of cigarette companies in 1914. More than 90 players were profiled on these felt squares. (Author's collection)

possession," said Rickey in January 1914 — but Bobby suffered severe burns in a fire at his home that season and managed to participate in only 26 games.

Bobby recovered from his injuries and returned to the Browns in 1915, but left the team in May to take a position as a substitute umpire for the American League. He soon found out that life as an umpire was not for him. "I will confess that the players bothered me," remarked Wallace. "I had been a player myself so recently that I could easily get the viewpoint of the fellows.... It is a tough job, and I held it hardly long enough to get used to the care and worry."[16] The league released him in August 1916, and Bobby returned to the Browns, playing in 14 games, mostly as a defensive replacement. At age 42, Wallace was the oldest active player in the major leagues.

With his playing career at a standstill, Bobby signed on as manager of the Wichita Witches of the Western League in 1917. His tenure there didn't last long; after a rocky start, the team released Bobby in June of that year. His former Browns manager, Branch Rickey, who had left the Browns and joined the crosstown Cardinals, then signed Bobby as a coach and part-time shortstop. Bobby had jumped from the Cardinals to the Browns 16 years before. He played for parts of two seasons for the Cardinals, batting .100 in 1917 and .153 in the war-shortened 1918 campaign. Wallace played his last game on September 2, 1918, and then hung up his glove after a record 25 seasons as an active player.

He tried managing again a few years later, piloting the Muskogee team of the Southwestern League in 1921, and though his team finished in second place, Bobby did not return for the 1922 campaign. He remained in baseball, scouting for the Chicago Cubs, coaching one season for the Cincinnati Reds in 1926, and then joined the scouting staff of the Reds. He served as a scout for the Reds for the next 30 years, interrupted only in September 1937 when Bobby took over the Cincinnati manager's job on an interim basis after team management fired Charlie Dressen. The woeful Reds occupied last place when Bobby took over, and they won only five of their 25 games under Wallace's management. Bobby's managerial career was not as successful as his playing career; his 62–154 record is the worst in history of anyone who managed more than 100 major league games.

He invested his money well, and many reports say that Bobby Wallace was one of the wealthiest of all ex-ballplayers. In the 1940s Bobby moved to Redondo Beach, California, where he scouted prospects on the West Coast and enjoyed a long semi-retirement. A two-part article in *The Sporting News* in early 1954 showed the 80-year-old Wallace playing golf, fishing, building model ships, and generally enjoying himself in his golden years. The Cincinnati Reds listed him as their "chief of scouting" long after he had ceased to play an active role in the organization.

Bobby lived long enough to see major league ball come to his adopted home state in 1958, when the Dodgers and Giants took up residence in Los Angeles and San Francisco respectively. He enjoyed a comfortable life long into old age until his health began to deteriorate in the late 1950s. The Little Highlander died in a convalescent home in Torrance, California on November 3, 1960, one day short of his 88th birthday.

Bill James has commented that Bobby Wallace's presence in the Hall of Fame is "one of the game's little mysteries," and that Bobby is "probably the most faceless member of the Hall of Fame as far as the public is concerned."[17] That's too bad, because Wallace was the top shortstop in the American League in the first quarter of the 20th century. His hitting statistics do not stack up well against those of later shortstops such as Joe Cronin or Luke Appling, but Bobby played in the depths of the dead-ball era. His .267 lifetime average would certainly have been much higher if he had played twenty years earlier, or twenty years later.

Bobby played most of his career for a poor St. Louis Browns team, far from the media spotlight of the East Coast. Still, he was almost always named as the shortstop on the unofficial all-star teams in the newspapers every year for more than a decade. He was the highest-paid player of his time, reflecting the value that his bosses believed that he possessed, and his fielding prowess set the standard for all American League shortstops that followed him. Though Bobby Wallace is largely forgotten today, his election to the Hall of Fame in 1953 was a fitting honor for one of baseball's early stars.

8

♦ JOHN CLARKSON ♦

[John] Clarkson, I believe, was the game's greatest pitcher. He had terrific speed, [a] greater curve than Mathewson, and his control was perfect. Clarkson, of course, didn't use as much change of pace, but he was a tricky old fox at that. Clean, natty, well groomed, well educated, he was a credit to the game, at home in any parlor or at any banquet table. — Billy Sunday, 1909[1]

Early Wynn was a stocky righthanded pitcher who began his career with the Washington Senators as a teenager in 1939. After a rocky apprenticeship with the Senators, he joined the Cleveland Indians in 1949 and became one of the American League's most consistent winners. He won 20 or more games in a season four times for Cleveland, and then put together his best performance for the Chicago White Sox in 1959. He won 22 games that year, leading the Sox to the pennant and winning the Cy Young Award as baseball's best pitcher.

Wynn posted a 13–12 mark in 1960, giving him a total of 284 career wins and virtually assuring that he would soon join the exclusive 300-win club. Unfortunately for Wynn, injuries and advancing age limited him to eight wins in 1961. In 1962, the 42-year-old pitcher won only seven games while losing 15, giving him a career won–lost record of 299–242. The White Sox released Wynn in November of 1962, and it appeared that his major league career might end only one win short of the magic 300 mark.

At the time, there were 13 members of the 300-win club, but only eight of those 13 pitchers had gained election to the Baseball Hall of Fame. The newest addition to the club, Warren Spahn, was not eligible because he was still an active player, and the other four non-electees were nineteenth-century stars John Clarkson, Mickey Welch, Tim Keefe, and Pud Galvin.

Wynn's quest for his 300th win occupied the newspapers through much of the winter of 1962-63, and articles about the 300-win club appeared in many sports columns in those months. It also focused new attention on the lesser-known 300-game winners from the 19th century, and many observers wondered in print why Clarkson, Keefe, Welch, and Galvin had not yet been elected to the Cooperstown museum.

The Veterans Committee noticed the publicity for those four long-forgotten pitchers. On January 27, 1963, the committee elected John Clarkson, who had been dead for 54 years, to the Hall of Fame. On August 6 of that year, Frederick H. Clarkson Jr., a businessman from Meriden, Connecticut, accepted his uncle's plaque at the ceremony in Cooperstown.

In the next few years, the remaining 300-game winners took their place in the museum one by one. Keefe gained the honor in 1964 and Galvin in 1965, while Welch waited until 1973 for his enshrinement. Today, all eligible 300-game winners (including Wynn, who won one more game for Cleveland in 1963) are represented in Cooperstown, and a pitcher who wins 300 games is almost automatically guaranteed election to the Hall.

John Gibson Clarkson was born on July 1, 1861, in Cambridge, Massachusetts, the oldest of five baseball-playing brothers. John's father Thomas was a Scottish immigrant who built a successful jewelry business, and the Clarkson family was one of the most prosperous in Cambridge, home of Harvard University. John was a handsome and intense young man who stood five feet and ten inches tall and weighed about 160 pounds. He had dark, deeply set eyes and long fingers that enabled him to throw sharp-breaking curveballs, which he practiced by the hour. In 1878, John earned a spot on his high school team at Webster School in Cambridge as a catcher, but he moved to the mound later that season.

Most players at the time were poor and hungry young men who worked their way up through the ranks of semipro ball, but John Clarkson took a different route. While learning the jewelry-making trade from his father[2] and attending Comer's Business School in Cambridge, John played for a gentlemanly amateur team, the Beacon nine, for two years beginning in 1880. Young Clarkson was one of the best hitters on the team, but his baffling curveball made him a star in the amateur ranks. John, already looking forward to a professional career, sought and received pitching tips from Tommy Bond, star hurler for the National League's Boston Red Stockings, who coached the pitchers at nearby Harvard University in his spare time.

Soon, John Clarkson's name was known throughout the state of Massachusetts, and in May 1882, he joined the Worcester Ruby Legs of the National League, skipping over the minor leagues entirely. John wasn't ready for such a jump, but perhaps the Worcester team signed the well-known local pitcher as a gate attraction, since the ballclub found it difficult to attract more than a hundred fans per game. The franchise was losing money, and later that season the Ruby Legs played to "crowds" of six and 18 people.

Predictably, National League competition proved to be much faster than John had found in the amateur leagues in Boston. John pitched in three games for Worcester, winning only one and giving up 51 hits in only 24 innings. Within two weeks he came down with a sore arm, and the Ruby Legs released him. Apparently John would need to play in the minor leagues after all. He refused to be rushed back into action; instead, he rested his arm for the rest of the 1882 season.

He joined the Saginaw, Michigan, entry in the Northwestern League in 1883, and there John Clarkson learned to be a pitcher. They didn't keep pitching statistics in the Northwestern League that year, but Clarkson starred on the mound and batted .305 as an outfielder on days that he didn't pitch. In 1884 John returned to Saginaw and dominated the league with his tricky curveball. He struck out 19, 16, 8, 16, and 14 batters in five successive games from June 30 to July 14, and when the Saginaw team disbanded in mid–August John Clarkson owned a phenomenal won–lost record of 34–9.[3]

John, now a free agent, did not stay out of work for long. The Boston and Cincinnati teams made offers for his services, but Cap Anson, first baseman and manager of the Chicago White Stockings of the National League, signed John and brought him to Chicago. The White Stockings, fighting for the pennant, pitched the 23-year-old Clarkson in a regular turn for the last six weeks of the 1884 season. John pitched in 14 games, completing 12 and compiling a 10–4 record for the White Stockings. He also proved his versatility, playing eight games in the outfield, two at third base, and one at first, batting .262 with three homers and 17 runs batted in.

Larry Corcoran was Chicago's main pitcher, and at the age of 24 Corcoran had already won 170 games and thrown three no-hitters. Corcoran was the mainstay of the team that won three consecutive National League pennants from 1880 to 1882, and he compiled a 35–23 record in 1884. However, second-string starter Fred Goldsmith fell to a 9–11 mark, and the team's lack of capable starting pitchers other than Corcoran doomed the ballclub to a disappointing fifth-place finish. Anson auditioned several other young hurlers late in the 1884 campaign, but Clarkson made the best impression upon the manager, and so Clarkson replaced Goldsmith as the number two starter for the White Stockings.

The 1885 campaign started with high hopes for a pennant in Chicago, but disaster struck in the first few weeks of the season when Corcoran's arm became sore. He won five of the seven games he pitched, but when his arm showed no improvement, Anson unceremoniously released him and promoted John Clarkson to the number one position on the Chicago pitching staff. Anson had no choice but to place the team's pennant chances on the shoulders of a young man playing his first full major league season.

Clarkson rose to the challenge. He started 70 of Chicago's 113 games, completed 68 of them, and put together an astonishing 53–16 record. Clarkson led the National League in starts, innings pitched (an amazing 623), complete games, wins, strikeouts (318) and shutouts (10). In late May, Clarkson threw three shutouts in five days, and topped off the season with a no-hitter, winning 4–0 against the Providence Grays on July 27. If the league had given a Cy Young Award and a Most Valuable Player trophy in 1885, Clarkson probably would have won both of them unanimously.

Clarkson was not a one-man team. Jim McCormick, the new second-string pitcher, contributed a fine 20–4 record, including a 14-game winning streak, and the Chicago hitters led the league in runs scored, slugging average, doubles, triples, and home runs. Despite all this, the New York Giants, who absorbed the best players from the other New York team, the Metropolitans, and emerged as a strong challenger, pressed the White Stockings to the wire.

The Giants came to Chicago in late September, only two games behind with eight to play. On September 29, McCormick beat Mickey Welch and the Giants by a 7–4 score, and then Clarkson defeated Tim Keefe by a 2–1 count to stretch the Chicago lead to four games. McCormick won again the next day, and although Clarkson lost the last game of the series, 10–8, the Giants were finally vanquished and Chicago clinched the pennant a few days later.

The only down note in a successful 1885 season came in the "World's Series," a best-of-seven post-season matchup against the St. Louis Browns, champions of the American Association. Clarkson pitched the first game in Chicago on October 14, and the White Stockings escaped with a 5–5 tie when the game was called on account of darkness. The Chicagoans won the second game in St. Louis by forfeit when Browns manager Charles Comiskey pulled his team off the field in a dispute with the umpire. Clarkson pitched and lost the next day, evening the series. After the Browns defeated McCormick in game four, Clarkson pitched a 9–2 win in the fifth game, but he could not pitch again in the series, pleading exhaustion. McCormick lost the last two contests and, although the White Stockings and Browns each won three games with one tie, the Browns ignored the second-game forfeit and declared themselves the champions of the world.

Clarkson threw a good fastball, though it was not the fastest in the game. He began his pitching career at a time when hurlers were not allowed to bring the ball above their shoulders, so pitchers were required to throw with a sidearm or underhand motion. Clarkson, a sidearmer, dominated the hitters with his bewildering array of sweeping curveballs. He was able to impart an incredible amount of spin on the ball with his long fingers, and people claimed that he could toss a billiard ball on a table and make it trace a complete circle. Teammate and future evangelist Billy Sunday said that Clarkson "could put more turns and twists into a ball than any pitcher I ever saw."[4]

He also relied on his knowledge of opposing batters, gained by studying the opponents carefully and making mental notes of their weaknesses. He stood on the mound with supreme self-confidence, throwing deliberately and making the batters wait. "John Clarkson never had a superior as a pitcher, and never will," said teammate Fred Pfeffer many years later. "I have stood behind him day after day and watched his magnificent control, as confident of his success, especially in tight places, as if he had the United States Army behind him. He was a master of control and that was his long suit. In addition, he had everything a pitcher ever had in the way of curves, with a thorough knowledge of his opponents."[5]

"He was one man who was a star," said outfielder Jimmy Ryan. "The heaviest batters looked all alike to him. Clarkson was as resourceful and foxy as any pitcher who ever lived, and there have been few to equal, none to surpass him, in later years."[6]

Clarkson, perhaps because of his privileged background, was something of a dandy among major league players of the 1880s. "Clarkson was always a 'tidy' pitcher," stated the *Detroit Free Press*. "His uniform was always immaculate, his linen always possessed that fresh-from-the-laundry touch, he was always smoothly shaven, [and] his manners were always faultless."[7] Some of the opposition players taunted Clarkson when they saw him mop the sweat from his forehead with a neatly pressed, white silk handkerchief that he carried in his uniform pocket. "Hey, you," shouted Pittsburgh's Jake Stenzel one hot day, "put away that society rag and pitch ball!" Clarkson said nothing, but struck out Stenzel on three curveballs.

However, John's personal habits, and those of several of his teammates, caused headaches for manager Anson. John, who married a Cambridge woman named Ella Bar in March of 1886, was one of the many drinking men on the White Stockings. Catcher and batting champion Mike "King" Kelly was the most prodigious drinker on the team, but outfielder George Gore, shortstop Ed Williamson, and second-string starter Jim McCormick also liked their alcohol, a little too much for Anson's taste. The White

Stocking ballclub was so talented that it could win despite the poor condition of many of its stars. In the mid–1880s, team president Albert Spalding invented spring training when he took his players to Hot Springs, Arkansas, to "boil out the alcoholic microbes" in their bloodstreams.[8]

John Clarkson was a loner and a solitary drinker, unlike his hard-partying Chicago teammates, and one would say, if he were playing today, that he was "high maintenance." Clarkson was a quiet and intelligent pitcher, but so moody and sensitive to criticism that people called him "Black Jack" Clarkson. His icy, almost arrogant manner on the mound covered up what appeared to be a large amount of insecurity, and if a teammate or manager Anson offered any criticism of his performance, Clarkson would refuse to pitch for a while. "Many regard him as the greatest [of all Chicago pitchers]," said Cap Anson many years later, "but not many know of his peculiar temperament and the amount of encouragement needed to keep him going. Scold him, find fault with him and he could not pitch at all. Praise him and he was unbeatable."[9]

Clarkson was no roughneck, but he was as competitive as anyone. One day, so the story goes, Clarkson threw a lemon instead of a baseball to the plate to protest the umpire's refusal to call the game on account of approaching darkness. John also wore a large silver belt buckle on his uniform pants one sunny afternoon, in an attempt to reflect the sunlight into the batters' eyes as he pitched. Since he threw the lion's share of innings for the Chicago club, Clarkson sometimes coasted when he held a lead. "He was peculiar in some things," recalled Anson, "...and in order to get his best work you had to keep spurring him along, otherwise he was apt to let up, this being especially the case when the club was ahead and he saw what he thought was a chance to save himself."[10]

Clarkson also possessed a superstitious streak. One day the White Stockings fell two runs behind after six innings, and manager Anson was surprised to see the usually dour Clarkson smiling. "Now, Pop, don't go getting all fussed up about nothing," said Clarkson brightly. "Remember, this is the lucky seventh." Chicago scored three times and took the lead in that seventh inning and won the game. It's forgotten today, but for many years the "lucky seventh" inning was part of baseball lore.[11]

Anson was intelligent enough to recognize that he needed to avoid burning out John Clarkson at a young age, as he had Larry Corcoran. Accordingly, Anson spread out the pitching load more evenly in 1886 among three pitchers. Clarkson started 55 games, 15 fewer than the year before, while McCormick and newcomer Jocko Flynn filled in the rest of the rotation. By season's end, Clarkson owned a 35–17 record, with McCormick at 31–11 and Flynn at 23–6, as Chicago swept to its second consecutive pennant.

Once again, the White Stockings met the St. Louis Browns in a best-of-seven post-season showdown. On October 18, 1886, Clarkson won the first game of the "World's Series" with a 6–0 shutout, but the Browns bombed McCormick 12–0 the next day. Since both McCormick and Flynn came up with painfully sore arms, Clarkson was obliged to pitch the next two games, winning the first and losing the second to tie the series at two games apiece.

Anson could not ask the exhausted Clarkson to pitch a third day in a row, so he put shortstop Ed Williamson on the mound in game five. Williamson didn't make it through the second inning, so Anson sent outfielder Jimmy Ryan in to pitch the rest of the game, which the Browns won by a 10–3 score. Now it was all up to Clarkson.

The sixth game of the series, played at St. Louis on October 23, was one of the greatest games of the 19th century. Clarkson, as dominating as ever, took a 3–0 lead into the bottom of the eighth inning, and it looked as if Anson's men would stay alive for another day. Unfortunately for the White Stockings, Chicago left fielder Abner Dalrymple dropped a fly ball and ignited a St. Louis rally that tied the score at 3. Neither team scored in the ninth, and Browns pitcher Bob Caruthers set down the White Stockings in the top of the tenth.

Clarkson, pitching in his fourth game in six days, finally faltered in the bottom of the inning. Curt Welch led off with a single and moved to third on an infield hit and a sacrifice. With Doc Bushong at the plate, Clarkson heaved a wild pitch, far outside and past the reach of catcher King Kelly. As the ball rolled away, Welch slid happily across the plate to win the game and the championship. The sportswriters called it the "$15,000 slide" for the amount of winner-take-all prize money won by the Browns.

Some confusion exists over whether the errant toss should be charged as a wild pitch or a passed ball. "I signaled Clarkson for a low ball on one side," explained Kelly after the game, "and when it came it was high upon the other. It struck my hand as I tried to get it and I would say it was a passed ball. You can give it to me if you want to. Clarkson told me that it slipped from his hands."[12] John was devastated by the loss. After the game, said future Giants manager Bill Joyce several years later, "Clarkson went out that night and shoved enough Kentucky dew into his face to get an engagement in [the popular play] *Ten Nights in a Barroom*."[13]

Clarkson's wild pitch, and Welch's famous slide, marked a turning point in the history of the national game. It was the last hurrah for the American Association, which never won another post-season series and collapsed only five years later. It marked the end of Chicago's dominance of the National League, because the White Stockings would not win a pennant again until 1906, by which time they had changed their name to the Cubs. It ended Cap Anson's reign as baseball's greatest manager, for Anson led the team for 11 more years without winning another league title.

It also started the breakup of the White Stockings. Many of the Chicago players did not take the rematch against the Browns seriously, and some of them even appeared to be drunk on the field. McCormick, the losing pitcher in the second game of the series, was "so thoroughly soused, he could not have struck out the batboy," snarled team president Albert Spalding. Some reports say that John Clarkson sat out the fifth game, not because he was exhausted, but because he was inebriated when he arrived at the park that day. "We were beaten and fairly beaten," said Anson many years later, "but had some of the players taken as good care of themselves prior to these games as they were in the habit of doing when the league season was in full swim, I am inclined to believe that there might have been a different tale to tell."[14]

Anson and Spalding decided to rid the team of some of its worst offenders. They sent McCormick to Pittsburgh and Gore to New York, then pulled off their biggest deal of all. On February 14, 1887, Anson sold his popular catcher and batting champion, the hard-living King Kelly, to Boston for a then-astounding sum of $10,000.

Chicago, with several new players, finished in second place behind the Detroit Wolverines in 1887, as John Clarkson won 37 games and led the league in wins, strikeouts, complete games, and innings pitched once again. John also contributed at the plate that year, belting five triples and six home runs. He had pitched over 1,500 innings in the preceding three seasons, and many feared that Clarkson's arm would go lame from overwork. Perhaps Anson thought so as well. Anson had a crop of new pitchers vying for positions, and since Anson needed to rebuild his ballclub, he knew that his next pennant was at least a few years away. Clarkson's mercurial temperament

John Clarkson pitching for the Chicago White Stockings in 1887. (Author's collection)

was a bother to the club in the championship years, but might be a distraction to a rebuilding team.

In addition, John decided that he had played long enough in Chicago and longed to follow his friend King Kelly back east. Quarrelsome as ever in 1887, John made even more trouble for Anson that season and threatened to retire unless traded back to the east coast. He lived in a boarding house during the baseball season in Chicago, and he longed to return to Boston and set up a year-round household. "I am anxious to have a home of my own and to fit it up as a permanent residence," said John in October of that year. "In Chicago I am obliged to board, and no boarding house will ever seem to me like home."

In December 1887, he told *Sporting Life*, "I want to play here [in Boston] because all my family live here, and here are most of my dearest friends. I think it's about time that I should have something to say about where I shall play. Chicago won't release me. Very well, then, I shall not play ball at all next season. I will remain in Boston and work at my trade. I mean just what I say. I shall not play in Chicago under any circumstances."[15] His trade was jewelry making, the same occupation his father followed. Clarkson told the papers that if he could not get himself released to Boston, he would quit the game and join his father Thomas in the family jewelry business.

When the prosperous Boston Beaneaters, who bought Kelly for $10,000 one year before, expressed interest in John Clarkson, the White Stockings began negotiations for the services of their ace pitcher. The Chicago fans howled, but on April 5, 1888, after months of dickering, the Beaneaters bought Clarkson's release from Chicago for $10,000. John joined the Boston team, which played its games only a few miles from John's boyhood home in Cambridge.

John pitched well in his first few years in Boston. He was 27 years old when he joined the Beaneaters, though his arm was much older from all the innings and complete games that he had pitched in the preceding seasons. His fastball was no longer as effective as it had been, but

Clarkson on an Allen and Ginter card, 1888. (Library of Congress)

the intelligent Clarkson adapted. By this time the league had dropped most of its restrictions on pitching deliveries, so John developed a nearly unhittable overhand "drop" pitch, what we today call a sinker, to go with his sidearm curveball. This new pitch allowed Clarkson to continue his reign as the top hurler in the National League.

Though the Beaneaters finished fifth in 1888, John contributed a 33–19 record. Off the field, however, King Kelly caused headaches for Beaneaters manager John Morrill. The Boston owners named the popular Kelly captain of the team, mostly to placate the fans, but Kelly's drinking was so out of control that he often took the field in an intoxicated state. This led to friction with manager Morrill, but when it became clear that Kelly and Morrill could not coexist, the owners fired Morrill and replaced him with Jim Hart.

In 1889 Clarkson almost pitched the Beaneaters to the pennant single-handedly. John won 49 games, leading the National League once again in wins, strikeouts, complete games, earned run average, and shutouts and turning in perhaps the most dominating single-season performance in baseball history. He won 21 more games, threw 22 more complete games, and pitched 200 more innings than any other pitcher in baseball that year. He lifted a mediocre Boston team to within one game of the pennant, which was not clinched by the Giants until Tim Keefe defeated Cleveland on the final day of the season, October 5. Later that day, with the pennant already lost, John took the mound against Pittsburgh in an attempt to earn his 50th win, but lost to Pud Galvin by a score of 3–1.

Clarkson dominated the league so completely in 1889 that Boston manager Jim Hart could not resist using him. John started 72 games, completed 68, and threw an incredible 620 innings. The Beaneaters, perhaps fearing the Hart would destroy their expensive acquisition through overuse, fired Hart and replaced him with Frank Selee, manager of Omaha in the Western League.

After the 1889 season, the long-simmering animosity between the players and the club owners erupted into a full-blown player revolt. New York Giants star John Montgomery Ward announced the formation of the Players' League, a new competitor to the established National League and American Association circuits. Almost all of baseball's biggest stars immediately jumped to the new league, throwing the game into turmoil.

One of the few star players who remained in the National League was baseball's greatest pitcher, John Clarkson. John attended some of the early organizational meetings of the Players' League, but he showed little enthusiasm for the effort, and he rejected an offer of $6,000 per year to jump to the new circuit. When Boston team owner Arthur Soden offered John a three-year contract for $25,000 — an unheard-of sum at the time — John not only quickly returned to the Beaneaters, he also signed several replacement players for the Beaneaters on Soden's behalf. John insisted that he did not act as an agent for the Beaneaters until he rejected the advances of the Players League. "I acted in good faith," said Clarkson. "...As soon as I had made up my mind to join the League, I stopped all negotiations with the Brotherhood [the Players League] and removed myself from their councils."[16]

Most of John's fellow ballplayers did not see the matter the same way, since John had apparently voted in some of the early Players League meetings. In December 1889, the Players League formally expelled several "turncoats," including John Clarkson, and some of the more radical players publicly accused John of spying for the National League. Outfielder Dick Johnston, John's Boston teammate, lashed out at Clarkson in print. "I rather pity Clarkson, but I'll never forgive him," said Johnston. "I think he is a creature of circumstance to a great extent, but he should not have attended our meetings and voted when he knew he would be going back on us."[17]

One possible explanation for Clarkson's decision to stay with the Beaneaters concerns his wife Ella. *Sporting Life* reported that one of the Boston club's directors, William Conant, approached Ella Clarkson and asked her to convince her husband to stay in the National League. "I will do so under one condition," replied Ella. "The conditions are that I can take just as many lady friends to the game as I feel like." Conant and the other club directors agreed, according to the story, and John remained with the Beaneaters for the 1890 campaign.[18]

Even John's friend Mike Kelly, who turned down a large offer from Soden and jumped to the competing Boston Players' League team, publicly chastised Clarkson for his actions. It is not clear if John was really reporting secretly to the National League owners, but many players believed that he was, and for the rest of his career some players considered John a traitor to the Players League cause. This controversy made the mercurial Clarkson even more withdrawn and moody than ever, and he became noticeably more demanding and difficult as the 1890s progressed.

Selee, the new manager, resolved to limit Clarkson's workload. He brought his star pitcher from Omaha, Kid Nichols, to Boston, and Selee managed to divide the pitching three ways among Clarkson, Nichols, and Charlie Getzien. In 1890 Clarkson went 26–18, Nichols 27–19, and Getzien 23–17 as the Beaneaters finished in fifth position. Selee knew he was on the right track, and when the Players' League collapsed in late 1890, King Kelly and other former Beaneater stars returned to the fold. In 1891 both

Clarkson and Nichols passed the 30-win mark as the Beaneaters won their first pennant in eight years.

Despite John's fine 34–18 performance in 1891, it was clear that he was slowing down. He walked more people than he struck out in both the 1890 and 1891 seasons, and as he passed the age of 30 his arm no longer bounced back from each start as quickly as it once did. In early 1892, John's arm became too sore to take his regular turn on the mound. The Beaneaters nursed him along for a while, but Arthur Soden decided to cut Clarkson's huge salary, since he was no longer the team's leading pitcher. John balked at accepting a pay cut, so the Beaneaters promoted Jack Stivetts to the rotation and released Clarkson in June of 1892.

Clarkson's talents were still in demand, and the Cleveland Spiders signed him almost immediately upon his release from Boston. John joined a rotation with Cy Young and Nig Cuppy, winning 17 and losing 10 in Cleveland after going 8–6 for Boston. One of his 17 wins was the 300th of his career, making John the fifth 300-game winner in baseball. The National League that year operated under a clumsy split-season arrangement, in which the first-half winner and the second-half winner met in a post-season nine-game series to decide the pennant. Boston won the first half and Cleveland the second, which gave John Clarkson the distinction of pitching for both first-place teams.

The series lasted only six games. Cy Young and Jack Stivetts battled to an 11-inning scoreless tie in the first game, but John lost the second to Harry Staley by a 4–3 score. Boston won games three and four, and then the Spiders put Clarkson in the box for the fifth contest. The Spiders took a 6–0 lead, but then the Beaneaters raked Clarkson for 12 runs and won the game 12–7. The next day, Boston closed the series when Kid Nichols defeated Young, and the Beaneaters claimed the championship.

John Clarkson, at age 32, started fading in 1893. The bosses of baseball moved the pitching mound back ten feet in an attempt to generate more offense. John, along with other older pitchers who relied on sidearm deliveries, found it difficult to adapt to the new pitching distance. Younger overhand fastballers like Kid Nichols, Cy Young, and Amos Rusie continued to prosper, but the new field configuration hastened the end of the careers of the previous generation of pitchers. Clarkson, Tim Keefe, Pud Galvin, and many other older hurlers saw their major league tenures draw to a close between 1892 and 1894.

The aging Clarkson declined to a 16–18 record in 1893, easily the worst of his career. He also became estranged from many of his Cleveland teammates, some of whom may have still resented John's alleged double-dealing during the formation of the Players' League. Players on other teams rode

Clarkson in the *New York Clipper*, May 3, 1890. (Author's collection)

the sensitive Clarkson mercilessly in that period, calling him "traitor" and making John's life even more difficult. John got along well with some of the Cleveland pitchers— Cy Young, in later years, credited Clarkson with providing helpful advice — but John began drinking more and kept to himself off the field. It appears in retrospect that John suffered from bouts of depression and paranoia, growing ever more despondent as his baseball career drew to a close.

An off-the-field tragedy may have hastened Clarkson's mental deterioration. Shortly after New Year's Day in 1894, John and one of his best friends, Boston catcher Charlie Bennett, traveled to Kansas for a hunting trip. They rode the Santa Fe railroad to the eastern part of the state. When the train pulled into the station at Wellsville, Kansas, Bennett stepped off the still-moving train to speak to an acquaintance. Somehow, Bennett lost his footing on the icy platform and fell under the wheels of the locomotive. The train severed both of Bennett's legs. Bennett survived the accident, but spent the rest of his life in a wheelchair. John Clarkson may not have seen the accident, but he certainly dealt with the immediate aftermath, and some say that Clarkson's personality was never the same afterward.

John pitched well in the early part of the 1894 campaign, winning seven of his first eight decisions, but then lost three in a row before he defeated Chicago on June 20 for his final major league win. On July 5, John's old team, the Beaneaters, scored 11 runs in the third inning and knocked Clarkson out of the box on their way to a 22–7 win. In his next two appearances, the Spiders fell behind early and rallied after Clarkson had been removed from the game. The Spiders won those two contests, 16–15 over Washington and 20–10 over the Phillies, but John did not pitch well enough in either game to gain credit for the win.

By mid-season 1894, John became convinced that some of the Cleveland players were not giving their best efforts when he was on the mound. John told manager Patsy Tebeau that one of the outfielders on the team was trying his utmost to make the Spiders lose when John pitched. The offending player, claimed Clarkson, "would throw me down at critical stages of games whenever he had the opportunity. He would dodge flies under the pretext that the sun was in his eyes, and in this way lost many a game, which, of course, was always charged up to me."[19] Jesse Burkett played left field, which was the sun field in Cleveland's League Park, and Burkett was not a good fielder in his first few years in the league. Burkett had to work hard to make himself even passable in the outfield, but perhaps Clarkson saw Burkett's fielding woes as a personal affront. In any event, manager Tebeau soon realized that Clarkson's presence was a detriment to the chemistry of his ballclub.

In July 1894, Tebeau traded John to the Baltimore Orioles for pitcher Tony Mullane, though John claimed that he quit the team of his own volition. "I grew disgusted," stated Clarkson, "and one day told Tebeau that I guessed it was no use for me to pitch any longer, and so I packed my baggage and skipped."[20] Mullane joined the Spiders, but John demanded a higher salary than the Orioles were willing to pay, and refused to report to Baltimore. He retired from the major leagues at the age of 33.

As John departed the game, two of his brothers entered it. Arthur "Dad" Clarkson, five years younger than John, starred at Harvard University in the late 1880s and earned tryouts with the Giants in 1890 and the Beaneaters in 1892. He finally landed in St. Louis in 1893, and pitched for six years in the National League with a 39–39 record. Another brother, Walter, seventeen years younger than John, captained the Harvard team and then joined the New York Highlanders of the American League in 1904, posting a log of 18–16 in five seasons. Together, Arthur, Walter, and John won 384 major league games, a record for pitching brothers that lasted until Gaylord and Jim Perry broke it in the 1970s. Two other Clarkson brothers played ball as well; Fred was a fine amateur pitcher who had no interest in joining the professional ranks, while Henry played in the outfield for Harvard.

One might have expected John to retire to Cambridge, where his parents still lived, but in 1895 he pitched for and managed a team in Bay City, Michigan, in the Michigan State League. The league collapsed in August of that year, but John remained in Bay City and opened a cigar store. He kept pitching and managing teams in semipro and town ball for several years afterward, and a *Chicago Tribune* report in 1898 found John managing his brother Arthur on a semipro nine in Bay City. Details of his life after baseball are sketchy, but reports state that John's drinking habit matured into full-fledged alcoholism by the time the 1900s rolled around. He tried to expand his cigar business to Chicago, but the attempt ended in failure, so Clarkson remained in Bay City and occupied himself with his store.

His depression and alcoholism worsened in the next several years, and in May 1905, John Clarkson entered a sanitarium in Flint, Michigan, after he suffered what the newspapers described as a nervous breakdown. By December of that year he was committed to a hospital for the insane in Pontiac, Michigan. One newspaper report described him as "a mental and physical wreck," and stated that his condition was "absolutely hope-less ... [he is] in such poor health that even though his mental facilities had not deserted him, he can not live many months."[21] After a three-month stay in Pontiac, John's father brought him back to Massachusetts to live in the McLean Psychiatric Hospital at Waverly, near Cambridge.[22] He never recovered his sanity, though his wife Ella told the *Detroit Free Press* in early 1909 that the ex-pitcher's condition was improving, and that she hoped to bring John back to Bay City before long. Though John was only in his mid 40s, his physical health deteriorated quickly. In late January of 1909 he became ill with pneumonia and lapsed into a coma.

He died in the McLean hospital on February 4, 1909, at the age of 47, and was buried in the Clarkson family plot in Cambridge. Both the Boston and Chicago National League teams sent floral displays, and dozens of John's old teammates attended the funeral. Stated the *Boston Post* in a headline, "John Clarkson is with Kelly now," while a *Detroit Free Press* reporter wrote, "In the old school of balldom there was none greater than John Clarkson. Today there are many people who still regard him as the greatest pitcher that ever lived."

In May of 1939, the Old-Timers Committee of the Baseball Hall of Fame, a three-man body consisting of the baseball commissioner and the presidents of the two major leagues, named six players to the Hall. They tapped only one 19th-century pitcher for the honor, choosing Charley (Old Hoss) Radbourn, the man who pitched the Providence Grays to the 1884 pennant and won an unbelievable 60 games that year.[23]

Radbourn, who was Clarkson's teammate in Boston in 1888 and 1889, compiled career statistics that bear striking similarities to those posted by John Clarkson. Radbourn and Clarkson pitched almost exactly the same number of games and innings, though Clarkson won 17 more games and lost 19 fewer.

	Games	Innings	Wins	Losses	Percent	Shutouts
Clarkson	531	4,534	327	177 (+150)	.649	37
Radbourn	528	4,533	310	196 (+114)	.613	35

Radbourn, who began his major league career in 1880, also shared many other traits with Clarkson, who joined the Worcester club two years later. Clarkson and Radbourn each accumulated more than 300 wins in slightly more than 11 seasons, and both men suffered career-ending arm problems in their early 30s. Both were righthanded pitchers and good hitters who sometimes played the outfield. Both men could be difficult, moody, and petulant, and both were drinking men who died young. On the National League's all-time list of wins in a season, Radbourn holds the first and fourth positions, while Clarkson occupies the second and third slots.

Radbourn, Providence, 1884	60
Clarkson, Chicago, 1885	53
Clarkson, Boston, 1889	49
Radbourn, Providence, 1883	48
Buffinton, Boston, 1884	48
Spalding, Chicago, 1876	47
Ward, Providence, 1879	47
Galvin, Buffalo, 1883	46
Galvin, Buffalo, 1884	46
McCormick, Cleveland, 1880	45
Bradley, St. Louis, 1876	45

In 1945 and 1946, the Veterans Committee selected 21 old-time players to the Hall, but for some reason the committee ignored all pitchers who played most of their careers in the 1880s and early 1890s. Before the election of Clarkson in 1963, no pitcher from the 1880–1890 era, besides Radbourn, had been given a plaque in Cooperstown. Other pitchers, some with fewer than 200 career wins, gained the honor in this period, but the committee repeatedly passed over several 300-game winners including Clarkson, Tim Keefe, Mickey Welch, and Pud Galvin.

It seems inconceivable that Clarkson, whose career was the equal, and perhaps the superior, of Radbourn's, was not elected to the Hall of Fame until 1963. Charles Comiskey, who faced Clarkson in the "World's Series" in 1885 and 1886, summed up the career of the mercurial and talented curveball artist. "He was a wonderful pitcher," said Comiskey in 1909, "and there have been few like him. Twice my team (the St. Louis Browns) had to face him in world's championship series and he had us all guessing … Clarkson was a star for eight years and was a wonder while he lasted."[24]

In the years since John Clarkson's election to the Hall of Fame in 1963, his legacy has been tarnished by a false accusation — that he is the only murderer in the Cooperstown shrine. Sometime in the 1970s, information began appearing in books and articles that Clarkson, sometime around the time of his 1905 nervous breakdown, killed his wife Ella with a razor.

This alleged occurrence was presented as fact in Richard Scheinin's book *Field of Screams*, published by W. W. Dutton in 1994, and it also gained currency during the campaigns to put disgraced superstars Pete Rose and Shoeless Joe Jackson into the Hall of Fame. Several postings to web site message boards and in letters to the editors of various newspapers sought to minimize Rose's and Jackson's misdeeds by stating that the baseball museum already contains the plaques of known racists, heavy drinkers, and, in John Clarkson, a murderer.

The accusation appears to be false in Clarkson's case. The newspapers of the period make no mention of such an attack, and there is no evidence that Clarkson spent time in jail or appeared in a courtroom upon a charge of murder or manslaughter. Besides, the Boston newspapers reported that Ella Clarkson was at her husband's bedside when he died, and the pitcher's death certificate states that Clarkson was married at the time of his demise.

Clarkson's modern-day accusers probably have confused him with another, earlier pitcher for the White Stockings who did attack his wife. Terry Larkin, whose last name almost rhymes with that of Clarkson, won a total of 60 games for Cap Anson's Chicago team in 1878 and 1879, but drank himself out of the game within two seasons. Larkin, like Clarkson, was an alcoholic, and experienced profound mental problems that eventually required his confinement in a sanitarium. In 1883 Larkin shot his wife during an argument and then slashed himself in the neck with a razor. Both he and his wife recovered, but Larkin never managed to put his life back on track, and he died in 1894 at the age of 41.

It seems logical that the names of Larkin and Clarkson have become confused in the nearly 100 years since Clarkson's death. Though John Clarkson was a difficult individual, he was not a murderer, and he fully deserves his plaque on the wall in Cooperstown.

9

◆ ELMER FLICK ◆

Mr. [Branch] Rickey told me I had been put in the Hall of Fame, and I thought he was kidding. — Elmer Flick, 1963[1]

The Veterans Committee provided the only new Hall of Fame inductees in 1963, because at that time the Baseball Writers Association only held elections in even-numbered years. Commissioner Ford Frick empowered the committee to select up to four new members, two whose careers ended before 1931 and two whose careers ended between 1931 and 1943. The committee, which met on January 27, 1963, responded by electing John Clarkson and Elmer Flick from the pre–1931 era, and Sam Rice and Eppa Rixey from the more recent period.

Clarkson had been dead for more than half a century, but the other old-time electee was still living. Elmer Flick, an outfielder for Philadelphia and Cleveland who played from 1898 to 1910, was an 87-year-old retired builder and real estate agent, living with his daughter and son-in-law in Warrensville Heights, Ohio, a suburb of Cleveland. Flick played only ten full seasons in the major leagues, and his greatest claim to fame was the fact that the Detroit Tigers had once offered to trade a young Ty Cobb to Cleveland for him. Aside from a small flurry of attention paid to Flick in the newspapers when Cobb died in July of 1961, Flick had been almost totally ignored by the public for more than 50 years.

Branch Rickey, who championed Elmer's candidacy on the Veterans Committee, called Elmer at home that Sunday afternoon to inform him of his election to the Hall of Fame. "I thought he said his name was Rickey," mused the elderly ballplayer immediately afterward. "Maybe it was Branch Rickey. I know he's been in my corner. I played with him, you know." Rickey, who caught for the St. Louis Browns in the first decade of the 20th century, was one of the few committee members who had seen Flick play. "Rickey remembers me when I was good," said Elmer a few days later, "and I'm sure he was the one responsible for getting me in."[2]

Despite Elmer's .315 lifetime batting average, the baseball writers had barely acknowledged him in the Hall of Fame balloting throughout the years. He had gained only one Hall of Fame vote, which came in the 1938 election. This lack of past support made his selection by the Veterans Committee in 1963 a surprise not only to baseball fans across the nation, but also to the old ballplayer himself. "I didn't even know my name was being considered this time," said Flick to Cleveland reporter Bill Levy. "It came as a complete surprise to me."[3] It took a while for Flick's relatives to convince the old ballplayer that the phone call from New York that informed him of his election to the Hall was not a practical joke.

The octogenarian ballplayer was not in the best of health, but he made the journey to Cooperstown for his induction ceremony on August 5, 1963. "I was introduced as being still young," commented Flick in his induction speech, "but I don't think I look it, the way I walk with a cane. But I feel good today. This is a bigger day than any I have ever had before. I'm not going to try to find words to explain how I feel."[4]

Elmer Harrison Flick, the third child of Zachary and Mary Flick, was born on a farm near Bedford, Ohio, on January 11, 1876. He spent most of his youth in Bedford, though it appears that his family lived in Indiana for some period of time as well.[5] In the early 1890s Elmer played on the Bedford High School baseball team as a catcher, though he was already a fixture in the semipro circuits in the Cleveland area. Elmer received his introduction to semipro ball totally by chance. Bedford sported a town team, and one summer day in 1891 the 15-year-old Elmer went to the train station to see the Bedford team depart on a road trip to Streetsboro. Only eight players showed up, and the manager asked Elmer to fill in. Elmer was barefoot and did not own a uniform, but he boarded the train and played that day against Streetsboro.

"We played two games and I hit pretty well," recalled Flick more than 70 years later. "I remember the opposing pitcher from the morning game told the pitcher in the afternoon to watch out for the guy without a suit."[6]

After playing in semipro leagues around the Cleveland area in his teenage years, his success convinced Elmer that he could compete on the professional level. In the late summer of 1895, he traveled to Youngstown, Ohio, to collect a bill for his father and to inquire about a position on the local Interstate League team. The manager, Art Anderson, asked if Elmer carried any recommendations. He didn't, but Anderson told the young man that he looked like a ballplayer, and to wait for a letter the next spring telling him where to report.

Anderson kept his word. Elmer received the letter in the spring of 1896, and joined the Youngstown Puddlers shortly afterward. The Puddlers already had a catcher, so Elmer moved to right field. Though the young ballplayer had difficulty judging and catching fly balls, he pounded out a .438 average in 31 games. "The manager told me that as an outfielder, I wasn't so hot," said Flick. "Then he added, 'But you can sure sting that ball.'"

Anderson lost his job after the 1896 campaign, so Elmer signed for 1897 with one of Youngstown's rivals, the Dayton Old Soldiers. Elmer, a lefthanded batter and a righthanded thrower, played 126 games for Dayton, scoring more than a run per game and batting .386. Some of the Interstate League teams did not play on Sunday, so Elmer often participated in Sunday-only semipro leagues for a few extra dollars. Like other players of the era, he also played for several different semipro and town teams after the close of the Interstate League campaign.

In October 1897, he signed a one-game contract to play for a team in Bowling Green, Ohio, which was involved in a key Wood County League series against North Baltimore, a few miles to the south. The Bowling Green club signed Flick and another future Cooperstown honoree, 18-year-old Roger Bresnahan, who spent the 1897 season pitching for the Washington Senators. Elmer whacked three hits and made a fine running catch in center field that day, but North Baltimore bombed Bresnahan for 25 hits and defeated Bowling Green by a score of 18 to 13.

Elmer's hard hitting, speed, and fielding ability soon brought him to the attention of the Philadelphia Phillies of the National League. George Stallings, manager of the Phillies, attended a game between Dayton and New Castle, Pennsylvania, and saw Elmer Flick belt a triple and make several good plays in the outfield. Impressed, Stallings invited Elmer to spring training at Cape May, New Jersey, in March of 1898. The 22-year-old Flick arrived at Cape May carrying a canvas bag, inside which was a bat that he made himself in the woodshop at his parents' farm in Bedford.

The Phillies owned the hardest-hitting outfield in baseball with Dick Cooley in center and two future Hall of Famers, Ed Delahanty and Sam Thompson, on the corners. Elmer would have had no chance to make the team had not Thompson sat out most of the 1897 campaign with a sore back. Phillies manager Stallings liked the young outfielder, and kept Elmer around as insurance in case Thompson's back troubled him again. "Flick is going to make the outfielders hustle to hold their positions," wrote Francis Richter in *Sporting Life*. "He is the fastest and most promising young-ster the Phillies have ever had."[7]

Sure enough, Thompson played only six games before his back went out. He was unable to play against the Boston Beaneaters on April 26, 1898, so Stallings sent Elmer Flick to right field. In his first major league game, Elmer pounded out two singles in three trips to the plate against Boston's 26-game winner Fred Klobedanz. Thompson returned the next day, but on May 13 he surrendered to his painful back and announced his retire-ment, leaving the right field starting position to the hard-hitting rookie.

Elmer Flick was not a big man. He stood about five feet and eight inches tall and weighed no more than 160 pounds through most of his major league career. He was strong, and he hit sharp line drives in the outfield gaps, relying on his speed to stretch singles into doubles and doubles into triples. Elmer was considered a power hitter in an era when power referred to triples more than home runs. He hit only 46 home runs in his 13-year career, but reached double figures in triples in every full season that he played. He also hit for average, with a .318 mark in 1898, .344 in 1899, and .378 in 1900, and stole 20 to 40 bases a year as well.

Elmer hit 11 home runs (mostly inside-the-park shots) in 1900, but claimed to the end of his life that he whacked several others that year. Late in his life, he proudly showed off a silver cup given to him after that sea-son, inscribed "Elmer Flick, champion home run hitter, 1900." "I had 14 or 15 that year and was awarded this cup. You know how records were kept in those days—not very good," insisted Flick. "A couple of years later Her-man Long, who had 11 homers in 1900, was given credit for being champ. They said he had 12. I was given 11 and he's in the books now as the fellow who led the league. Well, he's got the honor and I've got the cup."[8]

He worked hard to make himself into a good right fielder. The Phillies played their home games at the Huntingdon Avenue Grounds (later called the Baker Bowl) where the right field wall stood only 272 feet from the plate. Elmer learned to play line drives off the 40-foot wall and worked on throw-ing the ball quickly and accurately back into the infield. With such a short distance between the infield and the wall, Elmer played a shallow right field. He piled up assists because he was often able to field a sharply hit ball and throw the batter out at first.

The Phillies, meanwhile, fired manager Stallings in mid–1898 and replaced him with Bill Shettsline, who lifted the club to third place in 1899 despite the first serious injury of Elmer Flick's career. In early August of 1899, Elmer tripped over second base during a game against St. Louis and dislocated his knee. The Phillies thought that he would be sidelined for the remainder of the season, but Elmer re-entered the lineup after only three weeks. In his first game back, Elmer re-injured the knee while chasing a foul fly and put himself on the shelf for another three weeks. He returned as a pinch-hitter in mid–September, but did not play the field again until September 28. Elmer played the rest of the schedule, though his knee was still sore and hampered his ability to run. He lost more than 20 points on his batting average in the last few weeks of the season.

The Phillies expected to challenge for the flag in 1900, after the National League dropped four teams and continued as an eight-team circuit. Philadelphia owned some of the best young hitters in the league, including Elmer Flick and second baseman Napoleon Lajoie. Flick, at age 26, put together his best major league season as he led the league in runs batted in with 110 in 1900, and finished second to Pittsburgh's Honus Wagner in batting and slugging percentage. Lajoie, though slowed by injuries, also emerged as one of baseball's brightest stars as he batted .380 in 1899 and .346 in 1900.

One of Lajoie's injuries came in an altercation with Elmer. The two men had argued on the field on several occasions in the previous two years because Lajoie displayed so much range at second base that he often fielded balls in short right field and, as Elmer complained, "took away my chances." On May 31, 1900, an argument over the ownership of a bat between Flick and Lajoie escalated into a fistfight, which ended when Lajoie took a swing at his teammate. Elmer ducked and Lajoie smashed his fist into a wall, breaking his hand and virtually ending the Phillies' pennant hopes.

Lajoie was out of the lineup for more than five weeks, during which time the club management suspended him without pay. The Phillies were in first place by four games at the time of the fight, but played .500 ball the rest of the way and finished a disappointing third. The only beneficiary of the battle was Flick, who earned respect from his teammates for fighting the much larger Lajoie to a draw.

A healthy, intact Philadelphia club might have contended for the 1901 pennant, but the new American League came calling. Elmer remained with the Phillies, but Lajoie and pitchers Bill Bernhard and Chick Fraser moved across town and signed with Connie Mack's Philadelphia Athletics. Lajoie found immediate success in the new circuit, batting an incredible .422 with 145 runs batted in for the Athletics, and when the new league beckoned again in 1902, Elmer was ready to pack. He joined the A's in April 1902, along with third baseman Monte Cross and pitcher Bill Duggleby.

Elmer played only 11 games for Mack's ballclub. On April 21, 1902, the Phillies secured an injunction from the Pennsylvania Supreme Court restraining Lajoie, Fraser, and Barnhard from playing for the A's. Though he was not mentioned by name in the decision, Elmer was also covered by the injunction, as were Cross and Dugglesby. The Athletics appealed, but in early May the court denied the appeal and ordered the players to return to the Phillies.

Elmer did not appear on the field for the Athletics on May 7, and many of the fans in Philadelphia assumed that he had, indeed, jumped back to the Phillies. Instead, Elmer boarded a train that morning in a hurry to get out of town before the court officers could serve him with papers. Elmer beat such a hasty retreat that he left his baggage and baseball equipment behind. Connie Mack had foreseen this possible outcome of the court case; he had already worked out a plan to send Elmer to another American League team, the Cleveland Blues. Later that afternoon, Flick surfaced in Cleveland and signed a contract to play for the Blues. He played his first game in a Cleveland uniform on May 9 and drove in two runners with a single in his first trip to the plate. Three weeks later, Lajoie joined the Cleveland club as well.

Elmer was overjoyed at the opportunity to play before Cleveland crowds. In 1898, his rookie year, Cleveland fans came out to cheer him (and another Phillies star, Cleveland native Ed Delahanty) whenever the Phillies played a series there. Elmer could always count on a delegation of rooters from Bedford to make noise for their native son, and now the Bedford fans could watch Elmer all season long. Flick received several telegrams from his former Philadelphia manager Bill Shettsline, offering him more money to return to the Phillies, but Elmer preferred to play for the Blues.

Later that season, with the war between the leagues still raging in full fury, Elmer turned down a lucrative offer to return to the National League. John McGraw, who became manager of the New York Giants in mid–1902, sent Elmer a blank contract and invited him to fill in his own salary figure. Flick, however, liked the idea of playing only a few miles from home, and remained with Cleveland for the rest of his major league career.

The Cleveland team was called the Blues in 1901 and the Bronchos in 1902, but when the popular Lajoie arrived in June 1902 the papers started referring to the team as the Naps. The Naps received a jolt of adrenaline when two good hitters, Flick and Lajoie, joined the club, although neither man could play in the state of Pennsylvania for the remainder of the 1902 campaign. Lajoie and Flick might have been arrested for defying the court's order to return to the Phillies, so the two men stayed away from the ballpark when the Naps played Connie Mack's Athletics.

Elmer hit for a .295 average in 1902, in a season highlighted by his league record three triples in a game against Chicago on July 6. Several other men (including Napoleon Lajoie) have tied Flick's mark, but no twentieth-century batter in either league has ever bettered it. Flick also set a record, since broken, when he walked five times in a game on July 18 of that same season. Elmer scored four times in that game, won by the Naps 14–4 over Boston.

Flick had recorded several high batting averages for the Phillies, but he batted between .295 and .311 in his first six seasons for Cleveland. In 1905 Elmer enjoyed one of his best seasons, winning the batting title for the only time in his career, but his .306 mark was the lowest winning average in history until Carl Yastrzemski of the Red Sox batted .301 to win the 1968 title. "A lot of people remember me for that puny .306 average because it was in the record book," complained Elmer many years later. "But I hit .378 in 1900 with the Phillies and didn't win the championship."[9]

Elmer Flick in 1904. (Author's collection)

Averages tumbled throughout baseball in the first decade of the twentieth century, mostly because trick pitches like the spitball became a rage among the pitchers of the major leagues. The spitball broke sharply on its way to the plate, like an unusually good curveball, and most batters had problems catching up to it in time to hit it solidly. In addition, spitballs became wet and soggy as games stretched into the late innings, so base hits became harder to come by as a game wore on. Also, explained Elmer, "managers always checked the balls before the games and doctored them to perfection. Hitters had a nightmare … the balls would be smooth on one side and rough on the other. You wouldn't let your kids play with them, they were so bad."[10]

The Naps, with Lajoie and Flick supplying the offense and 20-game winners Otto Hess and Addie Joss on the mound, challenged for pennants in this era, but were undermined by injuries year after year. In 1905 Lajoie, who became manager of the club that season, suffered a spike wound to the leg; the blue coloring of his socks gave him blood poisoning, limiting him to 66 games and ruining the Naps' season. In 1906 Elmer batted .311 and led the league in stolen bases and triples, but Bill Bradley's broken wrist opened a hole at third base that the Naps could not fill. Lajoie moved himself to third and put Elmer at second base for a few games, but the experiment failed and the Naps finished five games behind the "Hitless Wonder"

White Sox. Neither Flick nor Lajoie could have known it at the time, but neither man would ever play for a pennant-winning ballclub.

In the spring of 1907, the Detroit Tigers held their spring training camp in Augusta, Georgia. Their young star, Ty Cobb, was not popular with his teammates, and manager Hugh Jennings worried that the team would never win a pennant with Cobb in the lineup, no matter how well he played. Before spring training was two weeks old, Cobb started a fight with the groundskeeper of the local ballpark, then slapped and choked the man's wife when she intervened. When Cobb's teammate, catcher Charley Schmidt, upbraided the young Southerner for his behavior, Cobb fought him as well. Manager Jennings restored order, then sent a telegram to Cleveland Naps owner Charles Somers at the Cleveland training camp in Macon.

Jennings, according to newspaper accounts of the period, proposed a trade to Somers: Ty Cobb for Elmer Flick, even up.

Though few teams would trade away a 20-year-old potential super-star, even for a hard-hitting performer like Flick, the offer made sense for the Tigers. Cobb was one of the emerging stars of the game, and he hit .320 in 1906 at the age of 19. However, Cobb had battled his teammates since joining the Tigers in August 1905, and Jennings feared that the young man would burn himself out within a few years. Flick was nearly 11 years older than Cobb, but got along well with his teammates, and appeared to have several more good years ahead of him.

Besides, Jennings knew that Flick might be available. Charles Somers was upset with Elmer, who was holding out for more money, and had not yet signed his 1907 contract. Elmer had spent the winter of 1906-07 playing ball in the California Winter League (where he faced a teenaged semi-pro pitcher named Walter Johnson for the first time) and was already in playing shape, so he felt no need to rush to training camp. Flick actively disliked the South, and often complained to the Cleveland newspapers about long train rides and unfamiliar Southern cooking. Flick had staged holdouts and delayed reporting to spring training in almost every season of his career, which did not sit well with the management of the Naps. Per-haps Jennings believed that the Cleveland ballclub might be persuaded to exchange a minor irritant for a more talented major one.

Tigers owner Frank Navin, in a letter to Jennings dated March 18, 1907, cautioned the manager against trading Cobb for Flick. "It seems hard to think that such a mere boy as Cobb can make so much disturbance," wrote Navin. "On last year's form, he has a chance to be one of the grand-est ballplayers in the country. He has everything in his favor. It would not surprise me at all to see him lead the league this year in hitting and he has a chance to play for 15 years yet.

"Flick is a dangerous man to bother with," Navin's letter continued, "for the reason that he has about all the money he cares for, does not care about playing ball, except as a means of livelihood, and is liable to quit on you at any time, besides being a great deal older than Cobb."[11]

Navin need not have worried about losing his young superstar, for Somers turned down the deal. "We'll keep Flick," he told Jennings. "Maybe he isn't quite as good a batter as Cobb, but he's much nicer to have on the team."[12] Somers then offered centerfielder Bunk Congleton, a .320 hitter in 1906, for Cobb, but Jennings rejected the offer.

Three days later, Flick signed his contract. Elmer

Flick warming up on the sidelines. (National Baseball Hall of Fame Library, Cooperstown, New York)

batted .302 in 1907, stole 41 bases, and led the league in triples for the third year in a row, while Cobb made a major leap to stardom. Cobb won the first of his record 12 batting titles and led the Tigers to their first of three consecutive American League pennants.

According to Baseball Hall of Fame historian Lee Allen, three other American League teams made offers to Jennings for Cobb's services, but Jennings decided to keep his troublesome outfielder. This makes it appear that Jennings' offer to Somers may have been made out of frustration. In the next few seasons Cobb became baseball's greatest player, and the proposed one-for-one trade of Flick for Cobb made Flick more famous than anything he did on the field of play.

Unfortunately for the Naps, 1907 was Elmer Flick's last productive season. He reported to spring training in 1908 severely underweight, a condition that he blamed on "train sickness," but it soon became clear that Elmer was seriously ill. "I don't know what it was exactly," said Flick many years later. "Acute gastritis is what many of the doctors called it.... There was a time in 1908 I was positive I wouldn't live another week." Despite medical attention from several physicians, the exact cause of the mysterious illness was never determined, and Elmer took pills for the condition for the rest of his life. He did not appear in the Cleveland lineup until July 24, and the condition kept him out of action for all but nine games in 1908.

The Naps put their strongest-ever team on the field that year and challenged Detroit for the pennant, but the absence of Flick in right field and in the batting order hampered the Cleveland ballclub, especially down the stretch. At season's end, both Detroit and Cleveland won 90 games, but Cleveland played one extra game when the Tigers were not required to make up a rainout. The Naps fought valiantly, but lost the pennant by mere percentage points. Twelve different men, including Flick, played right field for the Naps in 1908, and none of them hit well. It stands to reason that a healthy Elmer Flick would have won at least one game with his bat and led the Naps to their first American League pennant that year.

Elmer attempted to play again in 1909, but he began losing weight during spring training and failed to start the season with the Naps. His weight fell to 130 pounds before the illness subsided, and once again the doctors could not agree on a diagnosis. One doctor suggested that Elmer needed to have his appendix removed, but Flick rejected the advice, fearing the outcome of the then-dangerous procedure. By June his health had stabilized, but the illness robbed him of his speed, and he appeared in only 66 games with a .255 batting average.

In 1910 he made it through only 24 games before his mysterious malady put him on the sidelines once more. "My last three years—from 1908 to 1911—were awful," admitted Flick years later. "I had a nervous stomach that I never did get over. I shouldn't have played at all."[13] The Naps gave up on Flick and acquired a new right fielder, Shoeless Joe Jackson, in a trade with the Philadelphia Athletics. Jackson batted .387 in limited action in the latter part of the 1910 season and claimed the right field job on a permanent basis, ending Elmer Flick's career with the Naps. In mid-season 1910, the Naps released Elmer to the Kansas City club of the Western League, though Elmer chose to go home to Bedford rather than report to Kansas City.

Flick's health improved in the spring of 1911, but he was unable to find another major league job. He returned to the minors for two seasons with the Toledo Mud Hens of the American Association in 1911 and 1912, batting .326 and .262 with little power, before he hung up his spikes at age 36. Elmer returned to his hometown of Bedford, where he raised trotting horses and drove them himself every now and then at local racetracks. He wasn't through playing baseball, and The Sporting News reported in mid-1914 that Elmer was playing second base for an amateur team in Bedford called the Merchants. The 38-year-old Flick, in one Sunday game, belted a homer and four doubles in five trips to the plate.[14]

After leaving baseball, Flick entered the construction business, building houses and offices in the Cleveland area, and also occupied himself by farming and selling real estate. Elmer was a crack shot with a rifle, and stated proudly that his family never bought a turkey for Thanksgiving because he could bag one every November. Over the next few decades, he scouted local prospects for the Cleveland ballclub and enjoyed watching the Naps (who became the Indians in 1915) play at Cleveland's League Park, often attending with his old teammate and friend Cy Young. He and his wife Rosella, whom Elmer married in 1900, raised five daughters, who eventually produced six grandchildren.

A broken hip suffered in 1941, when he was 65, slowed Elmer down and obliged him to walk with a cane for the rest of his life, but he still offered scouting tips to the Indians on a part-time basis. The old ballplayer was past 80 when he recommended that the Indians sign a local teenaged infielder named Sal Bando. Bando signed with the Athletics instead, but he lasted for 16 seasons in the majors, validating Elmer Flick's estimate of his potential. In his later years, Elmer retired and moved in with a daughter in Warrensville Heights, a short distance from Bedford in the Cleveland suburbs. He and Rosella were living there when Elmer received word of his Hall of Fame election.

The *Cleveland Plain Dealer*, the city's major daily newspaper, was in the middle of a bitter strike at the time, but the other local papers sent reporters to interview the elderly ex-ballplayer. Elmer seemed rejuvenated by all the attention, and enjoyed sharing his memories after so many decades out of the spotlight. He also offered his own analysis of the plight of his old team, the Cleveland Indians, which had finished the previous season mired in the second division of the American League. Flick opined that the Indians were too predictable to their opponents. "Connie Mack used to like to mix it up—bunts, long balls, all kinds of things," insisted Flick. "That's the way to do it."[15] He, like most old ballplayers, did not like some aspects of the modern game, and remarked that he could not understand why modern players use bats with thin handles. "I get burned up every time I see one of those fellows with the skinny-handled bats," said Elmer, who turned his own bats on a lathe. "It's no wonder they can't hit or bunt. We used to get solid hits just off the handle alone."[16]

Despite his frail appearance at the 1963 Cooperstown ceremony, Elmer thoroughly enjoyed himself that weekend, and he returned to Cooperstown in the summer of 1964 to see the inductions of six new Hall of Famers. One of the museum's most touching legends concerns the 88-year-old Flick standing in front of his plaque with tears of pride rolling down his face. "I guess I was a pretty fair player at that," remarked Elmer that day. "I thought I had been forgotten."[17]

His health remained steady for several years after 1963 —"The doctors tell me I've got a lot of mileage left," said Elmer to the papers— and he diligently answered autograph requests from fans and well-wishers until he was well past 90 years of age. Elmer was proud of his advanced age, and signed his autographs with the date and his age underneath his signature. He outlived almost all of his teammates and contemporaries, and by 1970 Elmer was one of only four 19th century major league players still living.[18]

Elmer didn't travel much after 1964, but lived long enough to become the oldest member of the Hall of Fame. He died of a stomach ailment on January 9, 1971, two days short of his 95th birthday, and was buried at the Crown Hills cemetery in nearby Twinsburg. Rosella Flick, to whom Elmer was married for more than 70 years, died in November 1973 and was buried next to her husband.

Veteran writer Dan Daniel, reporting the election of Elmer Flick and three others to the Hall of Fame for *The Sporting News* in 1963, called the selection of Flick "quite a surprise" and suggested that "the old-timers group was actuated by a desire to honor outstanding eligibles who were still alive and able to glory in their new distinction as members of the Pantheon."[19] Joe King, in the same magazine a month later, put it more bluntly when he stated that the committee (which included Daniel as a member) "was aware of the race with the Grim Reaper."[20] Eight years later, Elmer's obituary in the January 23, 1971, issue of *The Sporting News* admitted that "Flick's credentials are considerably less impressive than many of the others in the Cooperstown shrine."

Did the long-forgotten Elmer Flick gain election to the Hall because he was a friend of Branch Rickey and happened to still be alive at the time? Perhaps, but Flick's qualifications may be greater than they appear at first glance. Flick led the league in triples three times and in stolen bases twice, led the National League in runs batted in once, and batted as high as .378 in a season. He won a batting title, no small feat in an American League dominated by Napoleon Lajoie and later by Ty Cobb. His batting average sank after he switched leagues, but so did almost everyone else's in that dead-ball decade. Elmer's lifetime batting average of .315 would probably have been much higher if he had played in almost any other era.

He never played for a pennant winner, never appeared in a World Series, and saw his career cut short by illness. Nevertheless, Elmer Flick was one of the most dangerous hitters of his time. He was not, after all, the equal of Ty Cobb, but he fully deserved his belated election to the Hall of Fame.

10

◆ EPPA RIXEY ◆

We should honor people like Eppa Rixey. His birthday, May 3, should be a national holiday for all those working stiffs who do nothing more admirable (and nothing less admirable) than shoulder their adequate talent and make a living. It would not be a celebration of the mediocre (mediocre folks don't play 21 years), but of those who do a fine if unremarkable job.— Mark Collins, *Pittsburgh Post-Gazette*, 1994[1]

On September 21, 1959, Milwaukee Braves pitcher Warren Spahn notched his 20th win of the season. National League fans throughout the country watched Spahn's performance closely, because the Braves and the Los Angeles Dodgers were locked in a tight pennant race at the time. Spahn's win enabled the Braves to move into a first-place tie with the Dodgers with only a week left in the regular season.

Spahn's victory was also the 266th of his career and enabled him to tie the record set by Eppa Rixey for wins in the National League by a lefthander. Five days later, Spahn defeated the Phillies for his 21st victory of the season and 267th of his career, breaking the mark that Rixey had held since his retirement in 1933.

Most baseball fans had long forgotten Eppa Rixey, who in 1959 was alive and serving as the president of an insurance agency in suburban Cincinnati. The baseball writers also ignored him, giving him scant support in the biennial Hall of Fame balloting throughout the 1950s. Rixey may have been the National League's winningest lefthander, but he gained only 27 votes (from more than 200 electors) in the 1956 Hall of Fame election and 32 votes in the 1958 ballot. "I'm glad Spahn broke [the record]," said Rixey to the newspapers. "If he hadn't broken it, no one would have known I'd set it."[2]

Rixey's name never appeared in the top ten of the ballot until Spahn's record-setting performance brought new attention to the old lefthander. On February 4, 1960, Rixey drew 142 votes from the baseball writers in balloting for the Hall of Fame. Though no one gained enough votes for election that year, Rixey finished third in the voting behind his old Cincinnati teammate Edd Roush and former Washington Senators star Sam Rice. In 1962, Rixey's last year on the writers' ballot, he fell to fifth place behind Roush, Rice, and the newly eligible Bob Feller and Jackie Robinson. Feller, Roush, and Robinson gained election, but Rice and Rixey remained outside of the walls of Cooperstown. Because Rice and Rixey had been retired from the game for 30 years, their candidacy for the Hall of Fame then passed from the writers to the Veterans Committee.

The Veterans Committee did not make either man wait long for baseball's highest honor. On January 27, 1963, the committee considered the merits of 28 players whose careers ended between 1931 and 1943. In the end, they elected Sam Rice and Eppa Rixey to the Hall of Fame. Reporters converged upon Rixey's insurance office, where the 71-year-old former pitcher expressed surprise at the news. "They selected me to the Hall?" asked the old pitcher modestly. "I guess they're scraping at the bottom of the barrel."[3]

Eppa Rixey Junior was born in the town of Culpeper, Virginia, on May 3, 1891. The Rixey clan was one of the most prominent families in Culpeper County; Eppa's ancestors had founded the town of Rixeyville, about eight miles from Culpeper, and Eppa's uncle John represented Virginia in the United States Congress for ten years. The ballplayer's father, Eppa Senior, was a prosperous banker.

Eppa Junior, the fourth of six children, was a good student as well as a fine athlete. His family moved to nearby Charlottesville when he was seven years old, and he spent his teenaged summers playing for the local town team against neighboring squads from Fredericksburg, Manassas, and other towns. In 1909 he graduated from high school and enrolled at the University of Virginia in Charlottesville to study chemistry, while making time for athletics. Rixey, the tallest man on campus at six feet and five inches, excelled in basketball.

The Virginia baseball coach, Cy Rigler, spent his summers as a National League umpire. One day the basketball and baseball teams worked out side by side in the campus gymnasium, and Rigler observed Rixey throwing fastballs to the catcher of the baseball team. Rigler asked the young man if he always threw that hard. "That isn't anything," remarked Rixey. "When I get outside, I throw much harder." The astonished Rigler suggested to Rixey that he had a future in professional baseball, and Rixey concentrated on baseball from that day forward.

Rigler worked with the tall lefthander, teaching him the basics of pitching and refining his delivery. Rixey, despite his large frame, did not possess an overpowering fastball, but Rigler worked with him on a devastating change of pace that became the young man's signature pitch. By 1912, Rixey was the best pitcher in Virginia college ranks, and Rigler recommended him to the Philadelphia Phillies, who promptly offered Rixey a contract. The team promised to pay a $2,000 bonus, to be split equally between Rixey and Rigler.

Eppa had intended to pursue a career in chemistry, but he was intrigued by the opportunity to play ball for a living and travel the country. He wanted to finish his degree work, but also decided to give baseball a chance before committing himself to life in a laboratory. Eppa signed the contract and reported directly to the Phillies in June of 1912, becoming one of the few pitchers to go directly to the majors without the benefit of minor league experience.

However, Eppa soon learned an unpleasant lesson about the business of baseball. Other National League teams complained about the apparent conflict of interest in an umpire serving as a scout for one of the league's teams. The league issued an order barring further scouting by its umpires, and the Phillies never paid either Rigler or Rixey their promised bonuses.

The young pitcher also learned how to handle his teammates. He pitched batting practice for the team shortly after his arrival, but each player in turn drove line drives back at Eppa in the pitcher's box. "I was just a green kid," related Rixey later, "and didn't know any better until one of the older pitchers took me aside and said, 'They're having fun with you.... They're making you skip rope. Throw a few at their heads and they'll quit.'

"I did, and they quit."[4]

By the time Rixey joined the club in mid–June, the Phillies had already dropped out of the pennant chase. Red Dooin, an old catcher who at the time was manager of the Phillies, put Rixey into the starting rotation right away. He lost his first game, a 7–0 defeat at the hands of the Brooklyn Dodgers on June 21, 1912, but Dooin wanted to see what the young man could do, and kept him in the rotation. By the end of the 1912 campaign, Rixey had made 20 starts, completing 10 of them and compiling a 10–10 record. Three of the 21-year-old lefthander's wins were shutouts, boding well for his future in a Philadelphia uniform.

The pitching star of the team was one of the all-time greats of baseball, Grover Cleveland (Pete) Alexander. The 24-year-old Alexander burst

Rixey (center) with teammates Tom Seaton (left) and John Dodge in early 1913. (Library of Congress)

upon the scene in 1911 with 28 wins, a rookie record in the 20th century. He fell to 19–17 in 1912 as the Phillies dropped to sixth place, but he and several other fine players were ready to move the Phillies back up the standings.

Eppa, after his promising beginning, took a while to establish himself. He compiled a 9–5 record in starting and relief roles as the Phillies bounced up to second place in 1913, but he slumped to 2–11 in 1914. Eppa's earned run average rose to 4.39 that year, and manager Dooin began to lose interest in the struggling lefthander. Rixey pitched in only 24 games in 1914 and spent weeks at a time sitting in the bullpen without getting into a game.

One problem was Eppa's conditioning, or lack of it. Eppa did not show up at spring training in 1913 because he was finishing his degree work at the University of Virginia, and *Baseball Magazine* reported that Eppa was not in good physical form when he joined the club in May. "Midnight hours poring over books," said writer J. C. Kofoed, "does little to aid an athlete's condition, and he was drawn and rather colorless when he came to Philadelphia."[5] As a result, Rixey was unable to pitch often, and the other Phillie pitchers were required to shoulder more of the burden. Eppa skipped spring training again in 1914 to do post-graduate work, and some of his teammates did not appreciate Eppa's apparent lack of dedication to his pitching career.

The Phillies were a talented, but undisciplined ballclub with players regularly ignoring curfew and fighting amongst themselves. Some of the rougher players made fun of Rixey's Southern accent, and liked to upset Eppa by whistling "Marching Through Georgia" and making snide comments about the Civil War. Rixey, a proud Virginian, would respond with a burst of swear words and some thrown bats and gloves. Most of the kidding was good-natured, but it escalated during Eppa's difficult 1914 season and became more mean-spirited in tone.

Eppa roomed with two other former college pitchers, Joe Oeschger and Stan Baumgartner, and some of the less educated players expressed their resentment of the "college boys." Once, teammate Sherry Magee dropped a bag of water on Eppa's head from a sixth-floor hotel window. The enraged Eppa charged into the building and dashed to the elevator. "Don't you be waiting for no one else," Rixey told the elevator operator. "You take me up to the sixth floor, and as fast as this damn thing will go."[6] Magee escaped and avoided a fistfight with the angry Eppa.

Magee was Philadelphia's best hitter, but he liked to cause turmoil, and manager Dooin failed to enforce discipline where Magee was concerned. Magee also feuded with Dode Paskert, with whom he traded punches on the bench one day, and Milt Reed, another Southern pitcher who fought Magee in the clubhouse. The constant bickering and fisticuffs soured the 1914 campaign and ended Dooin's term as manager of the team.

After the 1914 season, the Phillies traded Dooin to Cincinnati and appointed coach Pat Moran, a former Phillies catcher, to the manager's chair. This turned out to be a fortunate selection, both for Rixey and the team as a whole, because Moran was a skilled handler of pitchers. He also demanded discipline and attention, as the Phillies soon learned. One day Moran ordered Eppa, sitting on the bench, to study the opposing pitcher. Rixey joked around on the bench and ignored the assignment until Moran took a fungo bat and whacked Rixey across the toes with it.

However, Eppa grew to appreciate the attention from Moran. "It was Pat who made a pitcher out of me," said Eppa in later years. "Few men that I've ever known in baseball knew the fine arts of pitching as did Moran." Moran insisted that Rixey participate in spring training for the first time, and Eppa started the season in the best physical condition of his life. Eppa improved to an 11–12 mark in 1915 and lowered his earned run average by nearly two full runs. Moran's discipline gave the entire team a needed boost, and the rejuvenated pitching staff led the Phillies to their first National League pennant and a berth in the World Series against the powerful Boston Red Sox.

Moran decided to go with a three-man rotation of Alexander (31–11 in 1915), Erskine Mayer (21–10), and George Chalmers (8–9) in the Series, with Rixey in the bullpen. Alexander won Game 1 with a five-hitter, but the Red Sox carried the next three games over Mayer, Alexander, and Chalmers, all of whom threw complete games. In Game 5, with the Phillies down by three games to one, Alexander complained of a sore arm shortly before the game began. Moran was tempted to send the well-rested Rixey to the hill, but eventually started Erskine Mayer against Boston's 20-game winner Rube Foster. The Phillies took a 2–0 lead in the first inning, but the Red Sox scored once in the second and again in the third. Eppa entered the game in relief of Mayer with one out in the third and stopped the threat, and then Fred Luderus gave the Phils a 4–2 lead with a homer in the fourth. Eppa kept the Red Sox off the board for the next four innings, and after the seventh the Phillies held a 4–2 lead.

William F. Baker, owner of the Phillies, had expanded the seating capacity of his ballpark by installing temporary seats in front of the left and center field walls. Those seats made the tiny ballpark even smaller and contributed directly to the eventual defeat of the Phillies. The Red Sox finally solved Rixey in the eighth, when Duffy Lewis hit a fly ball to left field that bounced into the new stands. Balls that bounced into the outfield seats counted as home runs in those days, so Lewis' hit scored two runs and tied the game. In the ninth, Harry Hooper reached Rixey for another home run, which bounced into the temporary seats in center field and gave the Red Sox a 5–4 lead. Foster shut down the Phils in the bottom of the ninth, and the Red Sox were the champions of the world.

The Phillies finished in second place in each of the next two seasons, but Eppa Rixey never again pitched on a pennant winner. His only appearance in World Series play ended in a loss, though he pitched well for most of the game, and his final Series won–lost record stands at 0–1.

Eppa, perhaps bolstered by his World Series performance, finally blossomed as a pitcher in 1916. He won 22 games and lost 10, with a sparkling 1.85 earned run average, as the Phillies battled the Dodgers down to the wire for the pennant. Rixey ably supported Pete Alexander, who put together one of the greatest pitching seasons in history with a 33–12 record and an astounding 16 shutouts. Despite the fine mound work of Alexander and Rixey, the Phils finished in second place, mostly because Erskine Mayer dropped to a 7–7 mark. They finished second again in 1917 when Alexander won 30 games, though Eppa slid to a 16–21 log.

The Phillies played in the Baker Bowl, a tiny ballpark with a right field fence that stood only 272 feet from home plate. The short dimensions of the field greatly increased the number of runs scored in Philadelphia and made pitching difficult for all Phillies hurlers. Eppa liked to keep the ball low and outside against right-handed batters, but his opponents learned to go with the outside pitch and slap it against the 40-foot wall in right. Eppa was not an overpowering pitcher, and he needed almost perfect control to win games in the Baker Bowl. Rixey's won–lost record in the early part of his career would probably have been better if he had played his home games in almost any other National League park.

During his Philadelphia years, Eppa Rixey earned a reputation as one of baseball's gentlemen. As a college graduate and the son of a prosperous family, Eppa was more cultured than most ballplayers in that era. He liked talking to the sportswriters, who gave him good press in return and increased his popularity with the Philadelphia fans. Eppa liked to project the image of the slightly goofy lefthander. He once told writer F. C. Lane, "There are some 'nuts' among us left-handers. But look at all the right-handers who have their wires crossed. I tell you we are not properly appreciated, we left-handers. We are really a small and select circle … but among the limited number of left-handers, see how

Eppa Rixey warming up for the Phillies. (National Baseball Hall of Fame Library, Cooperstown, New York)

many are genuine stars. There are Babe Ruth and George Sisler and Tris Speaker and Jake Daubert…. What would baseball be without left-handers?"[7]

However, that is not to say that Rixey was not a competitive individual. He may have been the model of the Southern gentleman, but Eppa was known to smash up the furniture in the clubhouse after a tough loss. He wanted to win ballgames as much as any pitcher in the major leagues. This combination of friendliness and competitive zeal made Eppa one of the most popular players on the Philadelphia ballclub.

Eppa also gained a middle name in Philadelphia. Someone — perhaps a sportswriter, or maybe one of Eppa's teammates— decided that the young ballplayer should have a proper middle name. They settled on "Jephtha," a Biblical name that sounded both odd and memorable, and seemed to fit harmoniously between Eppa and Rixey. It probably started as a nickname, because the other Phillies were referring to the young pitcher as Jephtha as early as 1914, and so fitting did it sound that it stuck with Eppa for the rest of his life. Eppa tried to explain that he had no middle name, but to this day one still sees the pitcher identified as Eppa Jephtha Rixey, or at least as Eppa J. Rixey.

World War One changed the fortunes of the Phillies, and of Rixey's career as well. Pete Alexander held a high position on the draft list, and Phillies owner William Baker feared that Alexander might go into the service and never return. Accordingly, Baker sold Alexander and catcher Bill Killefer to the Chicago Cubs in November 1917 for $60,000 and two young players.

Eppa Rixey held a lower Selective Service number, and before the Alexander deal Eppa was content to take his chances on the military draft and continue pitching for the Phillies. Once the deal was made, however, Eppa knew that the Phillies would go nowhere in 1918. Eppa then enlisted in the Army, one of the first active players to do so. He served in Europe in the Army's chemical warfare division and earned the rank of captain. During Eppa's absence from the ballclub, the Phillies fell all the way to fifth place. He remained overseas until he was mustered out of the Army in May of 1919.

When Rixey returned to the Phillies, star players like Mayer, Alexander, and Killefer were all playing for other teams. What's more, Rixey's biggest supporter, Pat Moran, was dismissed as manager late in 1918 and signed with the Cincinnati Reds. While Moran led the Reds to their first World Series title in the infamous "Black Sox" series of 1919, the decimated Phillies dropped to the bottom of the standings. Eppa Rixey, finally the number one pitcher on the Philadelphia staff, suffered from a sore arm that season and won only six games and lost 12. None of the other Phillie pitchers did much better, as 13 different pitchers started games for the club that year, and no one managed to win more than eight games. The 1920 campaign was even worse, as Rixey returned to health but posted an 11–22 log, leading the National League in losses for the woeful Phillies. After eight seasons in the majors, Rixey's career record stood at 87–103.

Once again, Pat Moran stepped in to save Rixey's career. On January 16, 1921, Moran and the Cincinnati Reds traded outfielder Earle (Greasy) Neale and pitcher Jimmy Ring — two of the Reds' World Series heroes of 1919 — to the Phillies for Rixey.

Moran gave up two solid performers for a pitcher whose career was at a crossroads, but he recognized that the less-than-overpowering Rixey needed to play on a team with a solid defense. With outstanding glove men like Jake Daubert at first base and Edd Roush in center field, the Reds could offer Rixey the fielding support that the Phillies could not provide. After a 19–18 season in 1921, Rixey blossomed under Moran's tutelage. The Reds jumped to second place in 1922 as Rixey won 25 games, leading the National

League in wins for the first and only time in his career. "Everything I did that season was right," said Rixey many years later. "I just couldn't do anything wrong. I still wonder how I lost those 13 games."[8]

In 1923 the Reds finished second to the Giants once again, as Rixey compiled a 20–15 mark. He again settled into a subordinate position on the staff, as teammate Dolf Luque led the league with 27 wins and Pete Donahue chipped in 21. Luque and Donahue threw harder than Rixey, but Eppa won games with his control and knowledge of the hitters. People often said that Eppa liked to toy with the batters. He seemed to go to 3–2 counts more than any pitcher in the league, but he still averaged only slightly more than two walks per nine innings pitched in his career.

By 1923, Rixey had abandoned all pretense of being a strikeout pitcher. After topping the 100 mark in strikeouts three times with the Phillies, Rixey only once fanned more than 80 batters in any season for the Reds. He concentrated on putting the ball over the plate and letting his defense help him. He also learned to take advantage of the spacious Cincinnati ballpark. The outfield fences in Cincinnati were so far from the plate that home runs were a rare occurrence at Redlands Field; the park opened in 1912, but Pat Duncan hit the first over-the-fence homer there in 1921. After years of worrying about the short right field wall in Philadelphia, the huge Cincinnati outfield proved a blessing for Eppa's style of pitching.

As he aged, Rixey gained a reputation as an intelligent hurler. He knew that many batters lacked the patience to study the pitchers and look for certain pitches in certain situations. Years later, Rixey's old Cincinnati teammate Rube Bressler quoted Rixey's approach in the latter stages of his career:

> How dumb can the hitters in this league get? [said Rixey, as quoted by Bressler]… I've been doing this for fifteen years. When they're batting with the count two balls and no strikes, or three and one, they're always looking for the fastball. And they never get it. They get the change of pace every time — and they're just as surprised to see it as they were the last time.[9]

Eppa helped his own cause on the field by making himself into a good fielder. He committed only 30 errors in his 21 seasons of pitching, and compiled excellent fielding averages and range factors, combined with an unusually large total of assists. Many tall pitchers with large feet (Eppa wore size 13 shoes) prove awkward in fielding the position, but Eppa Rixey was one of the better fielding pitchers in the game in that era.

Baseball historian Bill James has remarked on Eppa's number of assists, many of which resulted from fielding sacrifice bunts. "Eppa," says James, "is the Babe Ruth of sacrifice hits allowed, allowing more than anyone else in history."[10] It appears that Eppa played the percentages and always took the out that the opposition made available. He didn't own a powerful throwing arm, and he didn't field a sacrifice bunt and throw it to second if there was any possibility that he might not be able to nip the lead runner. He simply took the out at first and went to work on the next batter. Since Eppa walked few batters and gave up few home runs, especially in Cincinnati, he knew that the opponents needed a lot of hits to beat him. If they were willing to surrender one of their 27 outs, then that was fine with Rixey.

Off the field, Eppa moved to Cincinnati and met a young woman named Dorothy Meyers, whom he married in October of 1924. They set up a household in the Cincinnati suburbs and raised two children, a boy named Eppa III and a girl named Ann. Eppa relied on Dorothy to keep him grounded. The ballplayer enjoyed telling a story of how, in a game in St. Louis on June 28, 1924, he belted two singles, a double, and a homer off Cardinal pitcher Jesse Haines. Eppa was never the greatest of hitters, and he excitedly called Dorothy, then his fiancée, with the news of his batting exploits.

"You hit a home run?" asked Dorothy. "Something dreadful must be about to happen in St. Louis."[11]

The lefthanded pitcher, who batted righthanded, hit only three home runs in his 21-year career, and the last one caused the Boston Braves to reconfigure their ballpark. In 1928, the Braves acquired Rogers Hornsby from the Giants and immediately built a "jury box" of seats in front of the left field wall, hoping that Hornsby would deposit his share of homers there. Hornsby did not hit many into the new seats, but opposing players did. In the first three days of June, three Cincinnati pitchers belted round-trippers into the jury box off Boston pitching. When the light-hitting Rixey connected against Joe Genewich on June 3, the Braves management took the hint and tore out the extra seats.

For the rest of the 1920s, Eppa Rixey remained as the second or third member of the Cincinnati rotation. The team's pennant chances in 1924 vanished in spring training, when manager Pat Moran died suddenly of Bright's disease. The Reds came in fourth under new manager Jack Hendricks, but the team suffered another tragedy in October of that year. First baseman Jake Daubert, a two-time batting champion and outstanding defensive player, died of appendicitis a few days after the end of the campaign. The Reds challenged for two more seasons before they dropped out of contention, passed by the rising Cardinals and Pirates.

The 1926 campaign ended harshly for both Eppa and the Reds. Cincinnati held a two-game lead in a four-team pennant race in mid–September, but on September 16 the Reds lost to the Giants in New York and fell back into a first-place tie with St. Louis. The next day, the Giants knocked both Dolf Luque and Pete Donahue out of the game and took a 4–0 lead. Eppa then relieved and held the Giants scoreless until the Reds could catch up. The score stood at 4–4 in the bottom of the tenth inning when Frankie Frisch finally solved Rixey. Frisch belted a home run to win the game and knock the Reds out of first place. The Reds never managed to reclaim the lead, losing the pennant to the Cardinals by two games.

After their second-place finish in 1926, the Reds began a long, slow slide to the bottom of the standings. Rixey went 12–10 in for the fifth-place Reds in 1927, then briefly regained his status as the number one starter with a 19–18 mark in 1928. After that, the aging lefthander shuttled between the starting rotation and the bullpen. The Depression hit the Reds especially hard, and team owner Sidney Weil was forced to declare bankruptcy and sell the ballclub. Before he did so, the Reds staggered along at a severe competitive disadvantage, unable to sign good young players or trade for established stars. The Reds, who dismissed Hendricks in 1929, fell with a thud to the National League cellar.

Eppa got older, but never mellowed. He showed the same competitive spirit that he had displayed during his career, and still made his feelings known after a tough loss. One of his catchers, Clyde Sukeforth, described him this way:

> He was a fierce competitor and a hard loser. When he pitched, you didn't have to ask who won the game, all you had to do was look at the clubhouse later. If he's lost, the place would look like a tornado had gone through it. Chairs would be broken up, tables knocked over, equipment thrown around. The ball club didn't like that, needless to say, but what were they going to say to Rixey? That fellow was an institution in Cincinnati.[12]

By 1933, Eppa Rixey was 42 years old, the oldest (and still the tallest) player in the major leagues, and was the only lefthander on the Cincinnati staff. For the last several years of his career, he served as the "Sunday pitcher" for the Reds. The Reds played the Pittsburgh Pirates often on Sundays in those years, because the Pirates did not play at home on the Sabbath and often skipped over to Cincinnati for a doubleheader, where they would face the well-rested Rixey. The Pirates fielded a mostly left-handed lineup, which suited Rixey to a T, and the old pitcher added several more games to his career win total against the Pirates.

One of Eppa's worst experiences in baseball came in a game against the Pirates, though he was able to laugh about it in later years. One day in

September 1927, Pittsburgh's Lloyd Waner lifted a lazy fly ball to left field that hit the chalk foul line and bounced into the stands for a cheap home run. The next batter, Paul Waner, swung at the first pitch and hit a fly ball in the same place. It also hit the chalk and bounced into the seats for a homer. "Those were the only two times in my life," said Rixey, "that I ever saw a ball hit in that spot and go into the stands. And it had to happen to me on two straight pitches, and by two brothers."[13]

Eppa fashioned a 6–3 record in 1933, with seven of his 12 starts coming against Pittsburgh, but he wanted to pitch more against other teams. When Larry MacPhail bought the Reds in 1934, Eppa asked the new owner to order manager Bob O'Farrell to pitch Eppa against other ballclubs. MacPhail replied that he would not interfere in his manager's handling of the pitching staff, so in March of 1934 Eppa announced his retirement. He left the game after 22 seasons with 266 wins and 251 losses, both National League records for lefthanded pitchers.

Rixey had been preparing for this moment for many years. His father-in-law, Charles Meyers, operated a successful insurance agency in Cincinnati and taught Rixey the ropes of the insurance business in the off-seasons. Eppa had joked about it often. "I am an insurance agent," he told F. C. Lane in the mid–1920s. "They told me it was a good job for a player and in a moment of weakness I yielded. The germs of a great salesman may be dormant in my frame and it's up to me to give them a chance."[14] By the time Eppa left the Reds, he was able to step in as a partner in the Meyers-Rixey Insurance Agency. Eppa became the proprietor after his father-in-law died, and the old ballplayer changed its name to the Eppa Rixey Agency. Eppa eventually brought his son, Eppa Rixey III, into the business.

He never felt that his degree in chemistry from the University of Virginia had gone to waste. "If I had my life to live over again," said Rixey one day late in his career, "I would do exactly as I have done. I would welcome an opportunity to play big league baseball. The old game has bestowed upon me a far wider reputation than I would ever have gained by holding test tubes over Bunsen burners in a chemical laboratory."[15]

Rixey built a fine Colonial home in Terrace Park, a suburb of Cincinnati, and lived comfortably there for the rest of his life. He was an outstanding golfer and enjoyed playing with his brother William, a doctor and top-notch amateur golfing star of the 1930s. The insurance business prospered, and Eppa spent many volunteer hours assisting in the formation of Knothole Baseball, a successful youth program in the Cincinnati area. He was an enthusiastic storyteller who gave interviews to sportswriters every now and then, but he mostly stayed out of the public eye until his Hall of Fame election.

Eppa had hoped to gain a place in the Hall for several years. In 1959 he visited Cooperstown, New York, bought postcards at the baseball museum and sent them to friends. "I made it to the Hall of Fame," wrote Rixey, "for only one day." Four years later, Eppa made it for real.

Eppa Rixey managed to enjoy his status as a Hall of Famer for only four weeks. On February 28, 1963, he suffered a heart attack and died at age 71. He was buried in the Greenlawn Cemetery in Milford, Ohio, and his widow and children accepted his plaque at the Hall of Fame induction ceremony in August of that year. The family insurance agency still operates in suburban Cincinnati, and Eppa Rixey IV, the ballplayer's grandson, now serves as the president of the company.

Does Eppa Rixey belong in the Hall of Fame?

His statistics pale beside those of many other Cooperstown honorees. Bob Feller, who entered the major leagues three years after Eppa retired, also won 266 major league games and, like Rixey, went straight to the majors without the benefit of minor league experience. Feller's won–loss record, however, was far superior, as was that of Jim Palmer, who won two more games than Rixey or Feller:

	Wins–Losses	Plus/Minus	Percentage
Eppa Rixey	266–251	+15	.515
Bob Feller	266–162	+104	.621
Jim Palmer	268–152	+116	.638

Eppa's winning percentage (.515) and plus–minus record (+15) are the lowest of any starting pitcher in the Hall of Fame.

It appears that Rixey rode into the Hall on the strength of his association with Warren Spahn, who passed Rixey's win record in 1959 and focused new attention on the long-forgotten pitcher. Nonetheless, Eppa Rixey's career bears little resemblance to Spahn's. When Spahn retired in 1965, he had won 363 games, 97 more than Rixey, while losing six games fewer (245 to Rixey's 251). Rixey's league total of 266 wins was also passed by another lefthander, Steve Carlton, in 1982. Carlton ended his career with 53 more wins and 25 fewer losses than Rixey in National League play. Though Rixey's total of wins now ranks third among National League lefties, his total of 251 losses still claims the top spot.

One can make the claim that Rixey's statistics were depressed by playing on poor teams, but other pitchers played for worse teams that Rixey did. The Phillies fell to the depths of the league in the latter part of Rixey's tenure with the club, but they won the pennant in 1915 and finished second three other times from 1913 to 1917. The Reds, for whom Rixey toiled from 1921 to 1933, never won the flag, but challenged several times, coming in second in 1922, 1923, and 1926. Walter Johnson, who won 416 games, and Tom Seaver, with 311 wins, also pitched for bad teams throughout their careers, with significantly more success than Rixey.

The most telling argument against Rixey's inclusion in the Hall of Fame remains the fact that he won only 15 more games than he lost. Every other starting pitcher in Cooperstown (except for those who were elected for their pitching in the Negro Leagues) compiled at least 24 more wins than losses. The bottom ten starting pitchers in the Hall in the plus–minus category are:

	Wins–Losses	Plus/Minus
Eppa Rixey	266–251	+15
Rube Marquard	201–177	+24
Ted Lyons	260–230	+30
Nolan Ryan	324–292	+32
Jim Bunning	224–184	+40
Robin Roberts	286–245	+41
Red Faber	254–212	+42
Don Drysdale	209–166	+43
Vic Willis	249–205	+44
Phil Niekro	318–274	+44

Even Hoyt Wilhelm, primarily a reliever throughout his career, finished at +21 in the win–loss department, six games better than Rixey. Babe Ruth, who pitched regularly for only the first six years of his career before he moved to the outfield, won 94 games and lost 46 for a +48 mark.

Several other pitchers have won over 250 games and have compiled better records, but are not in the Hall of Fame:

	Wins–Losses	Plus/Minus
Jack Morris	254–186	+68
Tommy John	288–231	+57
Jim Kaat	283–237	+46
Bert Blyleven	287–250	+37

Eppa Rixey was a good pitcher who lasted for an extraordinarily long time, but he was never considered to be the best pitcher in baseball. He led his league in wins once, in shutouts once, and in innings pitched once, and never led in any other positive pitching category. Rixey was the second or third starter on most of his teams, and compiled 266 wins mostly as a result of his longevity. His selection to the Hall of Fame, in retrospect, seems like an overreaction to the publicity that was generated when Warren Spahn broke his record.

11

♦ JAKE BECKLEY ♦

Beckley was one of the first of the lefthanded first basemen, and a good one, too. He was a quaint character, noted for his economy and original Missouri humor … and never stopped battling from the first inning till the finish. Off the field, Jake was good humored, peaceable, and popular. There were many like him long ago, and few of them survive today.— The Sporting News, 1918[1]

In the late 1950s and early 1960s, the Veterans Committee of the Hall of Fame selected several long-forgotten stars of the 1880–1910 period for induction. Two of them, Sam Crawford and Elmer Flick, were still living and able to enjoy the honor, but the rest of these old-timers had been dead for many decades. The committee, still catching up to players whose candidacies had been overlooked in the 1940s, selected 300-game winning pitchers (John Clarkson, Pud Galvin, and Tim Keefe), managers (John Ward) and batting stars (Crawford, Flick, and Billy Hamilton) from baseball's formative decades. This run of selections ended with the enshrinement of Galvin in 1965, and no additional 19th century stars were chosen in the next several years.

By 1970 the directors of the Hall of Fame realized that they still faced a backlog of qualified early candidates, and that not all of the deserving 19th century players had yet been honored with a plaque in the Cooperstown museum. In July of that year, the Hall authorized the Veterans Committee to choose up to four old-time stars for enshrinement. Because the committee was also charged with electing two men from the post–1925 period, along with one executive or umpire, the committee was empowered to choose up to seven new Hall of Famers at its next meeting in early 1971.

Most people believed that the term "old-time" meant "19th century," but the Veterans Committee emerged from its meeting on January 31, 1971, with a surprise. The committee chose seven men for induction, but elected only two 19th century players, longtime National League first baseman Jake Beckley and Baltimore Orioles slugger Joe Kelley. The other two old-timers were pitcher Rube Marquard and outfielder Harry Hooper, both of whom played in the major leagues as late as 1926. One of the post–1925 inductees, Dave Bancroft, ended his active career only four years after Marquard and Hooper ended theirs.

Hooper and Marquard are considered by most experts to be two of the weakest Hall of Fame selections, but their selections met with public approval. Each man had gained favorable public attention in 1966 when each was interviewed for Lawrence Ritter's popular oral history, *The Glory of Their Times*. Also, both were still living in 1971, which may have swayed the committee to elect them over others such as Sam Thompson, Roger Connor, and Mickey Welch, all of whom played in the 1880s and had been dead for many years. Nonetheless, it seemed odd that the committee had selected Marquard, winner of 201 major league games, only two weeks after the Baseball Writers Association had bypassed 300-game winner Early Wynn in its annual balloting. The veterans' panel paired Marquard with Hooper, a good but not great outfielder, after the writers had failed to elect Yogi Berra, considered by some to be the greatest catcher of all time.

The nods to Marquard and Hooper were criticized in the sporting press, but the attention of the sportswriters soon turned to a newly formed panel, the Committee on the Negro Leagues, which elected Satchel Paige to the Hall of Fame in June of 1971. This sparked a new controversy about the presence of Negro League stars, many of whom played major league ball only briefly or not at all, in the Cooperstown pantheon. Paige's election brought the total number of 1971 enshrinees to eight, the largest Hall of Fame class since 11 men gained induction in 1946.

Lost in all the confusion was the identity of a long-forgotten first baseman who still ranks as perhaps the most obscure member of the Hall of Fame. Jake Beckley was one of baseball's most celebrated players at the turn of the 20th century, but he quickly faded from memory after leaving the game in 1907. When Beckley entered the Hall of Fame in 1971, 53 years after his death, most baseball fans had no idea who he was or why he should be so honored.

Jacob Peter Beckley was born in the Mississippi River town of Hannibal, Missouri, on August 4, 1867.[2] He was the second oldest of the five children of Jacob and Mary Beckley, who owned a farm in Shelby County, a few miles west of Hannibal. Baseball mania swept the Midwest around the time he was born, and so young Jake played ball on sandlots and in pastures around town on breaks from his farm chores. Jake, a left-handed batter and thrower, was a good hitter and fielder, and as an older teenager he played for fast semipro teams whenever he could get away from his job in a machine shop.

Bob Hart, a former teammate of Jake's from Hannibal who by 1886 was pitching for Leavenworth, Kansas in the Western League, arranged for young Beckley's introduction to professional ball. The Leavenworth team needed players, and Hart recommended the 18-year-old Jake Beckley to his manager. Beckley traveled to Leavenworth and batted .342 in 75 games, playing mostly second base and the outfield. He won the crowd over in his first game when he belted three hits, including a homer.

Jake could hit — he batted over .400 in 1887 when walks counted as hits — but he did not show much range at second base, and his throwing arm was found wanting. Left-handed throwers still played second, short, and third in the 1880s, though fewer lefties did so with each passing year, and by the end of the decade three of the four infield positions became the virtually exclusive province of right-handed throwers. Beckley did not have the throwing strength or accuracy required to play at those infield positions anyway, or in the outfield either. The Leavenworth team moved him to first base in 1887, where being left-handed was an advantage, and Beckley played that position for the rest of his career.

The Leavenworth club sold Jake to another Western League team in Lincoln, Nebraska, in the middle of the 1887 campaign. He finished the season in Lincoln, then played winter ball for an independent team in Stockton, California. In early 1888, Lincoln sold the steadily improving Beckley to the Western Association's St. Louis Whites. Beckley's fine play at first base quickly attracted attention, and he played only 34 games in St. Louis before the Whites sold him to the Pittsburgh Alleghenies of the National League for $4,000.

The Alleghenies had finished second in the American Association two years before, but moved into the faster National League for the 1887 campaign. The team featured a few star players in pitcher Pud Galvin and outfielder Billy Sunday, but six different men played first in 1887 as the Alleghenies limped home in sixth place. Beckley arrived in June of 1888 and immediately closed the first-base hole. Still only 20 years old, Jake batted .343 and solidified the right side of the Pittsburgh infield with his defensive play. He was Pittsburgh's only .300 hitter and posted an average only one point behind league leader Cap Anson, though Jake did not play enough games to qualify for the batting title. He led the club's regulars in batting again in 1889, and soon earned the nickname "Eagle Eye" for his batting skill. The hard-hitting Beckley brought a dash of excitement to the Alleghenies, and it didn't take long for Jake to become the most popular player on the Pittsburgh team.

Jake interrupted his National League career when he, along with eight of his teammates and manager Ned Hanlon, bolted to the Pittsburgh entry of the new Players League in the spring of 1890. Beckley had become a member of the Brotherhood of Professional Baseball Players upon joining the Alleghenies in 1888, and when the Brotherhood created its own Players League in late 1889 Jake quit the Alleghenies and cast his lot with the new circuit. However, the Alleghenies made Jake a counteroffer, and Beckley angered his new compatriots when he jumped back to the National a few weeks later. The Brotherhood banned Jake and several others (including stars John Clarkson and Jack Glasscock) as "traitors" in December 1889, but the following March Beckley changed his mind again and rejoined the Players League. Beckley had considered remaining with the Alleghenies, but the new league needed the popular first baseman and made a higher salary offer. As Jake explained to the papers, "I'm only in this game for the money anyway."[3]

The new team was called the Burghers, and Hanlon brought the team home in sixth place despite Beckley's finest season to that point. Jake batted .320, with nine homers and 120 runs batted in, and led the Burghers in nearly every batting category. He belted 20 triples to lead the Players League, while the Alleghenies missed Beckley and their other stars so much that they fell all the way to last place. The Players League collapsed after one season, and Jake returned to the Alleghenies for the 1891 campaign. During that off-season, a multi-team dispute over the contract status of second baseman Louis Bierbauer prompted some rival newspaper columnists to dub the Pittsburgh club owners "Pirates," a term that became the team's permanent nickname.

The popular first baseman was Pittsburgh's main run producer and one of its leading run scorers. Despite his stocky build (he stood six feet tall and weighed nearly 200 pounds) he ran well enough to reach double figures in stolen bases and triples almost every year. Beckley was a fast base runner, but he didn't mind cutting across the infield if the umpire's back was turned. One day, when umpire Tim Hurst wasn't looking, Jake ran almost directly from second base to home, sliding in without a throw. Hurst called Jake out anyway. "What do you mean, I'm out?" demanded Jake. "They didn't even make a play on me!"

"You big SOB," shouted Hurst, "you got here too quick!"[4]

Beckley was a handsome man, though his right eye was slightly crossed, which might also have been the genesis of his nickname "Eagle Eye." His most noticeable physical feature was his impressive mustache, which he kept long after all but a handful of players had relinquished theirs. By the time his career was over, Jake was one of only three men in the majors who still sported facial hair. Popular with the female fans, Jake married a Hannibal girl named Molly Murphy in March of 1891, but she died only seven months later. He slumped badly after her death, with his batting average falling to .250 in 1892, before he righted his career and returned to the .300 level. Jake did not marry again for many years.

Beckley, like many players of his era, displayed a range of idiosyncrasies. He yelled "Chickazoola!" to rattle opposing pitchers when he was on a batting tear. He also perfected the unusual and now-illegal practice of bunting with the handle of his bat. As the pitch approached the plate, Beckley would flip the bat around in his hands and tap the

Jake Beckley playing for the St. Louis Whites in 1888. (Author's collection)

ball with the bat handle. Casey Stengel was a teenager when he saw Beckley perform the feat. "I showed our players," said Stengel 50 years later, when he was managing the Yankees, "and they say it's the silliest thing they ever saw, which it probably is but [Beckley] done it." Stengel tried the maneuver once himself in the minors, but the league fined him and warned him not to do it again.

Jake loved pulling the hidden-ball trick, and tried the stunt on every new player that entered the National League. Sometimes he concealed the ball in his clothing or under his arm, but he most enjoyed hiding it under the base sack and waiting for the unsuspecting player to wander off first. He nearly caused a riot in Baltimore one day in May 1893 when he caught the popular Oriole star Joe Kelley off the base that way. That trick backfired one other time when Jake forgot which corner of the base concealed the ball, and the runner strolled to second base as Beckley, on his hands and knees, searched for the missing ball. The hidden ball ploy worked often enough, however, and although every opposing player knew that Jake might be trying to trick them, Jake still caught more than his share of runners off base.

Another gambit ended more successfully. One day, with Louisville's Honus Wagner on first, Jake smuggled an extra ball onto the field and put it under his armpit, partially exposed so Wagner could see it. When the umpire's back was turned, Wagner grabbed the ball away from Beckley and heaved it into the outfield. Wagner lit out for second, but the pitcher still held the game ball and threw Wagner out.

Beckley was a fine fielder with good range and quick reflexes, and led the league's first basemen in putouts six times and assists four times. His only weakness was a poor throwing arm, and National League base runners always knew that they could take an extra base on Jake. He once fielded a bunt by Louisville's Tommy Leach and threw wildly past first base. Beckley retrieved the ball himself and saw the speedy Leach rounding third and heading for home. Rather than risk another bad throw, Jake ran all the way to home plate and threw a body block on the Louisville runner as both men slid into the plate. Beckley not only tagged Leach out, but also broke two of the smaller man's ribs in the collision.

Beckley with Pittsburgh in the early 1890s. (National Baseball Hall of Fame Library, Cooperstown, New York)

He was a friendly individual whom *The Sporting News* once described as a "bulky, gawky, playful Missourian," and he paid close attention to his statistics. One story relates how Jake was riding in a carriage when a group of fans called to him, asking him the outcome of that day's ballgame. "I got four hits," replied Jake proudly. "That was old-timer Jake all over," said *The Sporting News*, "not smart, just [a] big, natural guy ... [a] big, happy, healthy, good-natured, small-town boy."[5]

He wasn't the most popular first baseman in the league, however, among the opposing players. Cleveland infielder and manager Patsy Tebeau held a long-standing grudge against Beckley, dating from a spiking incident early in Jake's career. "Beckley has injured more men on the diamond that any three players," Tebeau once said. "He put me out of the game [with a spike wound] for three months in 1891, and the same injury has kept me on the bench from two to six weeks a season ever since."[6] Jake employed all the standard tricks of 1890s baseball; "he was no parlor ball player," remarked *The Sporting News*, "but believed in the old-school stuff— give 'em the leg when rounding first, grab 'em by the belt when the umpire wasn't looking."[7] During a contest in 1898, baserunner Bill Joyce of the Giants tangled with Beckley at first base and became so enraged that he grabbed the ball and threw it at Beckley, hitting him in the back.

Jake recovered from his 1892 slump and batted over .300 again the following year as the Pirates battled Boston for the pennant. Tensions ran high between the two ballclubs, especially after Boston's Herman Long crashed into Pirate catcher Connie Mack at the plate one day, shattering Mack's leg and virtually ending his playing career. In the end, Boston won its third consecutive league title by five games, and Jake Beckley never again came close to playing on a pennant winner. In the next season, the Pirates fell to seventh place and Mack replaced Al Buckenberger as manager.

"Eagle Eye" batted over .300 for Connie Mack's Pirates in 1894 and 1895, but when he slumped in 1896 the Pirates, over the loud objections of their fans, traded him to the New York Giants for first baseman Harry Davis and $1,000 in cash. Mack did not want to dispose of Beckley, but the Pirate front office made the deal without telling the manager, and Mack did not know that Jake had been traded until he saw Jake angrily packing his bags in the Pirate clubhouse.

"I didn't make the deal for Davis but I had to take all the abuse for it," said Mack to writer Fred Lieb many decades later. "Jake Beckley was about the most popular player in Pittsburgh; he was a powerful hitter and had a strong, loyal following. I still recall persons hollering at me from Pittsburgh windows: 'Why did you trade Jake Beckley?'"[8] Mack lost his job as Pirate manager at the end of the 1896 campaign, mostly because the Pittsburgh fans turned against him after the Beckley trade. The trade had one beneficial outcome for Mack, however. It introduced him to Harry Davis, who played and coached under Mack for many years thereafter and became Mack's trusted lieutenant with the Philadelphia Athletics.

Jake was not happy in New York. Beckley joined the Giants and found a team in turmoil, with star pitcher Amos Rusie sitting out the entire season in a salary dispute with the notoriously quarrelsome club owner Andrew Freedman. In 1895, Freedman hired and fired two managers (respected baseball men George Davis and Jack Doyle) before giving the job to Harvey Watkins, a sometime Broadway actor and political hanger-on with no baseball experience whatsoever. Watkins was probably the least qualified manager in the annals of the game, and many historians call Freedman the worst team owner in history. He turned the once-proud Giants franchise into a laughingstock, and Beckley was not the only player who longed to get out of New York.

Beckley batted .302 for the Giants in 1896 after hitting only .239 in Pittsburgh, but he made no secret of his displeasure with the Giants. When Jake began the 1897 season poorly (hitting only .250 after 17 games) the Giants surprised the baseball world when they released Beckley without even trying to trade him. Most observers thought Beckley's career was over, but the Cincinnati Reds needed a first baseman and signed Beckley a few weeks later. His bat came alive again in Cincinnati, and on September 26, 1897, Beckley belted three homers in a 10–4 victory at St. Louis. No major leaguer performed that feat again until Ken Williams did it in 1922. On May 19, 1898, Jake smacked three triples against the best pitcher in baseball, Kid Nichols, in a 5–4 Cincinnati victory over Boston.

For the next seven years Beckley played first base for the Reds, batting over .300 in every season except one. The Reds, however, were almost as dysfunctional as the Giants had been. Reds owner John T. Brush also owned the Indianapolis team in the Western League, and for several seasons Brush shuttled players back and forth between Cincinnati to Indianapolis, depending on each club's pennant chances. If the Reds dropped out of the National League race, they might find some of their players transferred to Indianapolis for the remainder of the campaign, if the Hoosiers were still in the Western League chase. The Hoosiers won pennants in 1897 and 1899 as the Reds fell steadily down the standings.

Brush played managerial musical chairs with the Reds. Buck Ewing was fired after a sixth-place finish in 1899, and Brush promoted Indianapolis skipper Bob Allen to the Cincinnati manager's chair in 1900. Allen lost his job after a seventh-place finish and a serious drop in attendance in 1900, and in an effort to win back the fans Brush gave the manager's post to the popular former second baseman Bid McPhee. Attendance perked up a bit in 1901, but the talent-poor Reds finished dead last in the National League, and by mid–1902 McPhee was sent packing.

Brush also displayed a stunning insensitivity when it came to dealing with his players. On May 28, 1900, a fire gutted the Cincinnati stadium and destroyed all the players' uniforms and equipment. Brush quickly moved to rebuild the ballpark, but he demanded that Jake and the other Cincinnati players cover the cost of replacing their uniforms. The players refused, and public pressure forced Brush to reconsider and pay for the new uniforms himself.

Jake ignored the turmoil and kept pounding the ball. He batted .299 in 1898, when the Reds held the league lead into August, but his season ended on August 27 when he collided with Philadelphia's Napoleon Lajoie at first base. This injury dropped the Reds out of contention, and the Boston club passed the Reds, winning the pennant with 31 wins in its last 36 games. In 1899 Beckley batted .333 and put together hitting streaks of 25 and 18 games, and the next season he led the team in batting with a .343 average. His career nearly ended on July 8, 1901, when Giants pitcher Christy Mathewson hit Beckley in the head with a fastball, knocking Jake unconscious for more than five minutes. Beckley recovered, missing only two games, and hit .307 for the last-place Reds that season. He was "Old Eagle Eye" by now, but still a solid fielder and run producer.

Beckley pitched for the only time in his career on the last day of the 1902 campaign. The Reds were in Pittsburgh on a rainy, muddy day, and Pirates owner Barney Dreyfuss insisted on playing even though the Pirates had clinched the pennant weeks before. To show his dismay, Reds manager Joe Kelley tapped the notoriously scatter-armed Jake Beckley as his starting pitcher, and played other Reds out of position. Jake allowed nine hits and eight runs in his four innings of work, and the game degenerated into a farce. Catcher Rube Vickers, normally a pitcher, committed six passed balls and didn't even bother chasing several of Beckley's wild pitches. The Pirates won the game 11–2, but the irate fans forced Dreyfuss to refund all the gate receipts.

"Old Eagle Eye" was popular with the Cincinnati fans, but by 1902 Jake was disgruntled with the Reds and longed for a way out of town. In mid–1902, Reds owner John T. Brush bought the Giants and sold his stake in the Reds to local investors, who tapped former Baltimore slugger Joe Kelley as their new manager. Kelley, who no doubt still remembered how Jake had embarrassed him with the hidden-ball trick nine years before, wanted to play first base himself, so the new owners promised to trade Jake to the Brooklyn Dodgers. They could not consummate the deal, however, and so Jake played for the next two seasons with Kelley looking over his shoulder.

The veteran first baseman batted .327 in 1903, but manager Kelley wanted to get back into the lineup, so in February 1904, the Reds sold the 36-year-old Beckley to St. Louis. He hit well in his first two seasons with the Cardinals, though some of his off-field habits caused headaches for his new manager, Kid Nichols. On July 30, 1904, rumors swept the city of Pittsburgh that the game that day between the Pirates and Cardinals had been fixed by gambling interests. In that game, Cardinal pitcher Jack Taylor walked seven batters and threw three wild pitches as the Pirates pounded out a 5–2 win. After an investigation, the National League determined that no game fixing had occurred. The local gamblers had wagered heavily on the Pirates that day because Taylor and Beckley had gone on a public drinking spree the night before, and all the gamblers in town knew that both the starting pitcher and the cleanup hitter of the Cardinals would be severely hung over at game time.

Jake was the victim of one of baseball's most controversial plays on May 7, 1904. The Cardinals were leading the Giants 1–0 in the bottom of ninth when New York's Roger Bresnahan doubled home pinch-runner John McGraw to tie the game. Most of the Giant players bolted from the bench and congregated near third base in the excitement, while Bresnahan took third on the throw back to the infield. While Jake held the ball at first, someone in a Giants uniform made a dash from third to home. Jake, naturally assuming that the runner in question was Bresnahan, threw wildly to the plate. The runner was not Bresnahan, but another Giant who noticed that the plate was uncovered and fooled Beckley into throwing home. Bresnahan trotted home with the winning run while the embarrassed Beckley raged at the umpire.

Cardinal manager Kid Nichols protested the game, citing a phrase in the official rulebook that stated "if one or more members of the team at bat stand or collect around a base for which a base runner is trying, thereby confusing the fielding side and adding to the difficulty of making such play, the base runner shall be declared out for the interference of his teammate or teammates." One report stated that Beckley, the Cardinal defensive captain, marched the umpire all the way to the clubhouse to show him the rulebook. However, league president Harry Pulliam disallowed the protest, and the result stood as a 2–1 Giant win.

Though Jake was one of the National League's oldest players by 1906, he saw no reason to think about life after baseball. "I'm still too young to think of retiring," said Beckley to Sporting Life magazine in May 1906. "Me for a few more years in the big league before I put my mitt away.... Why, I'd rather play a game of base ball than start a race with the best horses in the country entered."[9] Horse racing was his favorite hobby, but he believed that he still had a lot of baseball left in him. However, Jake's batting declined quickly as leg injuries robbed him of his speed. He began to fade at the age of 39, batting .247 with only three stolen bases, and by mid-season was relegated to the bench by new manager John McCloskey. Jake served briefly as a substitute National League umpire late in the 1906 season while on injury leave from the Cardinals. He tried to play again the following spring, but batted only .209 in 32 games, and in June 1907, the Cardinals put rookie Ed Konetchy on first and released Beckley, ending his 20-year major league career.

Beckley was nearly 40 years old, but he was not yet finished with baseball. He signed with the Kansas City Blues of the American Association shortly after the Cardinals let him go, playing there for three years and managing for one. Jake won the batting title of the Association in 1907 with a .365 average, but age began to affect his performance, and he never reached the .300 mark again. After an unsuccessful managerial stint in 1909, the Blues cut Beckley loose. Jake was not much of a manager, and one story about his decision-making ability made the rounds. In early 1909 a batter asked Beckley if he should bunt or swing away, and Jake told him to "do what you think is best." Jake then smiled at his benchmates and said, "Well, that lets me out, don't it, boys?" Some say that the Kansas City ownership let Jake go soon after and looked for a more proactive manager.[10]

He landed with Bartlesville of the Western Association in 1910, managing the team until the club went bankrupt and disbanded in late July. He then spent the rest of the season on the last-place Topeka club of the Western League, in which he had begun his professional career 24 years earlier.

Beckley returned in 1911 to his hometown, where he managed the Hannibal Cannibals of the Central Association to a last-place finish. He also played first base and batted .282 at age 44. In late 1911 he moved to Kansas City and retired from professional ball, though he managed and played on semipro and amateur nines for several more summers; according to The Sporting News, Jake was "still a great hitter and no slouch as a fielder when nearing his fiftieth year."[11] He helped coach the team at nearby William Jewell College and umpired for the independent Federal League in 1913, the year before the circuit became a short-lived major league.

Jake Beckley worked as a starter at horse race tracks and also operated a grain business in Kansas City after he stopped playing ball. Jake once placed an order with a Cincinnati company, which cabled back, "We can't find you in Dun and Bradstreet." Beckley replied, "Look in Spalding Baseball Guide for any of the last 20 years."[12] Beckley suffered from a weak heart, and was only 50 years old when he died in Kansas City on June 25, 1918. He was buried in Riverside Cemetery in Hannibal, where he was virtually forgotten until he gained election to the Hall of Fame. On August 11, 1971, two days after his induction, the citizens of Hannibal celebrated "Jake Beckley Day" and unveiled a small monument to his memory on North Main Street.

Beckley's reputation within the game suffered because he never played on a pennant winner, and only one team he played for (the 1893 Pirates) finished as high as second place. Still, Jake compiled a .309 lifetime average, hit .300 or better in 13 of his 20 seasons, and retired as baseball's all-time leader in triples. Beckley still stands fourth on the all-time list of three-baggers, behind only Sam Crawford, Ty Cobb, and Honus Wagner. He held the career record for games played at first base until 1994, when Eddie Murray passed him, but Beckley still leads all first basemen in putouts and total chances. He finished his career only 70 hits shy of the 3,000 mark, though almost nobody paid attention to such statistics during Beckley's lifetime. Beckley probably never realized that he stood second on the career list of hits (behind only Cap Anson) at the time of his retirement.

The Veterans Committee selected Beckley in 1971 despite his poor performance in previous Hall of Fame voting. Jake gained only one vote of 59 participating writers in the 1936 old-timers poll, and he received one vote in the 1942 balloting. However, the Veterans Committee examined his statistics and found a 20-year veteran with nearly 3,000 hits, a batting average over .300, and the career leader in games played at his position. There are many position players in the Hall who cannot claim any of those distinctions, and Jake's stats added up to a powerful argument in favor of his induction.

Some may wonder why the committee focused its attention on Jake Beckley when other qualified men from the same era such as Roger Connor, Bid McPhee, and Sam Thompson were still unacknowledged, but Beckley fully deserved to be honored in Cooperstown. This obscure first baseman was only the third most famous citizen of Hannibal, Missouri (behind novelist Mark Twain and Titanic heroine Margaret "The Unsinkable Molly" Brown) but the Veterans Committee, for once, made a good selection in Jake Beckley. The committee fulfilled its mission by giving recognition to one of the long-forgotten stars of 19th century baseball.

12

♦ ROGER CONNOR ♦

*I used to nail the horsehide over the fence into the tall grass, and that
would tickle some of the old New York stock brokers.* — Roger Connor[1]

On July 18, 1921, Babe Ruth of the New York Yankees hit his 36th home
run of the season and the 139th of his career against the Tigers at Detroit's
Navin Field. With this blow, Ruth became baseball's all-time home run
leader.

However, no one knew this at the time because statistics were not
then as important as they are now. While most people figured that Ruth
was probably the all-time home run champ, no one had yet compiled a
definitive record of career statistics, and no one knew who held the record
before the Babe. In the early 1920s, several attempts were made to codify
all-time records and career statistics, but such efforts proved difficult due
to a lack of reliable data. Some writers misidentified former National League
slugger Gavvy Cravath as the all-time home run leader before Babe Ruth,
while others nominated 19th-century stars Harry Stovey and Sam Thompson for the honor.

The real pre–Ruthian home run king was a 65-year-old resident of
Waterbury, Connecticut, who had recently retired from his post-baseball
career as a maintenance inspector for the local city schools. Roger Connor
was a hard-hitting first baseman and cleanup batter of the New York Giants
in the 1880s. Connor hit more triples and home runs than any other 19th
century player, but in the early 1920s he was almost totally forgotten by
writers and fans. He was one of the most celebrated and popular players
of his time, but when he died in 1931 he was buried at Old St. Joseph's

Roger Connor. (National Baseball Hall of Fame Library, Cooperstown, New York)

Cemetery in Waterbury in an unmarked grave. Connor's descent into obscurity was so complete that he never received a single vote in any Hall of Fame election.

Connor remained a forgotten man for more than 40 years after his death, until Henry Aaron passed the 700-homer mark and put pressure on Ruth's cherished record. Aaron belted 40 homers in 1973 and left himself only one behind the Babe at season's end, and articles about Ruth and Aaron appeared in the newspapers on a daily basis in the winter of 1973-74. With Aaron about to pass Ruth's total, people naturally wondered who held the record before the Babe. This brought the long-forgotten Roger Connor back to the attention of baseball fans and sportswriters. Two years later, on February 2, 1976, the Veterans Committee elected Connor to the Baseball Hall of Fame.

Roger Connor was the son of immigrant parents from County Kerry in Ireland. He was born on May 1, 1857, in Waterbury, Connecticut, a town in which there were literally dozens of families named Connor and O'Connor. Waterbury was a gathering point for Irish families who came to America to find jobs in the mid–1800s, and Roger grew up in a neighborhood full of families like his own. He grew into a strong and powerful young man, and as a teenager he stood about six feet and three inches tall and already weighed nearly 200 well-muscled pounds. He and his brothers attended school and worked in Waterbury's brass factories, but they also played sandlot ball, and Roger gained attention as the hardest hitter in town.

Roger's father Patrick was a laborer who did not understand why his strapping sons, especially Roger, preferred playing ball to working at a real job. Roger's enthusiasm for baseball caused some amount of friction in the household, and at 14 years old he left home to seek employment as a baseball player. He bounced around for a while, then returned to Waterbury to find that his father had passed away in his absence. Roger, the oldest of

11 children, then took a factory job to help support the family. He still dreamed of a baseball career, however, and played for town ball and semi-pro teams in New England over the next few years.

In 1876 Roger, a left-handed batter and thrower, entered professional baseball when he returned home to play for the Waterbury Monitors of the National Association. He played third base in an era when left-handed third basemen and shortstops were not a rarity. In those days, players did not wear gloves, and a fielder could stop the ball with either hand. Roger was almost always the biggest man on the field, and he put his large body in front of line drives, knocked them down with his hands or stopped them with his chest, and threw the runners out at first. Roger was fearless, a necessary trait in a third baseman of that time, and he displayed a strong throwing arm. He was also the leading hitter in the circuit, and after two years in Waterbury the 21-year-old Roger joined one of Waterbury's league rivals, the Shamrocks of Holyoke, Massachusetts.

The National Association left only fragmentary statistics from the late 1870s, but we know that Holyoke's Roger Connor was the hitting star of the circuit in 1878 and 1879. The Holyoke ballpark stood next to the Connecticut River, which ran behind the right field fence, and Roger thrilled the crowds with long home runs into the river. He hit many of his home runs against Holyoke's archrival Springfield, and the manager of the Springfield team, a former major leaguer named Bob Ferguson, was impressed with Connor's power. Ferguson became the manager of the Troy Trojans of the National League in 1880 and offered Connor a raise in salary to join his team. In the spring of 1880, Connor left the National Association for the National League.

Troy, New York, was the smallest city in the National League. The league had begun play with eight teams four years earlier, but the New York Mutuals and the Philadelphia Athletics were expelled after the 1876 season for refusing to complete their schedules. The circuit fielded only six teams in 1877, two of which folded at season's end, and in 1878 the league added new ballclubs in Milwaukee and Indianapolis. These failed, so in 1879 the league replaced those two western cities by expanding to eight teams with new franchises in Cleveland and in the New York cities of Buffalo, Troy, and Syracuse.

Troy finished the 1879 campaign in seventh place, and in 1880 new manager Ferguson brought in 16 new players. Among them was the hard-hitting Roger Connor, who anchored third base and batted .332 in his first major league season. Ferguson also signed three men who would one day share membership in the Baseball Hall of Fame with Roger. Pitchers Tim Keefe and Mickey Welch and catcher Buck Ewing provided an infusion of talent to the struggling franchise, and in 1880 the Trojans finished in fourth place with a 56–41 record.[2]

Connor hit well, but his fielding suffered in the move to the faster National League. He committed 60 errors (in only 88 games) at third, and his fielding percentage of .821 is one of the lowest in the history of baseball for a regular player. He had a strong, but not always accurate, arm, and many of his errors came on wild throws to first. In 1881 Ferguson moved Roger to first base, where being left-handed was an advantage. The tall Roger provided a large target for the other infielders, and he worked diligently to make himself into a good first baseman, though he also played a few games at second. Connor's replacement at third, Frank Hankinson, batted only .193 as the Trojans fell to fifth place.

Roger batted only .292 in 1881, but he hit one of baseball's most famous home runs late in the season. On September 10, in a game against Worcester played at Albany, New York, Connor came up in the bottom of the ninth inning with the bases loaded and the Trojans behind by a 7–4 score. Worcester pitcher Lee Richmond delivered a fastball, which Connor deposited over the right field fence for a grand slam home run, the first ever struck in the National League. The blow overcame a three-run deficit in one swing of the bat. Since then, only 22 other players have managed to end a game from three runs down with a grand slam. Babe Ruth of the New York Yankees hit baseball's next such walk-off grand slam home run 44 years later.

In that same month, Roger married a Troy girl named Angeline Meir. Roger had met her in the spring of 1880 when the Troy team discovered that he was too big to fit into any of the club's existing uniforms. The team sent him to a shirt factory to be fitted, and the blond Angeline was the seamstress who took his measurements and engaged Roger in conversation about his baseball career. Roger proposed marriage later that season, and the two remained together for more than 45 years.

In 1882 the 25-year-old came into his own as a hitter. He finished third in the league in batting with a .330 mark, scored 65 runs in 81 games, and led the National League with 17 triples. No other Troy batter managed to hit above .275, as the Trojans struggled to a seventh place finish despite the presence of four future members of the Hall of Fame on the roster.

Roger was big, the biggest man in the league (next to Buffalo's Dan Brouthers) at the time, but he was a fast and aggressive baserunner. He perfected what he called a "come-up" slide, which we now label a "pop-up" slide, in which he would slide into a base, unfold his legs, and quickly wind up on his feet again, ready to advance to the next base on a bad throw. Perhaps Connor did not invent the move, but he popularized it throughout baseball. New York player-turned-sportswriter Sam Crane called the big first baseman "the best base runner I ever saw, excepting Bill Lange, and it behooved the baseman to give Roger a clear path. With his weight catapulting him, with speed and force, he slid feet first and, as he landed, could bob up, like a jack-in-the-box."[3]

Late in the 1882 season, it became apparent that the National League, to ensure its own survival, needed to return to the nation's largest cities. A game between Troy and Worcester in September of 1882 drew only 18 fans, and a game between the same two teams the next day attracted only six paying customers. The league dropped the Troy and Worcester franchises after the 1882 campaign in favor of new teams in New York and Philadelphia. The primary investor in the New York Gothams, a

Connor in the mid-1880s. (National Baseball Hall of Fame Library, Cooperstown, New York)

manufacturer named John B. Day, bought the best players from the defunct Troy team and signed them to contracts to play in New York in 1883. Day also owned a competing ballclub, the New York Metropolitans of the American Association, who played virtually across the street from the Gothams in upper Manhattan. Day sent pitcher Tim Keefe to the Metropolitans and assigned Connor, Buck Ewing, and Mickey Welch to the Gothams. Roger Connor received the largest salary on the team, $1,800, with $300 worth of incentives for a total package of $2,100.

Roger paid dividends on his contract in that first New York season. He batted .357, second in the league to Cap Anson, and compiled a .957 fielding average at first base. The Gothams, despite Connor's heroics, finished sixth in the eight-team league. The Gotham second baseman, Dasher Troy, batted only .215 in 1883, so the manager decided to put Alex McKinnon on first base and move Roger Connor to second for the next season. The move was a disaster; Roger batted .316 but committed the astounding total of 71 errors in 67 games at second. Roger also played 37 games in center field and 12 at third base that season, but he fielded poorly wherever he played, and the Gothams finished a disappointing fourth. In 1885, new manager Jim Mutrie moved Roger back to first base, a position he fielded well, and Roger responded by winning the batting title with a .371 average. The steadily improving Gothams challenged Cap Anson's Chicago team for the flag that season, losing by only two games.

Mutrie, who managed from the bench in a suit and tie, was more of an enthusiastic booster than a baseball man, but in 1885 he gave the New York Gothams a new nickname. Mutrie's team featured several large men, most notably the six foot, three inch Roger Connor. Mutrie liked to boast about his team to the New York sportswriters, and one day, Mutrie grandly called his players "My big fellows! My Giants!" The writers liked the sound of that, and from then on the team was known as the New York Giants. Although the franchise now plays in San Francisco, the ballclub uses the name Giants to this day.

The most popular Giant, by far, was Roger Connor, particularly with the city's Irish population. Roger was a strikingly handsome man with a handlebar mustache and a confident, but not swaggering, manner. He wore a shamrock on the sleeve of his uniform to show his pride in his Irish heritage, and the fans affectionately called the big first baseman "Dear Old Roger." He was an intelligent and soft-spoken individual; as *Sporting Life* put it, "Roger Connor, the giant first baseman of the New York Club, is a very quiet man. He seldom has much to say, but when he does talk he generally knows what he is talking about."[4] He did not believe in showing off for the crowd or the sportswriters, but let his bat do the talking for him. The hard-hitting first baseman became a fan favorite, and the crowds cheered his every move in New York.

Roger was strong, and he used his strength to great advantage in the batter's box. "He was a lefthanded batter and took a long, free swing," wrote Sam Crane, "putting the whole force of arms and body into his swing so that when he did connect with a low ball down around his knees — his favorite — he could get full purchase. It was a case of breaking the back fences or clearing them."[5] Few batters swung for the fences in that era, and although Connor may have had the hardest swing in baseball, he made contact often enough to keep his batting average well above the .300 mark year after year.

The old Polo Grounds, situated between 110th and 112th streets in Manhattan, was the scene of one of Roger's most famous blows. On September 11, 1886, he belted a majestic home run far over the 20-foot high right field wall. It was the first ball ever hit completely out of the Polo Grounds, and many observers called it the longest homer ever struck in New

York City. It went over the grandstand and bounced down 112th Street, and one newspaper report said that pitcher Charley Radbourn gazed at Connor "in wonderment" as the ball sped upward "with the speed of a carrier pigeon" and disappeared.[6] Three years later, Roger helped inaugurate the new Polo Grounds at 155th Street and 8th Avenue when he became the first man to clear the center field fence with another memorable blast. According to *The Sporting News*, "several members of the New York Stock Exchange, occupying box seats, were so smitten by the Herculean clout that they took a collection for the slugger.... When the contributions were totaled, the fans were able to present a $500 gold watch to their hero."[7]

Connor in 1888. He did not wear a glove on the field until a few years later. (Library of Congress)

Off the field, Roger and his wife Angeline suffered a tragedy when their daughter Lulu, born in September 1886, died less than a year later. The couple remained childless for the next several years, but sometime around 1890 the Connors went to a Catholic foundling home in New York City and adopted a girl named Cecilia. Though Roger played ball in New York, the Connor family continued to live in Waterbury, where the townspeople held a banquet each winter to honor their favorite athlete. During the 1890s Angeline presented Roger with a weather vane made out of two of his bats. The Connors placed the vane on the highest peak of their house, and it remained as one of Waterbury's most distinctive landmarks for decades, even after Roger and Angeline no longer resided there.

The Detroit Wolverines won the National League pennant in 1887, but the steadily improving Giants were primed to mount a challenge. The Giants began slowly in 1888, but Roger set the tone for the season on May 9 when he belted three homers in a game at Indianapolis. Three other Giants hit home runs that day in an 18–4 victory, and the rout helped the Giants catch fire. They won 18 of 23 games in July, grabbed the league lead, and held on for the first pennant by a New York team in the National League. In October, the Giants met the St. Louis Browns of the American Association for the Dauvray Cup, a predecessor of the World Series, and won six out of ten games for the championship.

The Giants repeated in 1889 in a close race with the Boston Beaneaters, but all season long the players and club owners braced for a conflict that ultimately erupted at the end of the campaign. In October of 1885, Roger Connor and nine of his Giant teammates had founded a baseball trade union, the Brotherhood of Professional Base Ball Players, and by 1889 the union had become fed up with the dictatorial actions of the club owners. The breaking point came when the National League instituted a salary structure in which each of the league's players would be assigned a classification from A to E, with A-level players earning a maximum salary of $2,500 per year and other players receiving less. Roger's teammate John Montgomery Ward, head of the Brotherhood, then created a new league called the Players League to compete with the National. While Ward became the leader of a new team in Brooklyn, Roger and almost all of the other Giant stars formed a new Players League franchise in New York with Buck Ewing as manager.

Though the new circuit followed the National League's lead in banning Sunday baseball and retaining the prohibition on African-Americans, the Players League introduced some revolutionary ideas to the baseball world in 1890. The new league was owned and operated by the players themselves, and stars such as Roger Connor owned stock in their teams and stood to share in any profits earned by the club. The Players League also did away with the hated reserve clause, replacing it with a one-year contract with a two-year option, which allowed for more freedom of player movement. It banned the trade of any team member without his consent, and required a club's board of directors to approve a player's release.

By the spring of 1890 almost every National League star, save for Cap Anson, John Clarkson and a smattering of others, had abandoned the established league for the new one. John Day, owner of the Giants, traveled to Roger Connor's Waterbury home and invited his slugging star to "name your price" if he would return to the National League, but Connor rejected the offer and stood solidly behind Ward and his fellow union members. Some of the other Brotherhood players accepted offers and jumped back to the National League, but Connor earned great respect for turning down what was probably a large amount of money, and afterwards the New York fans added "The Oak" to Roger's list of nicknames. "The Oak of New York [is] as unbendable as ever," stated *Sporting Life* in admiration.[8]

Both New York teams called themselves the Giants, which made for a confusing summer for the city's sportswriters. Connor played well for the new ballclub, batting .372 in 1890 and leading the circuit in home runs with 14 as the team (called Ewing's Giants in the papers) finished third. Both leagues struggled financially all year long, especially after the National changed its schedule and forced the Players League to play its games in direct competition with the established circuit on the same dates and in the same cities. By the latter half of the season both leagues were staggering, and several Players League teams did not meet their payrolls in September.

Roger still held out hope for the Players League, even as the circuit began to fall apart late in the 1890 season. "Why, I am not one bit put out at the turn affairs have taken," proclaimed Connor to the *Philadelphia Press.* "Of course, we all expected to declare dividends at the close of the season, and we would have done so, too, if the [National] League had stuck to its first schedule...."

"Few of our clubs are behind, and I feel sure we will do much better next season. No, I can't say what the League will do, and candidly, I don't care. I know the Players League will be on deck and in a better condition than ever ... next season you will see some of the prettiest races you ever saw."[9] However, the Players League collapsed that winter, and in January 1891, it officially ceased operations. Connor and his New York Brotherhood mates returned to the National League for the 1891 season.

Roger's average fell to .294 that year, and in the following off-season he left the Giants and signed with the Philadelphia Athletics of the American Association. He never played for the Athletics, because the Association collapsed shortly after Roger signed his contract, and the National League awarded his services to the Phillies in the same city. After one year in Philadelphia Connor returned to the Giants, where he recaptured some of his old glory with a .322 average and 11 home runs in 1893. On August 7, of that year, the left-handed Roger decided to bat from the right side of the plate against a left-handed Brooklyn pitcher named George Sharrott. Connor whacked two homers and a single and led the Giants to a 10–3 win. He also won a "Most Popular Player" contest sponsored in 1893 by a local newspaper, which awarded Roger a gold watch that he wore for the rest of his life.

The big first baseman began his 15th season in the major leagues in 1894, but new manager John Ward wanted to turn the Giants into a younger, scrappier team. Roger soon lost his starting position to the younger Jack Doyle, and on June 1, 1894, the Giants handed the 36-year-old Roger his release. He signed with the St. Louis Browns shortly afterward, and on June 1, 1895, Roger stunned his old team, the Giants, when he pounded out six hits in six trips to the plate in a 23–2 St. Louis victory. Roger belted three singles, two doubles, and a triple that day as the Browns bombed the Giants with 30 hits. Two days later, Connor hit the 112th home run of his career against Brooklyn and, although no one was aware of it at the time, became baseball's all-time home run leader. He held this distinction for the next 26 years.

The Browns were one of the worst teams in the National League in the 1890s, finishing 11th out of 12 teams in 1895, and in early 1896 manager Harry Diddlebock was fired, reportedly for drunkenness. After team owner Chris von der Ahe and third baseman Arlie Latham filled in for two games each, von der Ahe offered the reins to Roger Connor. He became the manager of the Browns on May 12, 1896.

Connor did not have much talent to work with in St. Louis, and he won only eight of the 46 games he managed. He also had to endure the interference of von der Ahe, the German immigrant and self-styled baseball impresario who owned the Browns. Von der Ahe did not know much about baseball, but he liked to sit on the bench and second-guess his manager during games. One day he brought a pair of binoculars to the park and trained them on the field. "Vy are ze outfielders playing so far back, Roger?" demanded the owner in his thick German accent. "Zey look as small as ants from here! I can hardly see them!"

Roger patiently explained, with a sigh, "You're looking through the wrong end, Chris."[10]

Connor, like all three of his predecessors that season, did not last long in the manager's chair, and on July 7, von der Ahe dismissed Roger at the end of a 14-game St. Louis losing streak. The big first baseman remained with the team as a player, but he batted only .284 in 1896 when the league average was .292. He returned to the Browns in 1897 at the age of 39, but he batted .229 in 22 games and drew his release on May 18, of that season.

His major league career was over, but in early June Roger joined the Fall River, Massachusetts team of the New England League. He became the first baseman and cleanup hitter for Fall River, and caused a sensation when he wore glasses on the field, which he found necessary but apparently had not wanted to do in the majors.

He proved as popular with the Fall River fans as he had been in New York, but in 1898 he left the club and bought the Waterbury franchise in the new Connecticut State League. Roger served as first baseman, cleanup hitter, manager, and president of the club, while his wife Angeline handled the finances and their 10-year-old daughter Cecilia collected tickets. Roger also brought in his younger brother Joe, who later played six seasons in the major leagues, as a catcher. The bespectacled Connor hit well — he batted .319 in 1898 and won the league batting title in 1899 with a .392 average — but he never won a pennant as a manager, and after a sixth-place finish in 1901 he sold the Waterbury ballclub and shifted over to the Springfield team in the same league.

The Springfield fans were tough on umpires, and in one game a rookie arbiter named Bill Klem made one close decision after another against

Roger's Springfield ballclub. At the end of the game, which Springfield lost, Klem rushed to leave the field before the fans descended upon him, but Connor stopped him on his way to the dressing room. "Young man," said Connor, loudly enough for all the fans to hear, "let me congratulate you for umpiring a fine ball game." Roger then shook hands with the young umpire, an act which mollified the threatening crowd and turned Connor and Klem into fast friends. Klem, who never forgot Connor's kindness, later spent 35 years in the National League and became one of the first two umpires named to the Hall of Fame.[11]

Connor played for Springfield until 1903, when he batted .272 at the age of 46, then left baseball to take a position as a maintenance inspector for the Waterbury schools. For the next 16 years he supervised janitors, plumbers, and repairmen at several buildings. *New York Daily Mirror* sportswriter Dan Parker, who grew up in Waterbury and knew the older Connor, described the former ballplayer as "a tall, handsome, powerfully built man of about 60 whose majestic gray, handlebar moustache perfectly matched his regal bearing."[12] The old ballplayer remained one of Waterbury's most respected citizens; as Parker wrote in another article five years earlier, "There was nothing glamorous about this post ... but such was Roger's regal dignity and majestic aloofness that his commonplace job didn't diminish his effulgence by a single candlepower. The horse and buggy he drove around on his tours of inspection might have been a Roman emperor's chariot."[13]

The old ballplayer remained interested in baseball and enjoyed watching the Waterbury team of the Eastern League. About once a year, he traveled to Manhattan to take in a game at the Polo Grounds and see his friend, umpire Bill Klem, in action. He also renewed acquaintances with old teammates Amos Rusie, Mickey Welch, and Dan Brouthers, three former stars who all worked for the Giants as ticket-takers or night watchmen. Roger came and went quietly, and few writers or fans remembered that this gray-haired man with glasses was once the most popular athlete in New York City.

He worked for the Waterbury schools until 1920, when he retired at age 63 due to poor health. From then on Roger and Angeline spent winters in Florida and summered in Waterbury until Angeline's death in the fall of 1928. Roger's health deteriorated quickly after his wife's passing, and he battled throat cancer for the final three years of his life. An operation in mid–1930 proved unsuccessful in treating his cancer, and on January 4, 1931, Roger Connor died at the age of 74. His obituary in *The New York Times* called him "the Babe Ruth of the Eighties," but his death otherwise drew little notice from the sporting press.

Roger's illness drained his family's finances, and his estate could not afford to buy a headstone in the middle of the Depression. When Connor was elected to the Hall of Fame in 1976, he became the only deceased member of the Hall who was buried in an unmarked grave. This changed in 2001, when a group of Waterbury residents and baseball fans across the nation raised more than $6,000 for a headstone. The new grave marker was unveiled in a ceremony honoring Waterbury's greatest ballplayer on June 30, 2001, more than 70 years after his death.

The Permanent Committee elected 21 men to the Hall of Fame in 1945 and 1946, and although the panel chose Roger's New York Giants teammate Jim O'Rourke, it bypassed the big first baseman himself.[14] Bill Klem, the veteran umpire whom Roger had befriended in Springfield so many years before, campaigned on Connor's behalf, but few electors remembered the long-ago slugger, and he received no discernable support for the Hall until the 1970s. When he finally gained enshrinement in 1976, he set a new record as the "oldest" player ever elected to Cooperstown. Connor would have been 118 years old if he had been still alive at the time of his election.

One may wonder how the Permanent Committee ignored Connor, a .325 lifetime hitter and the career leader in home runs and triples at the time of his retirement, while several inferior candidates gained places in the museum. However, if the committee members were interested in making sure that a 19th century player represented each position, their decision looks a bit more defensible. In 1945 the panel elected Dan Brouthers, who (like Connor) was a big, slugging first baseman of the 1880s and 1890s. Brouthers and Connor have similar statistical records, though Brouthers' batting average is 24 points higher:

	Games	At Bats	Runs	Hits	Homers	Average
Brouthers, 1878–1904	1,678	6,725	1,507	2,349	106	.349
Connor, 1880–1897	1,987	7,807	1,607	2,535	138	.325

After the 1945-46 committee selections, the Hall contained the plaques of two 19th century first basemen in Brouthers and Cap Anson. Since the pre–1900 era was represented in the Hall at the time by only one shortstop (Hugh Jennings), one catcher (Buck Ewing) and no second baseman, perhaps the panel did not want to elect another first sacker. No additional 19th century first basemen entered the Hall for another 25 years, when the Veterans Committee bypassed Roger once again and chose Jake Beckley in 1971.

Connor was a power hitter, a popular man with the fans and sportswriters, and played for more than a decade for a pennant-winning team in New York. This combination usually turns a player into a household name, but Roger played in an era that was already fading from memory by the time the Hall of Fame opened its doors in the 1930s. Fortunately, the Veterans Committee rescued him from obscurity in 1976 when it finally recognized Roger Connor as one of baseball's earliest and greatest slugging stars.

13

◆ VIC WILLIS ◆

My point is, before you clutter up the Hall of Fame with more Early Wynns ... at least give a riffle to poor Vic Willis, now dead these 23 years and totally uninvolved. And to the many other Vic Willises who have been left lying in the litter of previous poor judgments. — Furman Bisher, 1971[1]

Vic Willis Junior, the son of a pitcher who won 249 games in the major leagues between 1898 and 1910, worked for more than two decades to put his father into the Hall of Fame. He wrote letters to sportswriters and members of the Hall of Fame's Veterans Committee, recounting the career of Vic Willis Senior (who died in 1947) and comparing his statistics favorably to those of pitchers who had already gained election to the Hall.

By 1986, nearly twenty years after the junior Willis began his campaign, his efforts appeared to bear fruit. On March 10, 1986, the Veterans Committee put the names of Willis and several other old-time players up for a vote; a player needed to gain 12 affirmative votes from the 15 committee members to be elected to the Hall. When the votes were tabulated, Vic Willis, Ernie Lombardi, and Bobby Doerr all gained 12 or more votes. Unfortunately for Willis, the committee was only allowed to name two men at a time to the Hall of Fame, and both Lombardi and Doerr led Willis in the balloting. Lombardi and Doerr received plaques on the wall in Cooperstown, while Vic Willis remained outside the doors of the baseball shrine.

During the next few years, his candidacy stalled in the Veterans Committee, and other players passed the 12-vote barrier while Willis fell short year after year. Vic Willis Junior died in 1989, but the senior Willis' grandson, Ben Decker, continued the effort to enshrine Willis Senior in Cooperstown. Stephen Cunerd, a member of the Society for American Baseball

Research, also championed Willis' candidacy for the Hall in an article that appeared in the 1989 *Baseball Research Journal.* "Willis has more career victories than 22 of the pitchers already elected," wrote Cunard. "He has a better earned run average than 28 of them and more shutouts than 33 of them…. He ranked with contemporary pitchers like Iron Man McGinnity, Three Finger Brown, Jack Chesbro, and Rube Waddell. So why isn't Vic Willis in the Hall?"[2]

Willis' baseball legacy suffered a setback in 1991 when researcher Richard Tourangeau revealed that Willis may have been credited with a no-hitter by mistake. On August 7, 1899, Willis, pitching for the Boston Beaneaters, defeated the Washington Senators by a 7–1 score. He allowed six baserunners that day; four reached base on walks, one was hit by a pitch, and the other beat out a slow roller to third baseman Jimmy Collins. For more than 90 years afterward, the baseball record books stated that Collins committed an error and that Willis did not allow a hit that day. Tourangeau, however, found that all four of Boston's daily newspapers reported the next day that the ground ball was a hit. Both *The New York Times* and *Sporting Life* magazine gave Willis credit for a no-hitter, but *Sporting Life* issued a correction a week later and marked the roller to third as a hit. The editors of *The Baseball Encyclopedia* discussed the matter late in 1991 and decided to retain Willis' no-hitter in the record books, but the tainted nature of the long-ago gem may have harmed Willis' candidacy for baseball's highest honor.[3]

In early 1995, the Hall authorized the Veterans Committee to select up to four men (two major league players, one executive or umpire, and one Negro Leaguer). Four years had passed since the controversy over Vic's 1899 no-hitter, and the committee found the old pitcher's other qualifications— his eight 20-win seasons, his 50 shutouts, and his 249 wins— sufficient for the Cooperstown museum. On March 7, 1995, the committee named Vic Willis, Richie Ashburn, Negro Leagues star Leon Day, and National League founder William Hulbert to the Hall of Fame.

Victor Gazaway Willis, born in Cecil County, Maryland on April 12, 1876, was the first child of a carpenter and a housewife who moved to Newark, Delaware, before young Vic was four years old. Vic became an outstanding all-around athlete as a teenager in Newark, the second largest city in the state, where he played sandlot and amateur ball and also managed to play college football and baseball despite never attending college. "In the nineties," explained Willis in his later years, "when Delaware College — the present university — had an enrollment of 95 to 100 students, there were times when it couldn't field a complete football or baseball team. So it scoured the streets of Newark for strong boys to fill in. That's how I happened to play fullback for Delaware College in 1893."[4]

At age 17, Vic was already a tall (six feet and two inches), slender, and hard-throwing pitcher in amateur leagues in and around Wilmington and Newark. He began his professional career in 1894, pitching for the Wilmington YMCA for five dollars a game. After some success there, he signed a contract in 1895 to enter organized ball with Harrisburg of the Pennsylvania State League. He pitched well in 16 games, though his statistics were lost when the league collapsed in August of that year. Willis finished the 1895 season with Lynchburg of the Virginia State League, and pitched well enough to earn a promotion to Syracuse of the Eastern League, one step below the majors.

In Syracuse, Willis polished his signature pitch, a knee-buckling overhand curveball. He threw his curve with an overhand motion that caused the ball to drop almost straight down just before it crossed the plate. The 20-year-old pitcher impressed the Syracuse fans in 1896 with a 10–6 record in 17 games, but his season ended abruptly when he contracted diphtheria and spent three weeks in the hospital. Healthy again in the spring of 1897, he returned to Syracuse and won 21 games for the pennant-winning ballclub.

At the end of the 1897 season, Vic Willis was one of the most sought-after minor league pitchers in the nation. The Baltimore Orioles expressed an interest in signing him late in 1897, but the Syracuse club demanded $3,000 for their star pitcher's release, and the Orioles passed on the opportunity. The Boston Beaneaters also pursued Willis. Billy Murray, manager of the rival Providence club, had recommended several outstanding ballplayers to Boston manager Frank Selee in the previous few years, including third baseman Jimmy Collins and outfielder Chick Stahl. Murray urged Selee to sign Willis, and in September 1897, the Boston club bought the young pitcher from Syracuse for $2,000. The Beaneaters, defending National League champions, signed Vic Willis to a contract for $1,800 per year.

Perennial 30-game winner Kid Nichols (31–11 in 1897) headed the Boston pitching staff, while lefthander Fred Klobedanz (26–7) and righthanders Ted Lewis (21–12) and Jack Stivetts (11–4) rounded out the rotation. The sore-armed Stivetts pitched only 18 games in 1897, spending most of his time in the outfield, and if Stivetts proved unable to pitch in 1898, Selee hoped that Vic Willis would be able to fill the void. Selee also recognized that a young pitcher like Willis would benefit from Boston's excellent team defense. "With the Boston team behind him," opined sportswriter H. G. Merrill, "Willis ought to be a terror."[5]

Vic was not in the rotation when the 1898 season began. He pitched his first game for Boston on April 20, 1898, entering a game in relief in the sixth inning with Boston losing to Baltimore by a 10–2 score. The nervous young pitcher struggled with his control; he walked three, hit two batters, and threw a wild pitch. Vic finished the game, but he allowed eight more runs as the Orioles won 18–2. His first starting assignment nine days later proved more successful, as he defeated the Washington Senators 11–4 with a 12-hitter.

Willis displayed an excellent curveball in his first season, though he could not always control it. On June 14, he struck out 11 batters in seven innings, but gave up 17 hits in a 9–0 loss to the Phillies. On July 8, Philadelphia's Frank Donahue no-hit the Beaneaters 5–0, while Vic Willis was once again afflicted with wildness. "The Phils were kept busy dodging around the plate," stated the *Philadelphia Record* the next day, "for the erratic Vic Willis, Boston's skeleton pitcher, was in the box. He gave up eight bases on balls, hit two batters and struck out seven."

Before long, Vic's control problems abated, prompting Selee to move Jack Stivetts to the outfield and Willis to the rotation. Vic responded with a 25–13 record, third best on the team behind Kid Nichols' 31–12 log and Ted Lewis' 26–8 mark. The Beaneaters repeated as pennant winners, and several newspapers touted Vic Willis as the unofficial rookie of the year.

Selee liked to fill his roster with well-behaved, dependable professionals, and the gentlemanly young pitcher fit well with Selee's team. Willis was a sober and dedicated player who kept himself in good physical condition and saved his money instead of spending it like too many players of the era. "Willis," stated an article in the *Boston Journal*, "in many ways is just the type of ball player Selee is constantly endeavoring to get into his team. He is modest and, on or off the field, is always a credit to the club."[6] Willis also built a stable home life. He wed Mary Minniss in February 1900, and remained married to her for the remainder of his life. The couple had two children, a daughter named Gertrude and, fifteen years later, a son named Victor Junior.

Early in his major league career, Vic began planning for life after baseball. The Washington House was the biggest hotel in his hometown of Newark, Delaware, and Vic decided that his future lay there after his pitching days were over. "I always wanted to own a hotel," said Vic many years later, "even when I was a kid in these parts, and it was always the Washington House that interested me. When I went into baseball, my goal was the purchase of that hotel."[7] He knew that the sale price of the hotel was about $40,000, which was not a small sum for a ballplayer making only a few thousand dollars per year, but Vic resolved to play baseball until he could save enough money to purchase the Washington House free and clear.

It took Vic some time to learn how to control his curveball, and contemporary accounts state that Jack Ryan, an old Boston catcher, built a wooden target for Vic to pitch against and polish his control of the ball. Vic also studied the pitching of Boston's number one starter Kid Nichols, who specialized in putting the ball over the plate, allowing the defense to help him, and not beating himself with walks. In 1898, Vic walked more men than he struck out, but his strikeouts-to-walks ratio improved over the next several seasons, and his curveball became even more formidable. By the end of the 1898 season, the nation's sportswriters were describing Vic's curve as the best in the National League. "Willis has speed and the most elusive curves," said the *Boston Journal* in admiration. "His 'drop' is so wonderful that, if anyone hits it, it is generally considered a fluke."[8]

When Vic Willis gained control of the strike zone, he ascended to the ranks of the National League's leading hurlers and gradually supplanted Kid Nichols as Boston's number one starter. In 1899 he improved to 27–8, leading the league in shutouts and earned run average, and pitched his only career no-hitter, defeating Washington on August 7, by a 7–1 score. The only Senator run scored on two walks and an error (though the no-hitter, as previously noted, became a source of controversy more than 90 years later). The Beaneaters battled the Brooklyn Dodgers that year for the pennant, and although Vic defeated the Dodgers four times in five tries, the Brooklyn team edged out the Boston nine by eight games at season's end.

One Brooklyn–Boston contest that year ended in a riot. Vic took a one-run lead into the ninth inning at Brooklyn on September 6, when he walked the Dodgers' Tom Daly with two men out. Bill Dahlen then drove a sharp single to center, which Boston outfielder Billy Hamilton misplayed. Daly tried to score all the way from first on the play, but Hamilton recovered and threw to the Boston catcher, who tagged Daly out on a close play to end the game. The enraged Brooklyn fans then charged out of the stands and attacked umpire Bob Emslie; order was restored only when the players of both teams surrounded Emslie and hustled him off the field, protecting him with their bats.

Vic credited much of his success to the handling of Marty Bergen, who was probably the best defensive catcher in baseball at the time. "Bergen was a great catcher and was my batterymate most of the time with Boston," stated Willis many years later. "He helped me considerably, as I was both fast and wild." Bergen, a talented but moody player, stunned the baseball world on January 19, 1900, when he murdered his wife and two children and then took his own life. His death, and the decline of stars like Kid Nichols and Billy Hamilton, began the destruction of Selee's Boston ballclub, which fell to a fourth-place finish in 1900.

Some onlookers blamed Bergen's mental troubles on the famously tight-fisted Boston management, though others insisted that Bergen's apparent instability could not be laid at the feet of the club owners. However, Vic Willis found out how cheap his bosses could be. In 1899 he earned the same $1,800 salary he drew as a rookie, with a $300 bonus for good conduct added on at the end of the season. The Boston owners sent Willis a contract for 1900 at the same amount, despite his outstanding 27–8 record. Willis, for the first time in his career, held out. "I held out for $2,400," said Willis in 1941, "and it wasn't until the 1900 season

Vic Willis in 1899, when he won 27 games for a fading Boston team. (National Baseball Hall of Fame Library, Cooperstown, New York)

was ready to start that Boston club officials decided they could afford to give me the $300 increase."[9]

It also didn't help the Boston pennant chances in 1900 when Vic Willis reported to training camp, after his holdout, in less than perfect shape. On opening day, the Philadelphia Phillies bombed Vic out of the box and took a 16–4 lead. The score was 17–8 in the bottom of the ninth when Boston, using three pinch-hitters and a record three pinch runners, scored nine runs and tied the game at 17. The comeback went for naught, however, as the Phillies won the wild affair, 19–17, in the tenth inning of the highest-scoring Opening Day game in baseball history.

Vic pitched poorly in the early months of the 1900 campaign and soon came down with a sore arm. He struggled all year and posted his first losing record at 10–17, but bounced back in 1901 with 20 wins and a league-leading six shutouts. When Kid Nichols left the Beaneaters at the end of the 1901 campaign, Vic became the team's undisputed number one starter.

Many other Boston players chafed under the financial restraints of management, and they listened when the American League came calling. Connie Mack, manager of the new Philadelphia Athletics, offered Willis a salary of $3,500 to jump to the new league in 1901. Willis agreed at first, but signed again with the Beaneaters when the Boston management matched the offer. However, several other Boston stars decamped for the new league. The team lost five future Hall of Famers in 1901 and 1902 when Hugh Duffy and Jimmy Collins joined the new league, Kid Nichols took a managing post in the Western League, Billy Hamilton retired from the game, and manager Frank Selee moved to the Chicago Cubs. In 1902 Vic, Boston's sole remaining good pitcher, took on a greater share of the pitching load after the departure of Nichols. Willis pitched 411 innings and set a 20th-century National League record with 45 complete games, posting a credible 27–20 record for a seventh-place team.

Vic Willis and first baseman Fred Tenney were the only Boston regulars from the 1900 season who remained with the Beaneaters by 1903, and the decimated team fell quickly to the bottom of the standings. Despite the downtrodden state of the Boston franchise, Willis turned down a two-year offer from the Detroit Tigers in early 1903 for $4,500 a year when the Boston club again matched the new league's salary figure. "They met the $9,000 bid by giving me $4,200 in cash outright and $400 a month," related Willis many years later. The cash most likely went into the bank, earmarked for the eventual purchase of the Washington House, but Vic's record suffered for his loyalty to the Beaneaters. The 1903 season marked the first of three losing campaigns for Willis; he went 12–18 in 1903 and 18–25 in 1904, and then posted a disastrous 12–29 log in 1905. His 29 losses set a 20th century major league record for losses in a season.

Vic was present at the scene of one of baseball's greatest tragedies. On August 8, 1903, he pitched the Beaneaters to a 5–4 victory in the first game of a doubleheader at Philadelphia. "I was in the dressing room, changing my clothes during the second game," recalled Willis, "when I heard a terrific crash. I discovered the overhanging gallery in the left field bleachers had collapsed, carrying with it several hundred fans."[10] Vic and all the players on both teams helped pull victims from the wreckage, but 12 people were killed and nearly 300 injured that day.

Willis was still one of the best pitchers in the game, but he got little support from his team. The Beaneaters, winners of five National League pennants from 1891 to 1898, became one of the worst teams in baseball by 1903, and their defense was especially awful. Ben Decker, Willis' grandson, told a newspaper reporter in 1995 that the seasons from 1903 to 1905 "were the worst years of [Willis'] life. He said those outfielders couldn't catch a fly ball in a peach basket."[11] Willis was the kind of pitcher who needed a strong defense behind him, but the 1903–05 Beaneaters stood near the bottom of the league in fielding average and close to the top in errors. They also scored the fewest runs in the league in both 1904 and 1905. The Bean-eaters were so depleted of talent that they played Vic Willis, who was not a particularly good hitter, at first base for 12 games in those years.

All four of the starting pitchers on the 1905 Boston club lost 20 games or more, and the talent-poor Beaneaters realized that they needed to obtain good players in quantity if they hoped to escape the league basement. Accordingly, they decided to part with their best player in a three-for-one trade with the Pittsburgh Pirates. On December 15, 1905, Pittsburgh traded infielders Dave Brain and George Howard and pitcher Vive Lindeman to Boston in exchange for Vic Willis.

Boston remained in the second division for another eight years, but Willis joined one of the leading teams in the National League. The Pirates possessed the league's premier player in shortstop and batting champion Honus Wagner, as well as manager and left fielder Fred Clarke and a solid corps of starting pitchers. The Pittsburgh rotation included veterans Sam Leever and Deacon Phillippe and 22-year-old Lefty Leifield, but Clarke moved Vic ahead of the others into a slot as the team's number one starter. On opening day, Willis won his first game as a Pirate with a 2–1 win over St. Louis, and in May he threw three shutouts in a row against the Giants, Dodgers, and Beaneaters. Vic also managed to pitch the entire 1906 season without giving up a home run. The Boston team finished last again in 1906, but the Pirates, fortified by Willis' 22 wins, ended the season in third place.

For the next several years, the Pirates battled the New York Giants and the Chicago Cubs for supremacy in the National League. In 1907 Vic Willis led the Pirate pitchers with a 21–11 record and boosted the Pirates into a second place finish, setting the stage for the memorable 1908 pennant race.

Most people recall that the Giants and Cubs battled down to the wire and ended the season with a playoff game in 1908, but few remember that the race involved the Pittsburgh team as well. The Pirates, Cubs, and Giants fought for the flag in the final weeks of the season, trading first place back and forth almost every day. On September 18, the Pirates dropped a dou-bleheader to the Giants, which left the Pirates five games behind New York and one behind Chicago. The Pirates then ran off 13 wins in their next 14 games. Vic defeated Christy Mathewson of the Giants, 2–1, on September 21, for his 21st win of the season, bringing the Pirates to within three games of the lead. He then defeated Brooklyn 6–1 on the 24th and came back two days later with a 5–0 shutout of Boston. This win left Vic with a 23–10 record and vaulted the Pirates into second place, one game behind New York.

The Giants stumbled, losing two games to the Reds and three to the

Phillies, while both the Pirates and the Cubs closed the gap with winning streaks in the following week. Pittsburgh captured a tie with the Giants for first place on September 30, in a wild game that saw the Cardinals score five runs and knock Vic Willis out of the box. Howie Camnitz relieved Willis and held St. Louis in check as the Pirates rallied for a 7–5 win. Both the Giants and Pirates were off the next day, October 1, but the Cubs won and created a three-way tie for the lead.

The Pirates then won three more games at St. Louis, and on October 3, they held a half-game lead over the Cubs and a one and a half game advantage over the Giants. The Pirates and Cubs had been rained out earlier in the campaign, and the two teams scheduled a make-up game, the Pirates' last of the season, for Sunday, October 4, at Chicago. A win would eliminate the Cubs and give the Pirates at least a tie for the pennant, so manager Fred Clarke sent Vic Willis to the mound against Chicago's Mordecai (Three-Finger) Brown.

More than 30,000 fans, one of the biggest crowds of the season, saw Brown pitch the game of his life. The Cubs reached Vic for one run in the first and one more in the fifth for a 2–0 lead. Pittsburgh tied it in the sixth, but with two out in the bottom of the sixth Joe Tinker doubled off Willis. Brown, the Chicago pitcher, then drove in Tinker with a single with what proved to be the game-winning run. Brown outpitched Willis the rest of the way, and the Cubs beat the Pirates by a 5–2 score and knocked Pittsburgh out of the race. Four days later, after the Giants beat Boston three games in a row to force a playoff, Brown defeated the Giants' Christy Mathewson to clinch the pennant for the Cubs.

Chicago won its third pennant in a row in 1908, but star catcher Johnny Kling held out all the next season in a contract dispute and opened the door for the Pirates to ascend to the top of the league. Pittsburgh and Chicago battled for the flag in 1909, but the loss of Kling hurt the Cubs, and the Chicagoans could not get to within six games of the Pirates after July. By September, the Pirates stretched their lead to 10 games and coasted to the pennant with a 110–44 record. It was Pittsburgh's first pennant since 1903 and Vic's first since 1898, and it gave the Pittsburgh team a berth in the World Series against Ty Cobb and the Detroit Tigers.

Vic Willis, still the Pirates' number one starter, received the honor of pitching the first game in the new Forbes Field on June 30, of that season, though he lost the game 4–3 to the Reds. Despite a fine 22–11 record in 1909, the Pirates sensed that the 33-year-old curveball specialist was slowing down. He won 11 games in a row in a streak that ended in the opening game at Forbes Field, but pitched at a .500 level for the remainder of the season. Vic struck out fewer men than the prior year for the fifth season in a row, and ended the 1909 campaign with an uncharacteristic losing streak. In September, he came down with quinsy, a serious bacterial infection of the throat, and pitched in only two of Pittsburgh's last 17 games, losing both.

His last win in a Pittsburgh uniform was a memorable one. Vic took the mound at Forbes Field on September 18, against Brooklyn for his first appearance in eight days. He overcame the impact of his illness by stopping the Dodgers on only one hit, an infield grounder that Zack Wheat beat out for a single in the third inning. Willis finished the day with a 6–0, one-hit victory. No pitcher ever managed to throw a no-hitter at Forbes Field in the 62 years that the Pirates played there, but Vic Willis came the closest that day.

The infection put Vic on the sidelines when the 1909 World Series began, but newcomer Babe Adams took his place and pitched a six-hitter, winning the first game of the Series 4–1. Willis made his first Series appearance in relief of Howie Camnitz in game two, but failed to stop the Tigers in a 7–2 defeat that featured a steal of home by Ty Cobb. In the third inning, Cobb stood on third with George Moriarty at bat when Willis relieved Camnitz. On Vic's first pitch to the plate, Cobb stunned the Pirates when he dashed for home. He slid around catcher George Gibson and scored.

"That's one thing I'll never forget as long as I live," remarked Willis later. "I didn't think Cobb could beat the throw. I often got razzed for letting Ty get away with that theft, but I don't think anybody could have prevented it."[12]

The Pirates and Tigers split the next two contests, while Adams won again in the fifth game to put the Pirates ahead three games to two. Clarke sent Willis out to clinch the championship in game six, but Vic, still weakened by his illness, surrendered five runs and seven hits in six innings as the Pirates lost by a 5–4 score. Vic did not pitch again in the Series, won by the Pirates when Babe Adams pitched an 8–0 shutout in the seventh game. Vic Willis and the other Pirates each received $1,825.22 for their winning efforts.

The emergence of Babe Adams and the World Series failures of Vic Willis convinced the Pirates to replace Willis in the rotation with the younger and cheaper Adams. In December 1909, the Pirates sold Vic to the St. Louis Cardinals for $5,000. He struggled for the seventh-place Cardinals in 1910, winning nine and losing 12, and on September 5, 1910, Vic pitched in his last major league game, a relief appearance against the Pirates. After the game, St. Louis manager Roger Bresnahan, who wanted to try out some new pitchers in September, paid off the remainder of Vic's contract and sent him home to Newark, Delaware.

The Cardinals sold Vic to the Cubs later that year, but with $40,000 now in the bank, he retired from the game and bought the Washington House in Newark. "I might have been able to go along for three or four more years—with a good team behind me—but I didn't want to gamble on it with all my money tied up in the hotel," stated Willis in later years.[13] Jack Dunn, owner of the Baltimore Orioles, offered him a contract in 1911, but Vic Willis was finished with baseball and never looked back. He ended his career with 249 wins, 205 losses, and 50 shutouts in 13 seasons. He set an unwanted 20th century record with 29 losses in the 1905 campaign, but left the game with eight 20-win seasons, a no-hitter, and a World Series championship to his credit. At the time of his retirement, he stood eighth on the all-time National League list in wins and third in shutouts.

For the next thirty-six years, Vic Willis operated the Washington House, serving as proprietor, business manager, desk clerk, bellboy, and barkeep. He and his wife Mary raised their two children: Gertrude, who married and gave Vic two grandchildren, and Victor Junior, who grew to be six feet six inches tall and played college baseball at the University of Maryland. Vic Junior was scouted by the Washington Senators, but was not interested in a career in professional ball. Instead, he earned a degree as a chemical engineer, married, and produced four more grandchildren.

In 1941, *The Sporting News* devoted a full-page article to the 65-year-old former pitcher, still happily operating his hotel and enjoying his life out of the spotlight. The article revealed that the hotel's stationery featured an eagle, symbolic of Washington, standing on a baseball. It was the only indication that the owner of the establishment was once one of the game's outstanding players.

He stayed in touch with major league baseball and often took his grandson Ben Decker to games in nearby Philadelphia. "We'd have a catch every Sunday or so. I was half scared to death trying to catch some of his pitches," related Decker, even though Vic had been retired from the game for many years at the time. Vic also volunteered his time and energy to youth and college baseball programs and did some impromptu coaching for nearby minor league teams, where he advised another future Hall of Famer, pitcher Waite Hoyt. He coached young ballplayers and managed his hotel until his health failed in the late 1940s. Vic suffered a stroke in the summer of 1947, and died in a hospital in Elkton, Maryland on August 4, 1947, at age 71. He was buried in St. John's Cemetery in Newark.

In later life, Vic Willis wondered why none of the sportswriters mentioned his name in the Hall of Fame balloting. Perhaps he saw that pitchers like Jack Chesbro (198 wins) and Ed Walsh (195 wins) entered the Hall in 1946 while Willis, with a 249–205 career record, received no votes at all from the participating writers in the elections of the 1930s and 1940s. "He was disappointed he had not been elected into the Hall of Fame," says his grandson Ben Decker. "He played with another Hall of Famer, Honus Wagner, for years and years, and though he was not boastful at all, [he] thought he deserved to be in the Hall of Fame."[14]

Vic Willis pitched in hard luck for much of his career. His sojourn in Boston started well, with four 20-win seasons in his first six years, but the Boston team fell apart and left Willis with 18, 25, and 29 losses in successive campaigns. His career record, after eight years in Boston, stood at only four games above the break-even mark at 151–147. Willis then rejuvenated his career in Pittsburgh, with four 20-win seasons in a row and the 1909 World Series title. All told, Vic spent about half of his career playing for good teams and the other half playing for poor ones. It stands to reason that his career record of 249–205 might be significantly better if he had jumped to the American League in 1901 or 1902.[15]

Does Vic Willis belong in the Hall of Fame? In *The Politics of Glory*, Bill James compares Willis' career record to that of Red Faber, who pitched for the Chicago White Sox from 1912 to 1933. The records of the two pitchers are also similar to that of another White Sox pitcher, Ted Lyons, who played from 1923 to 1946. Lyons was elected to the Hall of Fame in 1955, and Faber was selected in 1964.

	Wins–Losses	Percent	+/–	20-win seasons
Willis	249–205	.548	+44	8
Faber	254–212	.535	+42	4
Lyons	260–230	.525	+30	3

Based on raw statistics, it appears that if Faber and Lyons belong in the Hall, Willis probably does as well, although James suggests that neither Willis nor Faber should be there.

Willis' main qualification for the Hall of Fame rests with the fact that he won 20 or more games in a season eight times. Only eight pitchers in the history of the game have won 20 games more often than Willis, while great pitchers such as Bob Feller (6 times), Tom Seaver (7 times) and Bob Gibson (5 times) failed to match Willis in that regard. Hall of Fame pitchers Don Drysdale and Whitey Ford won 20 games only twice apiece in their careers, while Jim Bunning and 324-game winner Don Sutton managed the feat only once apiece.

There are eight starting pitchers in the Hall of Fame with a lower plus–minus rating than Vic Willis, and there are 27 pitchers in the Hall with fewer wins. He was the greatest curveball pitcher of his time, and his 50 shutouts put him in 20th place on the all-time list. Willis might not be overwhelmingly qualified for Cooperstown, but his 249 wins and eight 20-win seasons made a strong case for his enshrinement. Though the Hall of Fame electors forgot about him after his career ended in 1910, his belated election by the Veterans Committee was a well-deserved honor for one of the premier starting pitchers of the first decade of the 20th century.

14

♦ WILLIE WELLS ♦

The Hall of Fame is a great honor. It's as high as you can go, like being president. I think they'll put more of us [Negro Leaguers] in there. Just let me see it while I'm living. — Willie Wells, 1977[1]

Ted Williams, who was elected to the Hall of Fame in 1966, surprised the baseball world when he used his induction speech to state publicly what many people had been discussing privately. "I hope," said Williams, "that Satchel Paige and Josh Gibson somehow will be inducted here as symbols of the great Negro players who are not here because they were not given a chance."[2] Williams' plea appealed to the sense of fairness of fans and sportswriters across the nation, and in 1971 Commissioner Bowie Kuhn appointed a new panel, the Committee on the Negro Leagues, to select worthy candidates for induction. In June of 1971, the new committee chose Satchel Paige as the first player selected to the Hall of Fame for his performance in the Negro Leagues.

The Committee on the Negro Leagues selected eight more players to the Hall over the next six years, then voted to disband after its 1977 meeting. The responsibility for electing pre-integration African-American stars to the Hall then passed to the Veterans Committee, which selected only two more Negro League players in the following 18 years.

By the mid–1980s, additional information on the Negro Leagues had become available through such books as Donn Rogosin's *Invisible Men* and John Holway's *Black Diamonds*. These works, among others, helped to convince the public that there were many more Negro League stars who deserved Hall of Fame consideration. Those players gained a voice on the Veterans Committee when the Hall of Fame appointed former Negro League player

189

and manager Buck O'Neil to the panel in 1981. O'Neil, who was joined on the committee by ex–Negro Leaguer Monte Irvin in 1983 and by Ted Williams in 1986, began to push for more recognition of pre-integration African-American ballplayers by the Hall of Fame.

One player who drew strong support for induction was Willie Wells, who was considered by most observers to be one of the two greatest Negro League shortstops along with previous inductee John Henry Lloyd. Wells was both an outstanding fielder and a high-average hitter who set the Negro Leagues record in 1929 for home runs in a season with 27. "Willie was one of the greatest baseball players who ever lived," declared Negro Leagues historian James Riley. "If you can visualize Ozzie Smith hitting .350, that's what Willie Wells was like. He is the caliber of player who ordinarily would be elected to the Hall on the first ballot."[3] Monte Irvin agreed, calling Wells "the greatest player of Negro League baseball alive who isn't in the Hall of Fame."[4]

The committee named Wells' longtime teammate, third baseman Ray Dandridge, to the Hall in 1987, but could not agree on any other Negro Leaguers for the next eight years. "It was hard to get the black guys into the Hall of Fame because they were competing with white major leaguers," O'Neil explained. "There are stats for the major league players, but not for the Negro Leaguers. There wasn't anybody on the committee who knew much about Willie Wells."[5] Wells himself hoped to be elected during his lifetime, but died in January 1989, without receiving the call from Cooperstown.

The Veterans Committee finally began honoring Negro League stars again when two outstanding pitchers, Leon Day and Bill Foster, gained induction in 1995 and 1996 respectively. On February 6, 1997, the committee elected Willie Wells to the Hall of Fame, eight years after the shortstop's death. His selection was met with praise, but its timing was bittersweet for Wells' fans and family. "It's a shame that he didn't go into the Hall of Fame 12 years ago so he could have had the opportunity to smell the roses," said James Riley. "You can point a finger at the Cooperstown board of directors and the Veterans Committee. They're the ones who control who gets in."[6]

Willie James Wells was born on August 10, 1905, (some sources say 1906) in Austin, Texas. He was the youngest of five children of Lonnie Wells, a Pullman porter, and his wife Cisco, who worked as a laundress and homemaker. Austin was the capital of Texas, but it was then a dusty little town of about 22,000 people with only one paved street. It was also tightly segregated, and most of the African-American residents lived on the south side of town.

The African-American population of Austin almost never interacted with the white majority, and each side of town had its own restaurants, businesses, and entertainments. Among the most popular diversions of black Austin was baseball, and traveling African-American teams passed through Austin and played at Dobbs Field. Willie Wells, from a young age, came home from elementary school, finished his chores quickly, and then caught the trolley out to the park on game days. He became a regular at Dobbs Field where he caddied for the local team, the Austin Black Senators, carrying equipment into the park, running errands, and making himself useful to his heroes. He was an outgoing young man, and got to know many of the star players from other cities.

When Willie was about twelve years old, the San Antonio Aces came to town and Willie met Raleigh (Biz) Mackey, one of the greatest catchers in black baseball. Mackey took a liking to the enthusiastic Wells and got him free tickets whenever the Aces came to Austin. Before long, Mackey invited young Willie to sit on the bench with the team.

This early exposure to baseball made Willie Wells determined to create a career for himself in the game, and he absorbed all the knowledge and tips that he could gather from Mackey and other great players. He decided to become a shortstop, and he practiced diligently until he became one of the best high-school players in Austin. He starred in both baseball and basketball at Anderson High School, the city's segregated African-American school. It appears that he played a few games for the San Antonio Aces in the summer of 1923, though no statistics survive from that year.

In the spring of 1924, Willie was invited to join a Texas all-star team in a series of games against clubs from the Negro National League. The Chicago American Giants and the St. Louis Stars spent spring training in Austin, and both teams came away from their matches with the Texas all-stars impressed with the 18-year-old Willie Wells. Both teams made offers for his services, and some reports say that the Chicago club offered the most money. However, St. Louis was only a one-day train ride from Austin, and Willie's mother wanted him to play close to home. He signed with the Stars for the sum of $300 per month.

Willie soon discovered that professional pitchers threw better curveballs than the high schoolers in his hometown. He was a right-handed batter in a league with mostly right-handed pitchers, and Willie found himself chasing outside curveballs unsuccessfully all season long. "That curve ball was disastrous to me," remembered Wells years later, "and every pitcher in the league knew it. When I'd come up to bat, the guys in the other dugout would stand up and yell, 'Hey, Wells, here comes that curve ball!' Why, I'd just about run up into the stands to try to hit it."[7] Willie was so discouraged that when the season ended, he returned to Austin and enrolled in Huston College (now Huston-Tillotson College) to prepare for a career in business.

Willie began taking classes at Huston, but fate intervened before he decided to forget about baseball. A group of black all-stars traveled to California that winter for a barnstorming tour, but their regular shortstop broke his leg during one of the early games. The manager of the team sent Willie a telegram and offered him $400 a month to join the all-star team if he could get to California immediately.

"That was like $4,000 today," recalled Wells in 1979. "My mother wanted me to finish college, but I looked at her taking in wash and working so hard, and I saw that I had a chance to help her."[8] Willie dropped out of school and went to the West Coast to resume his baseball career.

In California, a teammate taught Willie how to hit the curveball. Fellow all-star Hurley McNair put Willie in the batter's box, and then "tied my leg to a stake near home plate so I couldn't run," as Willie later recalled. McNair then went to the mound and threw one curveball after another to the young shortstop. Unable to bail out, Wells learned to stay in the batter's box and judge the flight of the ball. "I learned to wait for the curve ball — then I could hit it," he said.[9]

Willie, who stood five feet and nine inches tall and weighed about 160 pounds, already knew how to field. He was fast and sure-handed, and his speed enabled him to cover more ground than other shortstops. He cut down the amount of area he had to cover by playing an extremely shallow position, almost on the inner infield grass, and studied the batters to figure out where to position himself for each opponent. "If you ever saw me dive for a ball," remarked Willie, "you know I misjudged the hitter."[10]

He suffered an arm injury in his early years in St. Louis, but learned to release the ball quickly to compensate for his weakened throwing arm, which was his only flaw on the baseball field. Fellow Negro League star Buck Leonard once joked that "you could run alongside the ball and watch it" when Willie threw it, but Wells still managed to throw runners out by inches. Teammate Max Manning once remarked of Wells' throwing, "Everybody thought they could beat it out. 'He just got me by a step that time. If I run a little harder, I'll beat him.' But they never did. It would be the same way the next time. It was always just by a step."[11]

Wells used a glove no thicker than a pancake with a hole cut into the middle of it. He, like major league shortstops Rabbit Maranville, Leo Durocher, and others, believed that he could get the ball out of his glove more quickly if it hit his bare palm and not a layer of leather. He was bow-legged, a source of teasing from opposing players, but he was so smooth in the field that people remarked that he played as if he was wearing a pair of roller skates. James (Cool Papa) Bell, who played the outfield behind Wells in St. Louis, ranked Willie on top of the all-time list of shortstops. "Wells could cover ground better than any of them," said Bell, who entered the Hall of Fame in 1974. "Willie Wells was the greatest shortstop in the world."[12]

On a personal level, Willie married an Austin girl named Lorene Sampson when he was still a teenager, even before he joined the St. Louis Stars. The couple produced two children, a son named Willie Brooks Wells, whom everyone called Willie Junior, and a daughter named Stella.

He struggled at the plate in his rookie season, but in 1925 Willie began to hit for both power and average. He used a thick-handled, heavy bat, and he was strong enough to bring the bat around and make good contact. He seldom struck out, and his line drives often went for triples and home runs, especially in the small St. Louis ballpark. Wells usually batted second in the St. Louis lineup behind the speedy Cool Papa Bell, even as his home run totals rose with each passing year. In 1929 Willie belted 27 homers in 88 games, the all-time Negro League record for a single season. He also won the league batting title in 1929 with a .386 average and again in 1930, when he hit .404.

With Bell, Wells, and power-hitting first baseman George (Mule) Suttles in the lineup, the Stars became a perennial contender in the first Negro National League. The Chicago American Giants and the Kansas City Monarchs won all of the first eight league titles from 1920 to 1927, but the Stars won the league championship in 1928, finished second in 1929, and won again in 1930 and 1931. The 1930 St. Louis team was one of the best in Negro League history, with a record .741 winning percentage. That season also marked the emergence of catcher Ted (Double-Duty) Radcliffe, so named because injuries to the St. Louis pitching staff forced the Stars to put Radcliffe on the mound for a few games. He performed so well that he became the team's best pitcher in the stretch run. The Stars closed the 1930 campaign by defeating the Detroit Stars in the league playoffs.

During the winter months, Willie and many other star players gravitated to the Cuban Winter League. Willie batted .322 for Cienfuegos in the winter of 1929-30, leading his team to the pennant and winning the Most Valuable Player award. He hit over .300 seven years in a row in Cuban Winter League play. Ten years later he hit .328 and led Almandares to another Cuban Winter League pennant and won a second Most Valuable Player trophy.

The Great Depression hit the Negro League teams hard, and the Negro National League collapsed at the end of the 1931 season. Some teams, like the Kansas City Monarchs, took to barnstorming and filled their summers with exhibition games, but the St. Louis Stars folded, leaving Willie Wells a free agent.

The 1932 campaign was the most difficult of Willie's career. He joined the Pittsburgh-based Homestead Grays early that year, but found that their barnstorming schedule was too much for him. In one three-day stretch the Grays played in Pittsburgh, Toronto, and Detroit, traveling by bus between cities, and after the third game Willie quit the team. Club owner Cumberland Posey offered him more money, but Wells replied, "I don't want no more money. I want my health and I want to live."[13] Later that year he joined the Chicago American Giants, but when the team ran out of cash the owner offered to pay Willie his full salary if he could persuade his teammates to play without compensation. Willie refused to participate in the scheme and quit.[14] However, the Negro National League resumed play in 1933 and Willie rejoined the American Giants.

Willie spent three years with the American Giants, and led the team to the best record in the new Negro National League in 1933. The pennant was disputed when some of the teams in the circuit did not complete their schedules, and the dictatorial league president, Gus Greenlee, awarded the flag to his own Pittsburgh Crawfords. However, the American Giants dominated the first annual East–West All-Star game, played in Comiskey Park on September 10, 1933. Seven of the starting West players were members of the American Giants, including Wells, and the West defeated the East by an 11–7 score. The East–West All-Star game became black baseball's biggest showcase over the next several years, and Wells was named to the all-star team seven more times in the next 11 seasons.

Perhaps Willie's greatest success came in exhibition games against white major league players. Statistics of such contests are maddeningly incomplete, but some knowledgeable sources say that Wells batted between .392 and .410 against white all-star teams in that era. He and the other Negro Leaguers played a hard, aggressive game; the white players saw the games as exhibitions, but the African-American players took the contests as a professional challenge and as a way to prove themselves. After Wells stole home to beat a Major League all-star team, the *Chicago Defender* wrote, "They dug up their big leaguers but the Giants were loaded. A good big team of brown baseball men beat a good big team of white baseball men and the white fans went down hook, line and sinker Sunday, half of the 4700 fans being pale faces."[15]

Baseball historian John Holway described a typical Wells performance. "In 1929 he bedeviled a team of American League all stars," wrote Holway. "In game one his two-out triple in the ninth tied the game, and a moment later he stole home with the winner. The next day he slammed two more triples and stole home again as the blacks won 10–1. In game four Wells came up in the ninth tied 6–6 and smashed a single over third to beat the big leaguers for the third time in four games."[16] One report states that in 1934, while touring with the Satchel Paige All-Stars, he took the mound against a white all-star team and held them to a 4–4 tie in a game called by darkness. It was the only pitching performance of Willie's career.

There were a few unpleasant incidents between black and white players at the time, and many still recall an ugly stream of racial epithets directed at Wells by pitcher Early Wynn in Cuba one winter. However, Willie preferred not to dwell on the negative. "I played against all of them, black or white," said Wells many years later. "A lot of those white players were gentlemen. The guy I admired was a shortstop for the Brooklyn Dodgers, Pee Wee Reese."[17] Reese was the man who played beside Jackie Robinson in 1947 and helped smooth the way to success for the majors' first 20th century African-American player. Wells was fourteen years older than Robinson, but few had any doubt that, had the color line fallen a decade earlier, Willie Wells would have become a major league star.

The American Giants withdrew from the Negro National League following the 1935 season, but Wells remained in the circuit as shortstop for the Newark Eagles. The Eagles came into being in 1936 when two ailing franchises, the Brooklyn Eagles and the Newark Dodgers, were combined by gambler Abe Manley and his wife Effa, who ran the team as the first woman chief executive of a Negro League club. The Eagles featured their "million-dollar infield" with Ray Dandridge at third, Willie Wells at short, Dick Seay at second, and Willie's old St. Louis teammate Mule Suttles at first. The powerful Pittsburgh Crawfords won the pennant year after year, but statistics say that Willie batted .294, .404, and .355 for the Eagles from 1937 to 1939.

In 1939, a 20-year-old shortstop named Monte Irvin joined the Eagles, but the 34-year-old Willie was not yet ready to relinquish his position to the younger man. "My first day," said Irvin, "Willie pointed to shortstop and told me, 'That's my position,' then he pointed to center field and told me 'That's your position. With your arm and your power, that's where you belong.' He did me a favor."[18] Irvin played for the Eagles until 1948, then played for two pennant winners in the majors with the New York Giants before he gained election to the Hall of Fame in 1973.

After four years in Newark, Willie quit the Eagles after a salary dispute with Effa Manley and took off for Mexico, where he signed with the Veracruz Blues of the Mexican League. Veracruz took advantage of the low pay and poor playing conditions that existed for African-American players in the United States and made offers to many Negro League stars. The result was the formation of one of the strongest teams in Latin American history, with Willie and four other future Hall of Famers in Ray Dandridge, Cool Papa Bell, Josh Gibson, and Leon Day. These five stars led Veracruz to the Mexican League title.

He enjoyed playing in Mexico, partially because society there was not segregated as it was north of the Rio Grande, and also because the fans took to Wells immediately. They called him "El Diablo," meaning "The Devil," a name he carried for the remainder of his career. Opposing batters told their teammates, "Don't hit it to shortstop. The Devil is out there."

They also called him the Devil for his style of play. Willie was a like-able man off the field — his teammate Lenny Pearson once said that "He was always there when you needed his help. Willie Wells was a hell of a man" — but he was a hard-nosed, tough competitor. "Intense. That's what I was," declared Wells shortly before his death in 1989. "I just wanted to be the best. I never wanted to lose."[19] Some people say that Willie kept two sets of baseball shoes, one normal pair and another with extra-long spikes to frighten opposing infielders. The pitchers tried to keep Willie honest at the plate with close pitches, and in July 1942, Baltimore's Bill Byrd beaned Willie at Yankee Stadium, knocking him out. Two days later Wells returned to the lineup wearing a mineworker's helmet. "Wells was the kind of player you always wanted on your team," Detroit Tigers star Charlie Gehringer once said. "He played the way all great players play — with everything he had."[20]

Willie was a widely respected veteran who took pride in his image and his appearance. "[Willie] was flamboyant in terms of dress," said his Newark teammate Max Manning. "Suits and handkerchiefs and stuff. I never saw Willie Wells look tacky."[21] "I always tried to look my best," said Wells late in life. He never forgot the kindness that Biz Mackey displayed to him many years before, so Willie befriended many young Newark fans, some of whom ran errands and shagged balls for their heroes as Willie had done back in Austin. In 1939 Mackey, 42 years old but still a fine catcher, joined the Eagles and played as Willie's teammate for that one season.

Wells led the Newark Eagles to a third-place finish in 1942, but the next year he returned to Mexico after another dispute with Effa Manley. The Manleys did not take kindly to losing their star shortstop and manager, and they moved to revoke the military draft exemptions held by Willie and third baseman Ray Dandridge, who joined Willie in the Mexican League. This would have forced the two men to return to the United States, but the attempt failed, and Wells and Dandridge spent the next two seasons south of the border.

Wells played for Tampico of the Mexican League in 1943, and in 1944 he joined the Mexico City Reds, managed by former St. Louis Cardinals star Rogers Hornsby. Hornsby was said to resent the presence of Wells and three other black players on the team, though the four men were the only English-speakers on the club and were the only ones who understood Hornsby's directions. In the early stages of the 1944 season Hornsby, so the story goes, demanded the dismissal of the four African-Americans, but the team owners fired Hornsby and installed Wells in the manager's chair instead.[22] Hornsby always denied that such an incident occurred, but Wells managed the Reds for the remainder of the 1944 season.

Willie loved playing in Mexico, and in 1943 he wrote a letter to *Pittsburgh Courier* sportswriter Wendell Smith that explained why. "I am not faced with the racial problem in Mexico," wrote Wells. "When I travel with the

Willie Wells with the Newark Eagles. (National Baseball Hall of Fame Library, Cooperstown, New York)

Veracruz team we live in the best hotels, we eat in the best restaurants, and can go any place we care to. We don't enjoy such privileges in the United States. We stay in any kind of hotels, far from the best, and eat only where we know we will be accepted. Until recently, Negro players in the United States had to go all over the country in buses, while in Mexico we've always traveled in trains....

"I've found freedom and democracy here, something I never found in the United States. I was branded a Negro in the States and had to act accordingly. Everything I did, including playing ball, was regulated by my color. They wouldn't even give me a chance in the big leagues because I was a Negro, yet they accepted every other nationality under the sun. Well, here in Mexico, I am a man. I can go as far in baseball as I am capable of going. I can live where I please and will encounter no restrictions of any kind because of my race. That also had a lot to do with my decision to return here."[23]

In 1945 Willie made peace with the Manleys and returned to Newark as player-manager. He was now 40 years old and slowing down, but he still performed well enough to earn his eighth berth in the East–West All-Star game. He spent much of the year tutoring young players like Don Newcombe, Monte Irvin and Larry Doby, who became stars in the major leagues when the color line fell two years later. Doby had joined the Eagles as a 17-year-old in 1942, during Wells' first term as manager, and Wells quickly moved to shore up the teenager's confidence. "You're here because you can play," Wells said to Doby. "Don't let anybody intimidate you because of your age."[24]

Doby, who broke the American League color barrier when he signed with Cleveland in June of 1947, appreciated the tutoring and encouragement he received from Wells. He also admired Wells as a player, though he did not see Wells play until Willie was long past his prime. "As a shortstop," said Doby, "I'd rank him with Phil Rizzuto, Pee Wee Reese, and Marty Marion. He had good hands, great range, and he could get rid of the ball as quickly as Rizzuto did."[25] In the East–West All-Star game in 1945, Willie played second base for the East while a newcomer, Kansas City's Jackie Robinson, played shortstop for the West team.

It didn't take long for Willie's relationship with the Manleys to disintegrate once again. In mid–1945 Abe Manley ordered Willie to pitch Terris McDuffie in a game against Baltimore, despite Willie's assertion that McDuffie was not in condition to pitch. The Baltimore team pounded McDuffie all over the lot that day, but Manley refused to let Willie take the pitcher out of the game. Wells objected to Manley's interference in the field management of the ballclub, and shortly afterward the Eagles traded Wells to the New York Black Yankees. They replaced Wells by putting Monte Irvin at shortstop and installing Willie's old idol Biz Mackey as manager.

In the spring of 1946 Willie visited with Jackie Robinson, the Kansas City Monarchs shortstop who had been signed to a minor league contract by the Brooklyn Dodgers. "Wells," said Robinson, "they got me playing second base, and I don't even know how to pivot." Wells spent part of the spring tutoring Robinson on how to make the pivot at second base, the position that he would play when he advanced to the Dodgers a year later. Willie was well respected as a teacher by this time; players he aided over the next few years included Ernie Banks, Don Newcombe, and others who streamed across the color line when integration finally came to major league baseball.

Willie batted only .258 in 1945, and when he started the 1946 season slowly, the Black Yankees released him in May. A few weeks later, Wells became player-manager of the Baltimore Elite Giants. The baseball color line was finally broken in 1947, but Willie Wells was too old to gain a place in the major leagues, especially after he batted only .226 in the 1946 campaign. He remained in the Negro Leagues, which slowly withered and died as most of its best players, such as Robinson, Doby, Irvin, Newcombe, and many others joined major league teams. The 1948 season found Willie in the uniform of the Negro American League's Memphis Red Sox, where he played mostly at third base and batted .328 at age 43. He also managed his son Willie Junior, who had joined the Memphis ballclub several years earlier and played second base, third base, and shortstop.

At the end of the 1948 season, the Negro National League collapsed, though the Negro American League limped along for two more seasons. Willie and his son bounced around in 1949, and then headed to Canada in 1950 to play in the independent Manitoba-Dakota League. Willie was one of the first black managers in any integrated league in the United States, and after spending four years in Winnipeg and Brandon, Manitoba, Willie Senior hung up his spikes in 1953. He had played professional ball for 31 seasons, not counting the many winters he spent playing in Mexico, Cuba, and Puerto Rico. Statistics, fragmentary as they are, credit Willie Wells with a .332 lifetime average in Negro League play, and his 128 home runs rank fourth on the all-time list.

He spent one more season in uniform as the non-playing manager of the independent Birmingham Black Barons in 1954, and then left the game for good as he neared his 50th birthday. Willie and his wife relocated to New York City where he worked in a Lower Manhattan delicatessen for thirteen years in the 1960s and early 1970s. In 1973 he and Lorene moved back to Texas to care for Willie's mother, and took up residence in the same South Austin house where he grew up more than six decades before. He spent his remaining years playing dominoes with old friends and following major league baseball, especially the Texas Rangers, on radio and television.

Willie Wells believed that he belonged in the Hall of Fame, but told his daughter Stella that he might not get in until after his death. He made sure, however, that the people in Cooperstown knew where to find him if necessary. "The Hall of Fame in Cooperstown knew where I was," said Wells, "because before I left New York, I told them I was coming back to Texas."[26] For the rest of his life, he waited for a phone call from the Veterans Committee every February.

An older Willie Wells in the early 1950s, when he played for and managed an independent team in Winnipeg, Manitoba. (National Baseball Hall of Fame Library, Cooperstown, New York)

His old teammates Cool Papa Bell, Ray Dandridge, and Monte Irvin were still alive when they gained election to the Hall, but Willie Wells did not live to see his plaque on the wall in Cooperstown. He suffered from diabetes and lost his sight in his last years, and in his final months he despaired of ever making the Hall of Fame. In 1988, shortly before he died, Wells remarked, "It doesn't make any difference. I know what I did."[27] He was 83 when he succumbed to heart failure in Austin on January 22, 1989. Eight years later, the Veterans Committee considered both Willie Wells and Biz Mackey before it elected Wells to the Hall of Fame.

Negro League stars still make up less than ten percent of the membership of the Hall, which may or may not be a fair share of the institution's total. One could make the argument that there are more great African-American stars who should be honored with a plaque, because several positions appear to be underrepresented by Negro Leaguers. There are no second basemen among the 18 honorees, along with only one first baseman and one catcher. On the other hand, the fragmentary nature of Negro League statistics make it difficult to decide which players deserve a place in Cooperstown and which men were merely well-known and popular.

In 2001 the Veterans Committee selected, among others, former Kansas City Monarchs pitching standout Hilton Smith to the Hall of Fame. Smith became the 18th player to gain entry to the Cooperstown museum for his playing in the Negro Leagues. However, he may be the last one for a while. The Veterans Committee underwent a radical transformation after its 2001 meeting, and the Hall of Fame decided to commission a study of

Negro League players and view the results before naming any more pre-integration African-American players to the Hall. A message on the Hall web site states, "A Hall of Fame-sponsored study of African American Baseball, 1860–1960, is underway. The Board will appoint a committee to review the results when the study is complete. After this review, a recommendation will be made to the Board concerning how to proceed with respect to Negro leagues candidates."[28]

It remains to be seen if any more Negro Leaguers will join the 18 men already present in the Hall of Fame, but time is running out for those who are still alive. The Negro Leagues went out of business more than 50 years ago, and the remaining men who played in those circuits are now in their 70s and 80s, if not older. Perhaps the Hall's study of African American baseball will identify other forgotten stars like Willie Wells and give them their rightful place in the museum in Cooperstown.

15

◆ FRANK SELEE ◆

*The success of the Boston team is due, more than any other thing, to
... a manager who is a thorough baseball general ... who knows what
should be done and how to do it, and is able to impress his advice upon
the men under his control.* —Sporting Life, *describing Frank Selee,
1893*

On March 2, 1999, the Veterans Committee selected four men to the
Hall of Fame. The committee's choice of Orlando Cepeda, the popular former National League first baseman, was met with general approval, but
the other three electees drew a collective groan from many of the nation's
sportswriters. In particular, many wondered why Frank Selee, a successful
but long-forgotten National League manager of the 1890s and early 1900s,
received a place in Cooperstown nearly 100 years after his final major league
game.

"He died almost 90 years ago. What's the point?" demanded columnist T. R. Sullivan of Knight-Ridder newspapers. "Did the Baseball Hall of
Fame's Veterans Committee suddenly dig up new information ... that
wasn't available 50 years ago? After all, the Hall of Fame has only been in
existence for 63 years. Surely if Selee is that deserving, somebody would
have made sure he was enshrined long ago."[1]

The Sporting News also expressed doubts regarding Frank Selee's election to baseball's highest honor. The paper described the selection of Selee,
umpire Nestor Chylak, and Negro Leagues star Joe Williams as "yet another
step toward turning Cooperstown into a gathering place for notable figures
and not a shrine for the game's truly elite ... Selee was a great manager to
be sure ... [but] there had been no groundswell of support for this man
over all these years. Why now?"[2]

Others, however, looked at Selee's record and found a man who managed five pennant winners himself, and then built another team that won four more titles with players that he had signed and nurtured. This made Selee responsible for nine National League flags between 1891 and 1910, an enviable record matched by only a handful of the game's greatest field leaders. Perhaps the Veterans Committee believed that if Al Lopez earned his place in Cooperstown by winning two pennants and Leo Durocher received his by winning three, then Frank Selee's election was not only desirable, but inevitable.

Frank Selee. (National Baseball Hall of Fame Library, Cooperstown, New York)

Frank Gibson Selee was born in Amherst, New Hampshire on October 26, 1859, the oldest child of Nathan and Annie Selee. Nathan Selee had attended Amherst College, then worked as a schoolteacher for two years before becoming a Methodist preacher one year before the birth of his first son. Nathan served as a minister for only six years, and in 1864 he left the pulpit and moved the family to Melrose, Massachusetts, where he entered the business world. Frank spent the remainder of his childhood in Melrose, about eight miles north of Boston, where he attended school and learned how to play baseball. The baseball fever that swept New England in the 1850s and 1860s reached Melrose, and the young Frank Selee became a ballplayer, one with more enthusiasm than talent.

Somewhere along the line, Frank realized that he did not possess the physical attributes of a successful professional baseball player. He was a delicate-looking individual of small stature and little strength, and he struggled with fragile health all of his life. As shown in available photographs, Frank appears to be about five feet and six inches tall, weighing not much more than 140 pounds. He played the outfield for the main town team in Melrose, the Alphas, but in his early twenties he decided to focus his talents on organizing, not playing, the game.

In 1884, when Frank was 24 years old, he left a job at a watch company to organize the new Waltham team in the Massachusetts State League.

"I was without any practical experience as a manager or player," confessed Selee years later, but he appointed himself president and manager of the club. He signed players and raised $1,000 to provide the playing field with seats and a fence. Despite Frank's hard work, the Waltham franchise collapsed after a few months, and he and several of his players shifted over to Lawrence to finish the season. He played a few games in the outfield that year, and those contests represent Frank Selee's entire professional playing career.

In 1885 Frank took over as manager at Haverhill in the New England League and led the club to a second-place finish, but the team directors released him midway through the following season. Frank was a non-playing manager, and the team leadership decided that it could not afford to pay Frank only to manage. However, he remained in the league long enough to notice several outstanding players on other teams. Tommy McCarthy, the Brockton centerfielder, won the batting title in the league that year, while pitcher Tom Lovett won 32 games for Newburyport and Lynn. When Frank became the manager of Oshkosh of the Northwest League in 1887, he convinced the team owners to sign McCarthy and Lovett and bring them to Wisconsin.

Selee, about whom people said, "he could size up a player in street clothes," took a chance on a young outfielder who had been rejected by several other teams. William Ellsworth Hoy was a 24-year-old from rural Ohio who left his trade as a shoemaker to play ball. He found it difficult to find a position on a professional team because he was completely deaf. He played for Oshkosh in 1886 but batted only .219. Frank Selee looked past Hoy's physical handicap and saw a speedy baserunner and excellent outfielder, so Selee retained Hoy for the 1887 season and devised ways to make it easier for Hoy to play. As an 1888 article explained, "[Hoy] is left handed, and when he bats a man stands in the captain's box near third base and signals to him decisions of the umpire on balls and strikes by raising his fingers."[3] This may have been the first use of ball-and-strike signals on the baseball field, years before umpires adopted the practice.

Hoy's teammates called him "Dummy," a term that was not considered so insulting at the time, and under Selee's guidance Hoy led the league in stolen bases and became a hit with the fans. Hoy played centerfield and batted .367, while McCarthy hit .345 as Frank won his first pennant by mere percentage points over Jim Hart's Milwaukee club.

The directors of the Omaha club in the Western Association noticed Selee's fine work and offered Frank a reported $3,000 to move his Oshkosh team *en masse* to Omaha. Pitcher Tom Lovett made the move to Nebraska, but Selee's other two stars, Tommy McCarthy and Dummy Hoy, advanced to the major leagues and left Frank with holes in his lineup. Though Lovett won 30 games, Omaha finished in fourth place in 1888 with a 55–48 record. This was a far better showing than the 41–66 mark they posted the year before, but Frank was not satisfied with fourth place. That winter, Selee wasted no time in searching for more talented players.

After three years with Selee, Tom Lovett joined the Brooklyn team of the American Association, but Frank trained his eye on another outstanding pitching prospect. Charles (Kid) Nichols was an 18-year-old righthander who posted a remarkable 16–2 record for Kansas City in 1888. Kansas City won the Western Association pennant that year, then joined the American Association for the 1889 campaign and, inexplicably, decided not to take Nichols to the major leagues with them. Selee quickly signed Nichols to an Omaha contract and installed the slender teenager as the team's premier starting pitcher.

Once again, Selee found a star in another team's reject pile. Nichols started 48 games for Omaha in 1889, finishing all of them and posting an incredible 39–8 record. He led Omaha to the Western Association pennant, Frank Selee's second as a manager. Omaha's 83–38 record and .686 winning percentage were the best in all of organized baseball that year. The Omaha club also gained a distinction on June 9, 1889, when infielder Johnny Crooks, another of Selee's signees, belted four home runs in one game. Crooks was the first player on any level of organized ball to perform the feat.

In September 1889, William Conant, one of the three main owners of the National League's Boston Beaneaters, scouted Nichols personally and signed the youngster to a contract for the following year. While observing Nichols, Conant became impressed with Frank Selee's managerial skill, and he began watching Selee closely. Conant was dissatisfied with Jim Hart as his manager, and he returned to Boston and persuaded the other owners to fire Hart and appoint Frank Selee as leader of the Beaneaters. In late 1889 Selee, who lived year-round in Melrose, became the manager of the nearby Boston ballclub.

Frank was not an imposing individual, and some in Boston wondered why the owners of the club hired this melancholy-looking man as manager. Selee, at the age of 30, was almost completely bald, and his impressive handlebar mustache merely accentuated the smallness of his other physical features. In team photographs of the period, the diminutive Frank wore a derby hat and bow tie and looked out of place among his strapping athletes. He looked like a haberdasher, which he was; he operated a men's clothing store in Melrose with former Phillies first baseman Sid Farrar in the off-season. Still, he possessed a first-rate baseball mind, and set to work rebuilding the once-powerful Boston ballclub.

The Beaneaters had nearly won the pennant in 1889, but Selee recognized that star pitcher John Clarkson had kept a mediocre team in the race almost single-handedly. Clarkson started 68 games, winning 49, and in September he pitched seven days in a row without a break. The Boston owners had fired Jim Hart mostly because they feared that he would destroy Clarkson's valuable arm through overwork, so Selee decided to install a three-man pitching rotation and lessen Clarkson's workload.

The 1890 season represented both peril and opportunity for Selee. Most of Boston's stars, except for Clarkson and catcher Charlie Bennett, jumped to the new Players League, leaving the Beaneaters bereft of talent. However, nearly every other National League team was in the same predicament, and the exodus to the Players League removed several strong-willed and hard-drinking veterans from Selee's roster. Veteran Mike (King) Kelly, the most popular player in the game, had undermined Jim Hart's authority as manager, and Kelly's jump to the rival league left Selee free to manage his ballclub with no interference from the game's biggest star.

Selee, the son of a Methodist minister, was not a drinker, in contrast to almost all other managers of his day. Frank was a soft-spoken man who relied on preparation, not force, to lead his players. "If I make things pleasant for the players, they reciprocate," Selee once explained. "I want them to be temperate and live properly. I do not believe that men who are engaged in such exhilarating exercise should be kept in strait jackets all the time, but I expect them to be in condition to play. I do not want a man who cannot appreciate such treatment."[4] He proposed to assemble a ballclub of dedicated professionals, and he turned the Beaneaters from a wild, hard-drinking crew into a team that relied on intelligence and execution to win games.

Frank had kept a close eye on the stars of other teams, and brought in several players from the Western Association to fill the void. Kid Nichols stepped in as a starting pitcher, and Selee persuaded the three Boston owners (the Triumvirs, the papers called them) to sign Milwaukee second baseman Bobby Lowe and Kansas City shortstop Herman Long. He then replaced first baseman Dan Brouthers with Tommy Tucker, the 1889 batting champion of the American Association. Long became a star at shortstop, Nichols won 27 games as a rookie, and Lowe filled in ably as a utility man in support of holdovers such as Clarkson and Bennett. While King Kelly and the Boston Players League squad won the pennant in the rival circuit, Selee brought the Beaneaters home in fifth place in the National League during his first season.

The Players League collapsed after only one season, and Selee went to work recruiting new men for the rejuvenated Beaneaters. Third baseman

Billy Nash and right fielder Harry Stovey returned to the Beaneaters, solidifying Selee's lineup and boosting Boston into the pennant race in the early stages of the 1891 season.

By August the Beaneaters stood alone in second place behind Cap Anson's Chicago squad, but later that month King Kelly returned to his old team and provided the spark that Selee's club needed. Chicago defeated Boston twice in mid–September, but then Selee's men ran off an 18-game winning streak (including one tie) and finished the race three games in front of Chicago. In Frank Selee's second season as Boston manager, he won the team's first league championship since 1883. When the American Association collapsed that winter, the Beaneaters acquired two future Hall of Famers, outfielders Hugh Duffy and Tommy McCarthy, the one-time star of Selee's Oshkosh pennant-winners.

Team chemistry was paramount to Frank Selee, and the manager made sure not to sign anyone who might disrupt the harmony of the ballclub. Reflecting upon his Boston experience, Selee once said, "It was my good fortune to be surrounded by a lot of good, clean fellows who got along finely together. To tell the truth, I would not have anyone on a team who was not congenial."[5] King Kelly was certainly an exception to Selee's general rule; he was a behavioral nightmare and a hard drinker, but by the end of the 1891 season the Beaneaters were Selee's team and not Kelly's any longer.

Kelly's presence electrified the fans and the local sportswriters for the last six weeks of the 1891 campaign, but he batted only .231, making it obvious that years of carousing had caused his once-prodigious skills to fade. The next year, Kelly, in his last season in Boston, batted only .189 as a part-time player. John Clarkson, too, was fading; he won 33 games in 1891, but he was slowing down, and Kid Nichols took Clarkson's place as Boston's ace pitcher. When Clarkson complained of a sore arm in early 1892, the Beaneaters released him and replaced him with Jack Stivetts, another signee from the defunct American Association. Stivetts and Nichols posted identical 35–16 records in 1892 as the Beaneaters won 102 games, becoming the first team in history to win 100 in a season.

The 1892 campaign marked the first and last instance (until 1981) of a split-season pennant race. Since there was only one major league at the time, the baseball bosses decided to divide the season into two parts and let the winners of each half-season battle in an October series for the official league championship. Boston easily won the first half, and most people expected them to run away with the second half as well, making the championship series unnecessary. Instead, the Cleveland Spiders rallied in mid-season and won the second half, despite griping from some quarters that

Selee's men had eased up and allowed the Spiders to win so that the post-season series could be played. In the end, Boston handily defeated Cleveland in their October matchup. Jack Stivetts and Cleveland's Cy Young battled to an 11-inning scoreless tie in the first game, but Selee's team won the next four contests and captured their second pennant in a row.

Selee valued players with brains as well as brawn, and two of his smartest men were outfielders Hugh Duffy and Tommy McCarthy. The papers dubbed them the "Heavenly Twins," and they strategized with Selee to devise new ways to win games. The Beaneaters may or may not have invented the hit-and-run, but they refined the play to a science in those years. With a runner on first, the batter would take a pitch as the runner faked a dash for second. This told the Beaneaters which infielder was assigned to cover first on a stolen-base attempt, and the batter would then flash a signal to let the runner know which pitch to run on. Then, the runner would break for second, leaving the batter free to slap the ball through the hole left by the covering infielder. Duffy and McCarthy worked this play to perfection, along with the fake bunt (to draw the infield in and allow the batter to swing away) and the double steal.

McCarthy also developed the trap play. On a short fly ball hit to left with runners on base, McCarthy sometimes let the ball hit the ground at the last possible moment. This allowed him to grab the ball and throw it into the infield to force runners out at second or third, sometimes both. The Beaneaters caught many runners napping with this ploy, and turned lazy fly balls into double plays. On August 15, 1894, McCarthy both started and ended the most unusual fielding play in history. With two men on and nobody out, the batter hit a short fly ball which Tommy let drop in front of him. McCarthy threw to Bobby Lowe to force the runner at second, and Lowe threw to first to retire the batter. While all this was happening, McCarthy dashed into the infield and, after a rundown, tagged the other baserunner out at the plate to complete a triple play.

McCarthy was "the chief schemer," as described by New York Giants manager John Montgomery (Monte) Ward, but men such as Lowe, Duffy, Long, and Nash spent hours devising batter-to-runner signals, defensive shifting, sign-stealing, and coverage schemes. Selee trusted his men to make the right decisions. "He was a good judge of players," said Bobby Lowe. "He didn't bother with a lot of signals, but let his players figure out their own plays. He didn't blame them if they took a chance that failed. He believed in place-hitting, sacrifice-hitting, and stealing bases. He was wonderful with young players."[6]

Monte Ward watched the Boston team with amazement. "I have never, in my twelve years' experience on the diamond, seen such skillful playing," said Ward in 1893. "The Boston players use more head-work and private signals than any other team in the country, and that alone is the reason why they can win the championship with such apparent ease.... 'Team-work in the field' used to be a prime factor in a pennant-winning team, but now 'team-work at the bat' is the latest wrinkle and the Bostons have it down fine."[7]

Frank Selee showed a flair for identifying a player's best defensive position. Selee moved Bobby Lowe from the outfield to second base in 1892, and Lowe teamed with Herman Long to form a keystone combination that stayed together for nearly ten years. They developed the 3-6-3 double play with first baseman Fred Tenney, a lefthanded catcher from Brown University whom Selee moved to first base. Pitcher Jack Stivetts, a 30-game winner in 1892, was also an excellent hitter, so Selee took the unusual step of playing Stivetts in the outfield whenever he needed another good bat in the lineup. Boston was also the best-hitting team in the league, and in 1894 Bobby Lowe became the first major leaguer to hit four home runs in a game, five years after Jack Crooks became the first minor leaguer to do so. Both men performed the feat under Frank Selee's leadership.

By 1893 the Boston Beaneaters so dominated the National League that fans in other cities cried, "Break up the Bostons!" Selee's men held off the Pittsburgh Pirates and won their third pennant by a five-game margin, but the fans around the league resented the Beaneaters' stranglehold on first place. In a mid–1893 game at Pittsburgh, Herman Long slid into Pirate catcher Connie Mack and shattered Mack's leg, which made the fans so incensed that they stoned the Boston players' carriages following the contest. The police declined to intervene, and only some fast whipping of the carriage horses saved the Boston team from serious injury. The Boston dominance ended in 1894, when injuries, holdouts, and the emergence of the Baltimore Orioles drove the Beaneaters to a third-place finish, eight games behind.

Selee convinced the Triumvirs not to tear the team apart, but to rebuild it around several of his existing stars. He put Fred Tenney on first base and kept Long and Lowe at short and second, but sent third sacker Billy Nash to Philadelphia for outfielder Billy Hamilton. On a trip to Buffalo, Selee noticed a fine young third baseman named Jimmy Collins and brought him to Boston. Collins stumbled early on, and the Triumvirs demanded that Selee get rid of the youngster, but Selee farmed him out to Louisville for more experience. In 1895 Selee brought Collins back to Boston, where the young man completed the new Boston infield.

Hugh Duffy remained in the outfield, but Tommy McCarthy began to slow down in his mid-thirties, and after a vicious hotel-room fight between McCarthy and Stivetts in 1895 Selee released his longtime favorite and put Hamilton in center, with Duffy in left and newcomer Chick Stahl in right. The pitching staff featured perennial 30-game winner Kid Nichols, along with Jack Stivetts and two new faces, lefthander Fred Klobedanz and righthander Ted Lewis, who attended divinity school in the off-season. The career of catcher Charlie Bennett ended with a train accident in 1894, but Selee found a talented replacement in Marty Bergen. The Orioles won three pennants in a row from 1894 to 1896, but the revamped Beaneaters stood ready to challenge again for the flag in 1897.

Selee's retooled ballclub jumped out to an early lead, but Baltimore stayed close all season long. In mid–September the two teams met in a three-game series to decide the pennant. Nichols won the first game for Boston, while Lewis lost the second and set the stage for one of the greatest games of the 19th century. On September 25, 1897, more than 25,000 people packed the Baltimore ballpark and watched Kid Nichols stagger to a 19–10 win over the Orioles. This victory virtually clinched Selee's fourth pennant and established Boston once again as the dominant team of the National League.

There was no World Series then, but for four years in the 1890s the first and second-place teams in the National League met in the post-season Temple Cup series. Boston appeared in the series only once, after the 1897 season, but the Beaneaters were exhausted after battling the Orioles all season long and played poorly, losing the Cup in five games. Selee came in for some rare criticism for his failure to rouse the Beaneaters into action, but the players did not attach much importance to the match. "We didn't have any interest in the series in 1897," explained Fred Tenney. "We had just beaten Baltimore in the competition that counted, and this was just something extra."[8] Because the series was carelessly played and poorly attended, the National League returned the Temple Cup to its donor and discontinued the annual October matchup between the top two teams in the league.

Jack Stivetts' mound career ended in 1898 with a sore arm, but Selee located another outstanding young pitcher, as he had found Kid Nichols a decade before. Vic Willis was a tall curveball specialist who posted a 20–17 mark for Syracuse in 1897, and Selee convinced the Boston owners to buy the pitcher's release for $3,000. Willis impressed the Boston observers with his overhand curve, but he needed work on his control, so Selee hired Jack Ryan, a retired catcher, who built a wooden target for Willis to practice against. Before long Willis began to get his pitches over the plate, and he joined the rotation in May. Willis posted a 25–13 record in able support of Nichols (31–12) and Lewis (26–8) as Selee's Beaneaters rolled to their fifth pennant in eight years.

Frank Selee and his 1899 Boston Beaneaters. Top: Nichols, Clarke, Killen, Willis, Bergen, Lewis, Hickman. Center: Tenney, Collins, Stafford, Selee, Duffy, Hamilton, Long. Front: Lowe and Stahl. (National Baseball Hall of Fame Library, Cooperstown, New York)

The core of the Boston team began to unravel in 1899. Kid Nichols fell to a 21–19 record, Billy Hamilton slowed down due to leg injuries, and stars such as Bobby Lowe, Herman Long, and Hugh Duffy faded with advancing age. When the owners of the Brooklyn Dodgers bought the Baltimore franchise outright and absorbed many of the Oriole stars, they created a superteam that ran away with the 1899 pennant as the fading Bostons held second place. Selee tried to rebuild again, but team management balked at spending money for minor-league players, and Selee had no choice but to play his aging stars. The ballclub suffered another crippling blow when catcher Marty Bergen, the backbone of the outstanding Boston pitching staff, committed suicide in January 1900, and left the Beaneaters short behind the plate. After a fourth-place finish in 1900, several Boston stars jumped to the new American League and doomed the Beaneaters to a sixth-place finish in 1901.

Frank Selee had won five pennants in 12 years with the Beaneaters, but he encountered resistance from ownership in his never-ending search for new players. At the end of the 1901 season the Triumvirs decided to make a change and hired Rochester manager Al Buckenberger to replace Selee.

Outfielder Hugh Duffy reacted angrily to the news of Selee's dismissal. "Selee should long ago have left this city," said Duffy, "and taken one of several good chances he had, instead of staying here at a very small salary."[9] Duffy was correct, because Selee earned about $3,500 a year as Boston manager, which was not nearly the highest managerial salary in the league. Chicago White Sox manager Clark Griffith also offered his opinion on Selee's departure from Boston. "That is a big mistake," said Griffith. "Selee is one of the few great managers in the business."[10]

Jim Hart, the man Selee replaced as manager of the Beaneaters in 1890, was the general manager of the National League Chicago Orphans in 1901 and contacted Frank almost immediately after Selee's firing hit the newspapers. In no time, Frank signed a contract to succeed Tom Loftus as manager of the Chicago ballclub.

The Chicago team had been known as the White Stockings when it entered the National League in 1876, and they became the Colts with an influx of young players in the 1890s. Perhaps no team in baseball was so thoroughly identified with one player, as the Chicago nine was, by Cap Anson, who played for the club for 22 years and managed it for 19 of those seasons. The team was known as "Anson's Colts" until Anson left after the 1897 campaign, and so bereft were the people of Chicago at his departure that the papers called the team the Orphans. The club wallowed in mediocrity for the first four years of the post–Anson era, and Jim Hart knew that the team needed a fresh identity for the new century. He turned to the most successful manager in baseball, Frank Selee, to provide it.

Once again, Selee built a team by studying young players and finding places for them to fit in. Frank Chance was a good-hitting catcher who joined the club in 1898 but struggled with his defense, especially his throwing. Selee put the better-fielding Johnny Kling behind the plate and transferred Chance to first base. Selee brought Bobby Lowe with him to Chicago, but Lowe suffered a series of injuries and relinquished the second base position to an intense young man from Troy, New York named Johnny Evers. During spring training, Selee looked at a dozen shortstops before giving the job to Joe Tinker. With the addition of veteran Doc Casey at third, Selee completed his infield and created the most famous double play combination of all time, Tinker to Evers to Chance.

Selee's infusion of youth gave the Chicago ballclub the new identity it needed. On May 27, 1902, the *Chicago Daily News* stated, almost in passing, "Frank Selee will devote his strongest efforts on the team work of the new Cubs, this year." That sentence turned the Chicago Orphans into the Chicago Cubs, a name the team still carries more than 100 years later.

The Cubs improved almost immediately under Selee's leadership. The team went 55–81 under Loftus in 1901, but Selee lifted them to within one game of the .500 mark in 1902 and then, with his crew of young stars in place, jumped to 82–56 and a third-place finish in 1903. After that season Selee pulled off one of his most daring trades, sending 20-game winner Jack Taylor to St. Louis for a young righthander from Indiana named Mordecai Brown. They called him "Three-Finger" Brown because his pitching hand was severely injured in a childhood accident, but he could throw unusual curveballs with the damaged paw, and Selee saw Brown as a future star. Selee, as usual, was correct, and Brown soon became Chicago's primary starting pitcher.

Frank Selee's strict attention to detail was one of his strongest traits as a manager, though his sharp eye cost the Cubs two games early in his tenure. On May 7, 1902, at Chicago, the Cubs defeated the Giants and Christy Mathewson by a 6–0 score, and followed that victory with a 10–4 win the next day. After the second game, Selee casually remarked to Giants manager Horace Fogel that the distance from home plate to the pitching rubber looked short. Fogel measured the distance himself and found that it was, indeed, 15 inches too short. Fogel then filed a protest with the league, and on June 3, of that year the league upheld Fogel's protest and ordered the two games replayed.

"To make a success," Selee once wrote, "a baseball manager must enter into his work with every bit of energy he can command."[11] By the early 1900s, Selee's increasingly poor health made it difficult for him to apply his usual energy to the task of building another baseball team. Frank contracted a severe cold during the last series of the 1902 campaign, and by mid–October he was diagnosed with pleurisy. He recovered, but his lungs remained weak, and he traveled to Colorado to spend the winter breathing the healthy mountain air. Selee spent the rest of his tenure with the Cubs battling health problems, and in late 1904 he returned to Colorado to rejuvenate his weakening lungs.

The Cubs advanced to second place in 1904 and prepared to challenge the New York Giants for the league title in 1905, but Frank Selee was not destined to lead the Cubs to the pennant. Never robust, Frank fell ill in 1905 during spring training at Santa Monica, California. He offered to give up the reins of the team, but Jim Hart convinced him to stay, so Frank opened the season as manager. His condition grew worse, and before long he developed both appendicitis and lung congestion. He stopped taking road trips with the team, leaving Frank Chance in charge while he stayed in Chicago and sought medical attention. In July 1905, Selee received the bad news that he was suffering from tuberculosis. As his health deteriorated, he realized that he could no longer lead the team, so on July 28, he took a leave of absence as manager of the Cubs. Frank Chance, who had been elected as captain of the team by his fellow players earlier that season, succeeded him on an interim basis.[12]

Selee fully expected to return to the Cubs for 1906, but in the fall of 1905 Jim Hart, who was ill himself, sold his interest in the Cubs to a group of Cincinnati and Chicago businessmen. Selee looked into the prospect of putting his own syndicate together to buy the team, but his health worsened again, and during the winter he severed his connection with the club, which left Frank Chance as full-time manager of the team. Selee could only watch from the sidelines as Chance led the Cubs to three consecutive pennants and two World Series titles.

In late 1905 Selee moved to Denver, Colorado, hoping that the environment would restore his health. He could not stay away from the game, however, and in 1906 he bought an interest in the Pueblo team of the Western League. Frank, despite his declining physical state, managed the team for three seasons but never finished higher than fifth in an eight-team league. He sold the team after the 1908 campaign when his physical condition took a turn for the worse.

He tried his best to stay active. He purchased and operated a Denver hotel, wrote articles for newspapers and followed baseball as best he could, but his lungs continued to decline. In 1909 he was confined to a sanitarium, the Elks Home for Consumptives in Denver, where he died on July 5, of that year. He was 49 years old and left a widow named Mary, but no children. Frank's parents, who were still living, brought his body back to Massachusetts and buried him in the town cemetery in Melrose, where Frank Selee grew up and learned the game of baseball. One year later, in 1910, Frank Chance managed the team that Selee built to its fourth pennant in five years. Six of the team's eight everyday players, in addition to two of Chance's starting pitchers, had been signed by Frank Selee.

When the Baseball Hall of Fame opened in 1939 Frank Selee had been dead for 30 years, and the nation's baseball fans and sportswriters had mostly forgotten the Boston powerhouse that he assembled. None of his Beaneater stars—Jimmy Collins, Bobby Lowe, Hugh Duffy, Tommy McCarthy, Kid Nichols—gained election to the Hall of Fame in the first few rounds of balloting from 1936 to 1939, and none of them garnered more than a handful of votes from the writers.

Commissioner Kenesaw M. Landis created the Permanent Committee specifically to rectify such omissions, and in 1945 and 1946 the committee recognized six of Selee's men. The committee selected Duffy, McCarthy, and Collins to the Cooperstown shrine, along with the Chicago double-play combo of Joe Tinker, Johnny Evers, and Frank Chance. Three years later, the committee added two of Selee's greatest pitching discoveries, Kid Nichols and Mordecai Brown. At present, 12 of Frank Selee's Boston and Chicago players are enshrined in the Hall of Fame.

Selee himself received a secondary honor of sorts when the committee emerged from its 1946 meeting with something that it called the "Honor Rolls of Baseball," a list of 39 managers, executives, umpires and sportswriters that formed a second tier of recognition within the Hall of Fame. It appears that the committee was not convinced that such non-playing personnel deserved full membership in the Cooperstown pantheon, but deserved to be honored in some way. Frank Selee was one of five managers so recognized, but the Honor Rolls concept was severely criticized in the sporting press, and the museum never put the names of Selee and the other 38 honorees on display in any way. No other names were ever added to the Honor Rolls, and the idea quickly sank without a trace. Another 53 years passed before the Veterans Committee put Frank Selee into the Hall of Fame, this time on an equal footing with all of the greatest managers and players of the past.

Though the Hall of Fame electors appeared to have forgotten Selee, the men who played for and against him held Selee in the highest regard. Bill Everitt, who played the infield for Chicago in the 1890s and competed against Selee's Boston teams, paid tribute to one of the game's greatest managers and team builders. "There is no question about it," said Everitt. "Frank was one of the brightest men baseball ever saw, and he was so acknowledged by such men as [National League president Harry] Pulliam and [Giants owner] John T. Brush. He was the greatest judge of ballplayers I ever saw. In fact, his word in every branch of the game was almost final. It was he who found Fred Tenney and made him [along with] Herman Long, Hugh Duffy, Bobby Lowe and Billy Hamilton. Selee made Frank Chance by putting him on first when he was barely making good as a catcher."[13]

Frank Selee may be the most obscure manager in the Cooperstown museum, but his record (five pennants and a .598 winning percentage, the fourth-highest of all time) makes a strong case for his enshrinement. He not only managed the turn-of-the-century Boston Beaneaters and Chicago Cubs, but he also built both teams, virtually from scratch, into champions. As a manager and team-builder, Frank Selee has had few equals in the history of the game, and his election to the Hall was a well-deserved, though long-awaited, honor.

16

♦ Bid McPhee ♦

[Bid] McPhee was utterly boring.... He played hard, but clean. In all his 18 seasons, he was never fined. He was never even thrown out of a game! At a time when rough and rowdy baseballers were providing a wealth of wicked anecdotes, McPhee showed up every day in shape, stayed sober, did his job, and went home to a good night's sleep. — John Thorn and Pete Palmer, 1991[1]

July 23, 2000, was a great day for fans of the Cincinnati Reds.

On that date, the Baseball Hall of Fame held its annual induction ceremony in Cooperstown, New York. The celebration began as longtime Cincinnati broadcaster Marty Brenneman received the Ford Frick Award and earned a place in the broadcasters' wing of the Hall of Fame. Master of ceremonies Ralph Kiner then introduced the five newest members of the Hall, three of whom were former Reds. Two were well-known baseball personalities: Sparky Anderson, who managed the "Big Red Machine" to four pennants in the 1970s, and Tony Perez, the sweet-swinging first baseman and key run producer for Anderson's teams.

There was one other Cincinnati Red inducted that day, but even the most rabid Reds fans struggled to recognize his name. John (Bid) McPhee was a second baseman who joined the Reds some 118 years before, when the team was still known as the Red Stockings. From 1882 to 1899 McPhee, one of Cincinnati's most popular players, batted in many different lineup spots and anchored the infield defense for the Reds. People looked at his photograph and found it hard to believe that this diminutive man led his league in fielding percentage nine times and in double plays 11 times. They found it even more incredible that he did so without wearing a glove for most of his long career.

Bid McPhee was the greatest second baseman and one of the outstanding batters of the 19th century, but his name was almost unknown outside of his family. As one of his grandnieces, Jean Ratcliff, told the *Cincinnati Post*, "We're very proud and gratified that he's going to be inducted into the Hall of Fame. Growing up, everybody in our family knew about Bid McPhee, but no one else really knew much about him."[2] That all changed for Bid McPhee on a sunny July afternoon in Cooperstown, 100 years after his retirement and 58 years after his death, as he finally took his place among the honored players of baseball.

John Alexander McPhee was born in Massena, New York, on November 1, 1859. His father John was a saddlemaker who died young, leaving his wife Maria without a husband and young John fatherless. When John was seven years old, he and his mother moved to Aledo, Illinois, a town in the western part of the state near to Maria's family.

Maria's brother operated a hotel in Keithsburg, a Mississippi River town a few miles from Aledo, and before long John McPhee found employment in the hotel kitchen. He ran errands, fetched things, carried messages, and generally did the bidding of whoever needed him at any particular time. The errand boy was usually called "Bid" or "Biddy" by the kitchen staff for this reason, and the nickname followed John McPhee into his career in baseball.

In his teenaged years, Bid McPhee excelled on the sandlot ball fields of Keithsburg. He started out as a catcher, with no mask or protective equipment, but a foul tip hit him in the face one day and caused Bid to move to the infield. He was small, but fast, and he played second base with a sure-handed grace. Bid McPhee wore no glove — no one did at the time, except for catchers — but he could stop the hardest hit grounders and line drives with his bare hands and throw the fastest runners out at first.

In 1878, when Bid was 18 years old, he joined a minor league team in nearby Davenport, Iowa. After two seasons there, he traveled to Denver, Colorado, where he played ball in his free time and worked as a clerk in a store. He might have given up baseball for life in the business world, but the owner of an independent team in Akron, Ohio, remembered him from Davenport. This owner offered Bid a position on his team, with a job as a bookkeeper in a lumber company thrown in for good measure.

Bid was an intelligent young man, with excellent penmanship and a head for numbers, but his hitting and fielding success for the Akron club convinced him to put his business career on hold. When the 1881 season ended, the Cincinnati Red Stockings of the new American Association bought his contract from Akron. In 1882, Bid McPhee made his major league debut for the Red Stockings at second base, a position he would play for the next 18 seasons.

The Red Stockings were the successors of baseball's first true all-professional nine, the undefeated 1869 Cincinnati Red Stockings. Managed by Harry Wright, the team steamrolled the opposition in that memorable season and caused a surge of interest in professional baseball throughout the Midwest and the East Coast. However, the Queen City fans became spoiled by the success of the Red Stockings, and the team fell on hard times shortly after its undefeated season. In 1870 the Red Stockings lost a few games and disbanded when fan support dwindled. Harry Wright and several of his Cincinnati stars decamped to Boston, where Wright organized a new team that dominated the first professional league, the National Association.

For the next five years, the Cincinnati fans contented themselves with amateur and semipro baseball. The city returned to the professional ranks when it entered the National League with a new Red Stockings team in 1876, but the Eastern clubs disapproved of the sale and consumption of beer in the Cincinnati ballpark. They also objected to the Cincinnati club renting its park out for other teams to play in on Sundays. The Red Stockings, who profited from Sunday park rentals and beer sales, refused to modify these practices, and in November 1880, the other National League teams expelled the Red Stockings from the circuit.

Cincinnati remained outside of the major league orbit for only one year. In early 1882, a new league, the American Association, accepted Cincinnati as a member. The management quickly gathered players, three of whom had played for the Red Stockings in 1880. Most of the other players were experienced major leaguers, with the exception of Bid McPhee, the 22-year-old second baseman from Akron. The hastily assembled new team struggled to find its form in the spring of 1882. The new Red Stockings played a few pre-season games against National League nines, losing most of them by lopsided scores and worrying the local fans.

On opening day, May 5, 1882, the Red Stockings played their first home game of the season. Despite the new league's bargain admission price of 25 cents, only about 1,500 fans showed up; perhaps the public wanted to see if the new Red Stockings were for real before offering their unqualified support. The fans in attendance that day caught a glimpse of one of the American Association's most bizarre innovations. Each player wore a different colored jersey, based upon the position each man played. McPhee, the second baseman, wore orange with black stripes, while pitchers wore light blue, catchers dark red, and so on.

The Red Stockings lost that first game to Pittsburgh by a 10–9 score, but the fans appeared to be satisfied with the play of their new home team. Bid McPhee, who handled several fielding chances cleanly, earned praise for his efforts in the papers the next day. So began a career that would find McPhee participating in over 2,200 games for the Cincinnati ballclub. Bid batted sixth or seventh in the lineup and hit only .228 in his inaugural season, but he solidified the infield with his steady fielding play. He led all Association second basemen in putouts, double plays and fielding percentage.

The Cincinnati ballclub coasted along under the .500 mark until June 2, when a game at Philadelphia turned their season around. The Red Stockings trapped the Quakers' Jack O'Brian in a rundown, and O'Brian crashed heavily into Bid McPhee at second base. McPhee tagged the runner out, but Bid's spikes cut a long gash in O'Brian's face and knocked out two of his front teeth. The bloody injury necessitated a 30-minute delay in the game. It was an accident, but the incident gave McPhee and the Red Stockings a reputation for toughness, deserved or not, and immediately afterward the Red Stockings went on a 10-game winning streak. Thanks in large part to the rookie second baseman, the Cincinnati club grabbed first place by the end of June and coasted to the pennant, winning by 11 and a half games in an 80-game season.

At season's end, the Red Stockings hosted the National League champion Chicago White Stockings in a two-game set. Some enthusiastic historians call this matchup the first "World's Series," though it was more correctly described as an exhibition, but it was the first post-season series between league champions in baseball history. More than 2,700 fans, a healthy crowd for the 1880s, filled the Cincinnati grandstand for the first game on October 15.

The Red Stockings, champions of a new league, entered the contest as decided underdogs. The confident Cap Anson, Chicago's player-manager, left his star catcher Mike "King" Kelly at home and put ace pitcher Larry Corcoran at shortstop for the first game. It appeared that Anson and his Chicago team did not take the Cincinnati nine seriously, but the Red Stockings battled the White Stockings to a scoreless tie for the first five innings of the contest. Cincinnati scored first off Chicago's second-string pitcher Fred Goldsmith, taking a 1–0 in the sixth inning with three consecutive singles. There were two men on and one out when the light-hitting Bid McPhee came to the plate. McPhee, who liked to belt the ball into the gaps in the outfield, pounded a line drive deep into right field, scoring both runners with a triple. Soon after, McPhee scored on a wild pitch, and the Red Stockings led by a count of 4–0, a score that held to the end of the game.

The next day, more than 6,000 fans overflowed the wooden ballpark to cheer their heroes, but the White Stockings returned Corcoran to the mound and won the game by a 2–0 score. Perhaps the Chicagoans had not planned on losing any games to the Red Stockings, because they left town without playing a deciding game because of previously scheduled commitments elsewhere.[3] The series ended in a tie, but the Red Stockings acquitted themselves well, and fans would long remember how Bid McPhee delivered the key hit in Cincinnati's first post-season game.

McPhee improved at bat and in the field with each passing year, though it took him a while to learn how to hit a major league curveball. The local papers remarked on how badly Bid looked when he went fishing for a breaking pitch outside of the strike zone. In 1883 Bid raised his average to .243, but the Red Stockings fell to third place, five games behind the Philadelphia pennant winners. In 1884 Bid's average rose sharply to .292, and he put together a 25-game hitting streak and scored 100 runs in a season for the first time. By the late 1880s, Bid was one of the most productive hitters in the Cincinnati lineup, using his speed to beat out bunts and steal bases. Though his career average never approached the .300 mark, Bid walked nearly 1,000 times and posted an excellent on-base percentage. He also developed a knack for hitting triples; he reached double figures in triples eight times, and pounded out 180 in his career. In 1886 he stretched out eight would-be triples into inside-the-park home runs, enough to lead the Association in round-trippers. Bid McPhee was probably the smallest home-run champion in the history of the game.

Despite his increasing prowess at the plate, it was McPhee's bare-handed fielding that made him a favorite with the Cincinnati fans. He spent several weeks each spring toughening up his hands for the season ahead, and expressed disapproval for his contemporaries who wore rudimentary gloves. "I never use a glove on either hand in a game," remarked Bid to the newspapers one day in 1890. "I have never seen the necessity of wearing one, and besides I cannot hold a thrown ball if there is anything on my hands.

"This glove business has gone a little too far. It is all wrong to suppose that your hands will get battered out of shape if you don't use them. True, hot-hit balls do sting a little at the opening of the season, but after you get used to it, there is no trouble on that score."[4] He was nothing if not stubborn, because Bid was the last major league infielder, at any position, to play without a glove. The Red Stockings sought to take advantage of Bid's sure-handedness, and their groundskeepers made the Cincinnati playing surface as smooth as possible by not putting grass in the infield. The Red Stockings had the last all-dirt infield in the majors, and it helped

Bid avoid errors in Cincinnati. One source claims that McPhee's fielding percentage at home was ten points higher than his percentage on the road.

With his speed, Bid exhibited far more range than any other second baseman in the league, which explains his amazing fielding statistics. He led his leagues in double plays 11 times and in fielding average nine times. In 1886, when second sackers played nearer to the bag than they do today, Bid recorded 525 putouts, a record that stands to this day. No other second baseman in baseball history has ever managed to record 500 putouts in a single season, before or since. His fielding and his knack for scoring runs — he averaged more than a run per game in 1887 — made Bid the most valuable player on the Cincinnati team. He was the king of the second basemen, and the Cincinnati sportswriters called him "King Bid" in their columns.

On a personal level, Bid McPhee behaved less like a ballplayer and more like someone who, as he did, lived

Bid McPhee in 1888. (Author's collection)

with his parents and followed the trade of bookkeeping in the off-season. The writers found Bid to be the most articulate member of the Red Stockings, and while he was not a teetotaler, he was also not a hard-drinking rowdy like so many players of the era. He kept himself in excellent physical condition year-round, and stayed at five feet eight inches and 152 pounds for his entire career. As his salary rose (to $2,300 a year by 1887, a large amount in those days) he became a sharp dresser. He never argued with the umpires, and played 18 seasons in the major leagues without ever suffering an ejection from a game. He was, in short, one of baseball's gentlemen in a wild and woolly era.

The St. Louis Browns dominated the American Association in the mid-1880s. The Red Stockings finished second to the Browns in 1885, a distant sixteen games behind, and despite Bid McPhee's record-setting fielding exploits in 1886, the Red Stockings fell to fifth place. They rose to second again in 1887, when Bid led the league in triples with 19, though they were never really in the pennant race, since the Browns defeated them by 14 games. By 1889 the Red Stockings had fallen to the middle of the pack in the Association.

At the conclusion of the 1889 campaign, the Cincinnati management quickly signed most of the Red Stockings, including star second baseman Bid McPhee, to contracts for the following year. This enabled the team to head off any challenges from the new Players League, which was created by disgruntled major leaguers as a protest against the policies of the club owners. By signing their players early, the Red Stockings, who soon became known simply as the Reds, managed to hold the team together. The biggest surprise of the winter months, however, came in December 1889, when the Cincinnati ballclub resigned its membership in the American Association and moved into the National League.

The Reds found much keener competition in the older circuit, but McPhee barely noticed the difference. In May of 1890 Bid tied a National League record when he belted three triples in a game against future Hall of Famer Amos Rusie of the Giants, and he whacked a career-best 25 three-baggers that season. The Reds, led by their diminutive second baseman, grabbed first place and opened up a five-game lead by the Fourth of July, though they faded in the stretch and finished a distant fourth. Though Bid McPhee still stole bases, hit triples, and scored more than 100 runs almost every year, the Reds fell to fifth in 1891 and sixth in 1892 (after the Association folded). Charles Comiskey, who led the old St. Louis Browns to four pennants in the 1880s, took over as Cincinnati manager in 1892, but the Reds dropped all the way to tenth place in the twelve-team league by 1895.

When Louisville Colonels third baseman Jerry Denny retired in 1894, he left Bid McPhee as the only major league infielder who still refused to wear a glove. Bid, at age 34, hit over .300 for the second time (not including 1887, when walks counted as hits), but his totals of putouts and assists fell and his fielding percentage, while still higher than the league average, was no longer good enough to lead the circuit. Bid's stubbornness about wearing a glove was beginning to hurt the team. On September 23, 1894, the usually sure-handed McPhee set a new National League record for second basemen with three errors in one inning.[5]

He finally changed his mind about wearing a glove in early 1896. Bid, now 36 years old, reported for spring training in New Orleans in April of that year and quickly developed a sore back. He blamed the popular Turkish baths of the city, and not his advancing age, for the problem. "I notice that Peitz, Gastright and Gray, and all the other players who indulged in Turkish baths the same way that I have, suffered," McPhee said, somewhat defensively, to the writers.[6] He also had to contend with a sore on his left hand that took an unusually long time to heal. The sore was more irritating than painful, and Bid tried to play through it, but the more he played, the worse it became.

Finally, in late April, Bid obtained his first fielding glove and wore it on the diamond. "McPhee, for the first time in his long career on the ball-field, is using a glove," reported the *Cincinnati Enquirer* on April 23. "He was forced to use it because (of) a little sore.... The ball coming in contact with it kept it irritated and it would not heal. The use of the glove protects the sore spot and it is now pretty nearly well." The glove paid immediate dividends. Bid, slowed by his sore back, fielded fewer balls in 1896, but the glove helped him to hold onto the ones he could reach. His .978 fielding percentage not only led the league, but set a new major league record that stood until 1925. Finally convinced, Bid used the glove for the rest of his career.

Bid's last years as a player were filled with frustration. The Reds were an aging team, with the oldest average starting lineup in the National League, and they made a practice in the 1890s of starting out each season quickly and fading in the stretch. In 1896, Cincinnati stood on top of the league by the end of July, but ran out of gas and fell back to third place, 12 games behind the pennant-winning Orioles. In 1897 Bid suffered his first serious injury, a severely broken ankle, in a collision at second base with Baltimore's stocky catcher Wilbert Robinson. Bid's spikes cut a gash in Robinson's knee and knocked the catcher out of action for the rest of the season, but McPhee's injury was so debilitating that most observers thought that he might never play again. On July 29, 1897, the Reds held a benefit game in his honor that raised more than $3,500 as a going-away present. After Bid's injury, the Reds fell out of contention and stumbled to a fourth-place finish.

McPhee rehabilitated his ankle and surprised everyone when he returned to the Reds for the 1898 campaign, though the ankle bothered him for the remainder of his career. His range was decreasing, but he was still one of the best defensive second basemen in the league, and his inspiring play helped boost Cincinnati into the league lead. The Reds held the top position in the standings from May 11 to August 16, but withered under the challenge of the streaking Boston club and faded away to third place. Bid, slowing down at the age of 38, batted only .246 in 131 games, and it was apparent that his career was coming to an end. He even played three games in right field that season, the first time (except for one appearance at third base in 1889) that Bid had played anywhere besides second base in a Cincinnati uniform.

Despite his advancing age, Bid McPhee performed one of the most spectacular defensive plays of the 19th century on July 3, 1898. Tommy Dowd, the speedy leadoff batter of the St. Louis Browns, whacked a sharp grounder to the right side of the infield. Bid caught up with it, but had no time to catch the ball and make a throw from shallow right field. Instead, Bid slapped at the ball with his bare hand, handball-style, and directed it to first baseman Jake Beckley for the out.

Bid participated in only 106 of the team's 156 games in 1899, batting .283 and slowly relinquishing the second base position to the younger Harry Steinfeldt. He played his last major league games on October 15, 1899, in a doubleheader against the talent-poor Cleveland Spiders, who won only 20 games and lost 134 that season. Bid belted four hits, including a triple, and scored five runs in the two games as the Reds walloped the Spiders by scores of 16–1 and 19–3.

He went to spring training in New Orleans with the team the following year, but his throwing arm was sore, and the pain persisted despite his attempts to throw through the discomfort. The Reds management offered Bid a contract and allowed him as much time as he needed to work his arm into shape, but Bid was now 40 years old, and he knew that he was at the end of the line. "I am uncertain about myself," said Bid to a reporter. "I still have a touch of rheumatism in my throwing arm, and I am fearful as to my ability to get into playing form before the season opens. I do not want the club to carry me as dead timber. If I feel that I can do myself justice after I have practiced some, I will sign a contract and give the team my best effort. However, should I feel that I can not give the Cincinnati club value received, I will retire from the game."[7]

McPhee, the off-season bookkeeper, believed that he could no longer play well enough to justify his salary, and on March 9, 1900, McPhee announced his retirement from active play and formally brought his 18-year career to a conclusion. "Bid McPhee's manly and voluntary retirement from the game," stated the *Washington Post* a few days later, "is in keeping with the sterling honesty that has marked McPhee's long and honorable career on the diamond."

Bid stayed away from the game for only one season. The Reds played poorly in 1900, and attendance dwindled with on-field mediocrity and off-field controversies filling the newspapers. The team management appealed to the still-popular McPhee to return to the Reds as manager, and Bid accepted the post in early 1901. As one of his first orders of business, he decided to move spring training to Cincinnati from New Orleans. The new manager told the newspapers that New Orleans provided too many temptations and diversions for his ballplayers, especially the younger ones.

McPhee's appointment as Cincinnati manager met with approval from the public, but it appears that Reds owner John T. Brush wanted to use McPhee's popularity to placate the fans and draw attention away from his own plans to sell the Reds. Brush had been negotiating to buy the New York Giants for nearly a year, and he made several moves to ensure the Giants' future success at the expense of the Cincinnati team. In the major league player draft of December 1900, Brush obtained a 20-year-old righthanded pitcher, Christy Mathewson, who had been left unprotected by the Giants. Many people wondered why the Giants exposed Mathewson to the draft; though he went 0–3 for the Giants in 1900, he posted a 20–2 log in the Virginia League, and most baseball men considered him a future star.

It soon became apparent that Brush drafted Mathewson as a favor to the Giants, who chose to protect other players on their team. The Reds claimed Mathewson to prevent any other National League team from doing so, and immediately traded him back to the Giants for Amos Rusie, the sore-armed former strikeout king who had not pitched in more than two years. Brush wanted to make sure that Mathewson would be pitching for the Giants when Brush finally completed his quest to buy the New York team. The Mathewson–Rusie trade, one of the most lopsided deals of all time, did no favors for the Reds or for manager Bid McPhee. Rusie pitched in only three games for the Reds, giving up 43 hits in 22 innings, and soon quit the team, while Mathewson became the league's premier pitcher for the next decade and a half.

The 1901 Reds, under McPhee, led the league on June 8, but suddenly collapsed, losing 13 of their next 14 games and dropping all the way from first place to seventh in less than two weeks. With only 32 wins in their last 105 games, the Reds finished the campaign in the National League cellar, 38 games behind the pennant-winning Pittsburgh Pirates. Brush had neglected the Cincinnati talent base; the ballclub owned an exciting young slugger in 21-year-old Sam Crawford, who led the league in homers with 16, but also employed a starting catcher (Bill Bergen) who batted .179 for the season. With only one effective starting pitcher in 22-game winner Frank (Noodles) Hahn, McPhee and the Reds found themselves overmatched against the better National League ballclubs.

Bid managed to elevate the Reds to fifth place during the early stages of the following season, but by mid–1902 John T. Brush had completed his plans to sell the Reds to local investors and buy the New York Giants. In early July, rumors abounded that the sale was close to completion, and that the new owners intended to fire Bid and replace him with former Baltimore Orioles outfielder Joe Kelley. Bid did not wait to be fired. He resigned as manager of the Reds on July 11, 1902, five days before Kelley signed to manage the club.

McPhee immediately began the next chapter of his life. In August 1902, less than one month after he left the Reds, he married a Chicago woman named Julia Broerman. Bid did some scouting work for the Reds until 1909, when he and Julia moved to Los Angeles. In 1916 they settled in Long Branch, near San Diego, where Bid spent his retirement years fishing and visiting the local racetrack.

Despite his unpleasant departure from the Reds, Bid still followed the team in the papers and kept their schedule posted in his home. Unlike most other old ballplayers, Bid praised the younger crop of major leaguers. The old-timers, said McPhee, were "great fellows, all of them, and great ball players too, but the younger generation is all right. Facts are, maybe they're better than us youngsters were back in the Eighties. Chances are the boys would bunt me out of the league if I were playing today."[8] In 1937 the National League honored the 77-year-old McPhee with a gold lifetime pass, granting him free entry into any league game for the remainder of his days.

McPhee had invested plenty of money from his baseball earnings, but he suffered two heart attacks in the late 1920s and the resulting medical bills exhausted his savings. By 1928 most of his money was gone, and the Cincinnati Reds offered financial assistance to their longtime star player and former manager. McPhee accepted the help, and he managed to live the rest of his life in relative comfort. Julia McPhee passed away in 1940, while Bid McPhee died on January 3, 1943, at the age of 83. He and Julia had no children, and nieces and nephews survived them.

In an era when most players bounced from one team to another and played multiple positions, Bid McPhee played his entire career for the Reds, and spent all but nine of his 2,127 games at second base. He batted only .281 for his career (though *Total Baseball* and other sources reckon his lifetime average as .271), but at the time of his retirement he stood third on the all-time list of triples, behind Roger Connor and Dan Brouthers. His total of 1,674 runs scored placed him third all-time, and he was fifth in hits with 2,342. However, he compiled his most impressive statistics as a fielder. Bid McPhee left the game as baseball's all-time leader in putouts, assists, total chances, double plays, and games played by a second baseman. Today, more than 100 years later, he still holds the career record for putouts and stands second (behind fellow Hall of Famer Eddie Collins) in total chances at second base.

Though Bid McPhee was one of the most popular players of his era, especially in Cincinnati, he was nearly forgotten by baseball fans by the time he died in 1943. He never received a single vote from the Hall of Fame electors of the Baseball Writers Association, and there is no evidence that the Veterans Committee, in its various forms, seriously considered McPhee for the Hall until the 1990s. As late as 1994, Bill James stated in his book *The Politics of Glory* that McPhee "has no realistic chance of being selected" to the Hall.[9] Even in Cincinnati, there was little distinction attached to his memory. He was not inducted into the Reds Hall of Fame until the summer of 2002.

There may be several reasons for McPhee's descent into obscurity. Many Hall electors were either not knowledgeable about the players of the old American Association, or discounted their statistics in comparison to those compiled by National League players. The American Association was considered the weaker of the two major leagues in the 1880s, and (until the year 2000) no player who spent any significant portion of his career in the Association had gained election to the Hall of Fame. It also may be true that McPhee's feats would have been more widely publicized if he had played in New York. Instead, McPhee spent his entire career in Cincinnati, moved to California in 1909, and remained there for the remainder of his life. His absence from the major league scene caused him to disappear from the memories of the baseball writers who voted in the annual Hall of Fame elections.

McPhee returned to the public eye in the 1990s, when baseball statisticians turned their attention to the stars of the 1800s and discovered, through statistical analysis, that McPhee was one of the greatest forgotten players in the history of the game. John Thorn and Pete Palmer, authors of *Total Baseball*, created a statistic called TPR (total player rating) and found, more than 100 years after the fact, that Bid McPhee was the most valuable National League player of 1890 despite his .256 batting average that year. They also discovered that McPhee owned one of the highest career TPR numbers of any player not in the Hall of Fame. He did not hit for a high batting average, but McPhee's baserunning and his defense made him the most valuable member of the Cincinnati Reds for nearly two decades.

Bid McPhee's election to the Hall of Fame is a direct result of the maturation of the field of sabermetrics, the analysis of statistics as applied to baseball. For more than 100 years, batting statistics such as home runs and batting average served as the measuring stick for all major league players, simply because those numbers are easily understood by even the most casual baseball fans. McPhee, who hit only 53 homers in his career, did not

Ghosts in the Gallery at Cooperstown

own the glowing hitting statistics necessary for him to be remembered by later generations as a great player. When sabermetricians developed formulae and methods that enabled them to attach meaning to fielding statistics, they were able to prove that Bid McPhee was, indeed, the greatest second baseman of the 19th century and a worthy addition to the Hall of Fame. His selection shows that the Veterans Committee now accepts the importance of fielding in the evaluation of a player's worthiness for the Cooperstown shrine, and may open the door for other outstanding glovemen to enter the Hall in the future.

♦ NOTES ♦

1. Morgan G. Bulkeley

1. Frederick Ivor-Campbell and Robert L. Tiemann, editors. *Baseball's First Stars* (Cleveland, Ohio: Society for American Baseball Research, 1996), page 15.

2. *Ibid.*

3. *Hartford Courant,* January 7, 1873.

4. *The Sporting News,* October 31, 1918.

5. Ken Burns and Geoffrey C. Ward, *Baseball: An Illustrated History* (New York: Knopf, 1994), page 24.

6. *The Sporting News,* October 31, 1918.

7. *Ibid.*

8. Tom Melville, *Early Baseball and the Rise of the National League* (Jefferson, North Carolina: McFarland & Company, 2001), page 100.

9. A thorough description of the controversy can be found in "Connecticut's Crowbar Governor," *Hartford Courant Magazine,* April 7, 1957.

10. Peter Levine, *A. G. Spalding and the Rise of Baseball: The Promise of American Sport* (New York: Oxford University Press, 1985), page 113.

11. Levine, page 114.

2. Candy Cummings

1. W. A. Cummings, "How I Pitched the First Curve," *Baseball Magazine,* August 1908.

2. Daniel Carter Beard, *The Outdoor Handy Book* (New York: Charles Scribner's Sons, 1896).

3. Cummings, *Baseball Magazine,* August 1908.

4. *Ibid.*

5. *Ibid.*

6. *Ibid.*

7. *New York Journal,* January 8, 1912.

8. Cummings, *Baseball Magazine,* August 1908.

9. *New York Clipper*, July 8, 1871.

10. Clipping from an 1870 issue of the *Brooklyn Union*, quoted in *The New York Times*, September 29, 1900. The game between the Stars and the Mutuals was played on May 7, 1870.

11. Article by Cummings in the August 1898 edition of *The Cottager*, Baldwinville, Massachusetts, found in the Candy Cummings file, National Baseball Library, Cooperstown, New York.

12. *New York Journal*, January 8, 1912.

13. Marty Appel and Burt Goldblatt, *Baseball's Best: The Hall of Fame Gallery* (New York: McGraw-Hill, 1980), page 120.

14. Baseball records state that Goldsmith was born in 1856, so if he showed the curve to the Yale team in 1866, he was only 10 years old at the time.

15. Clipping from *Sporting Life* in 1898, reprinted in *The Scrapbook History of Baseball* (Indianapolis: Bobbs-Merrill, 1975), page 43.

16. Clipping from *Sporting Life* in 1896, reprinted in *The Scrapbook History of Baseball*, page 38.

17. *The New York Times*, August 22, 1883. In that article, Mathews confirmed that he learned the curve from Cummings.

18. Spalding spelled Cummings' name wrong, but stated, "Arthur Cummins, of Brooklyn, was the first pitcher of the old school that I ever saw pitch a curved ball. Bobby Mathews soon followed." Albert G. Spalding, *Base Ball: America's National Game, new edition* (San Francisco, California: Halo Books, 1991), page 319.

19. Harry Grayson, *They Played the Game* (New York: A. S. Barnes and Company, 1944).

20. Undated clipping in Candy Cummings file, National Baseball Library, Cooperstown, New York.

3. Roger Bresnahan

1. John McGraw, *My Thirty Years in Baseball* (New York: Boni and Liveright, 1923), page 160.

2. Cappy Gagnon, "The Debut of Roger Bresnahan," *Baseball Research Journal* #8 (1979), page 41.

3. John P. Carmichael, "Roger Bresnahan," *Baseball Digest*, October 1943.

4. Bill James, *The New Bill James Historical Baseball Abstract* (New York: Free Press, 2001), pp. 377–378.

5. CMG Worldwide website, http://www.cmgww.com.

6. McGraw, page 160.

7. Gagnon, page 42.

8. *The New York Times*, September 24, 1908.

9. CMG Worldwide website, http://www.cmgww.com.

10. Allison Danzig and Joe Reichler, *The History of Baseball* (Englewood Cliffs, New Jersey: Prentice-Hall, 1959), page 174–175.

11. *Toledo Blade*, December 5, 1944.

12. Carmichael, *Baseball Digest*, October 1943.

13. *Toledo Blade*, December 5, 1944.

14. Bill James, *The Bill James Historical Baseball Abstract* (New York: Villard Books, 1986), page 315.

15. Bill James, *The Politics of Glory* (New York: Macmillan, 1994), page 42.

4. Jack Chesbro

1. *The Sporting News*, November 12, 1931.
2. Chad's occupation was listed as "shoe repairer" in the 1880 United States Census.
3. *Cooperstown (New York) Freemans Journal*, July 1896.
4. Undated interview in the Jack Chesbro file, National Baseball Library, Cooperstown, New York.
5. *New York World-Telegram*, December 22, 1938.
6. Undated interview in the Jack Chesbro file, National Baseball Library, Cooperstown, New York.
7. Chesbro's record of 15 errors was tied by Rube Waddell of the Athletics in 1905 and by Ed Walsh of the White Sox, also a spitballer, in 1912.
8. Fred Lieb, *The Boston Red Sox* (New York: G. P. Putnam's Sons, 1947), page 57.
9. Lieb, page 59.
10. Undated interview in the Jack Chesbro file, National Baseball Library, Cooperstown, New York.
11. *Sporting Life*, October 20, 1906.
12. *The Sporting News*, August 27, 1908.
13. F. C. Lane, "Should the Spit Ball Be Abolished?" *Baseball Magazine*, June 1919.
14. *Baseball Digest*, May 1970.

5. Jesse Burkett

1. *Baseball Magazine*, May 1911, page 84.
2. *The New York Times*, May 28, 1953.
3. The United States Census of July 1, 1880 lists "Jessie" Burkett as an 11-year-old, so the 1868 birth date is probably the correct one.
4. *Worcester (Massachusetts) Telegram*, January 11, 1953.
5. *Ibid.*
6. Clipping from an unidentified newspaper, dated September 13, 1890, in the Jesse Burkett file, National Baseball Library, Cooperstown, New York.
7. *Worcester Telegram*, January 11, 1953.
8. John Phillips, *The 1898 Cleveland Spiders* (Cabin John, Maryland: Capital Publishing Company, 1997), page 67.
9. Clipping from an unidentified newspaper, dated June 27, 1896, in the Jesse Burkett file, National Baseball Library.
10. Robert L. Tiemann and Mark Rucker, editors. *Nineteenth Century Stars* (Kansas City, Missouri: Society for American Baseball Research, 1989), page 124.
11. John Phillips, *The 1896 Cleveland Spiders* (Cabin John, Maryland: Capital Publishing Company, 1995), page 16.
12. Bill James, *The New Bill James Historical Baseball Abstract* (New York: Free Press, 2001), page 659.
13. F. C. Lane, *Batting* (New York: Baseball Magazine Company, 1925), pp. 18–19.
14. His National League hit record stood until Rogers Hornsby surpassed it in 1922. Burkett's total of 240 hits is still the sixth highest in National League history.
15. *Washington Post*, May 27, 1897.

16. John Phillips, *Chief Sockalexis and the 1897 Cleveland Indians* (Cabin John, Maryland: Capital Publishing, 1991).

17. Phillips, *Chief Sockalexis and the 1897 Cleveland Indians*, page 119.

18. In *Total Baseball: The Official Encyclopedia of Major League Baseball, 2nd Edition* (New York: Warner Books, 1991), editors and researchers John Thorn and Pete Palmer have recalculated the statistics for the 1899 season and assigned Jesse a batting average of .396, not .402, for that campaign. The Baseball Hall of Fame, which uses statistics from the Elias Sports Bureau, still recognizes the .402 average.

19. *Worcester Telegram*, August 18, 2002.

20. Hamilton was elected to the Hall by the Veterans Committee in 1961.

21. *Worcester Telegram*, January 11, 1953.

6. Kid Nichols

1. From Kid Nichols page at http://www.baseball-almanac.com.

2. *Buffalo Evening News*, June 10, 1949.

3. Undated 1941 clipping from *The Sporting News* in the Kid Nichols file, National Baseball Library, Cooperstown, New York.

4. *Buffalo Evening News*, June 10, 1949.

5. Harold Kaese, *The Boston Braves* (New York: G. P. Putnam's Sons, 1948), page 57.

6. *Ibid.*

7. *Boston Post*, March 24, 1901.

8. Kaese, page 57.

9. John Phillips, *The 1898 Cleveland Spiders* (Cabin John, Maryland: Capital Publishing Company, 1997), page 102.

10. Kaese, page 89.

11. Undated 1941 clipping from *The Sporting News.*

12. *Ibid.*

13. Robert Creamer, *Stengel: His Life and Times* (New York: Simon and Schuster, 1984), pages 40–41.

14. Frederick Ivor-Campbell and Robert L. Tiemann, editors, *Baseball's First Stars* (Cleveland, Ohio: Society for American Baseball Research, 1996), page 119.

15. *Buffalo Evening News*, June 10, 1949.

7. Bobby Wallace

1. John Thorn and Pete Palmer, editors. *Total Baseball: The Official Encyclopedia of Major League Baseball, 2nd Edition* (New York: Warner Books, 1991), page 389.

2. *The Sporting News*, October 7, 1953.

3. *The Sporting News*, March 31, 1954.

4. *The Sporting News*, March 31, 1954. September 13th fell on a Thursday in 1894, but Wallace always remembered it as a Friday.

5. Wallace's tombstone gives his year of birth as 1873, and he appears as a six-year-old in the federal census held on July 1, 1880.

6. John Phillips, *The 1898 Cleveland Spiders* (Cabin John, Maryland: Capital Publishing Company, 1997), page 82.

7. John Phillips, *Chief Sockalexis and the 1897 Cleveland Indians* (Cabin John, Maryland: Capital Publishing, 1991).

8. Al Kermisch, "Cy Young Not Proud of First No-Hitter," *Baseball Research Journal #28 (1999)*, page 142.

9. *The Sporting News*, April 7, 1954.

10. Honus Wagner, who is almost unanimously considered the greatest shortstop of all time, entered the major leagues in 1897 with Louisville, but did not move to shortstop on a permanent basis until 1903.

11. *Ibid.*

12. *Ibid.*

13. *The Sporting News*, March 31, 1954.

14. David Pietrusza et al., editors. *Baseball: the biographical encyclopedia* (Kingston, New York: Total Sports Illustrated, 2000), page 1189.

15. *The Sporting News*, April 7, 1954.

16. "The Oldest Player," *Baseball Magazine*, February 1917, pp. 15–16.

17. Bill James, *The Bill James Historical Baseball Abstract* (New York: Villard Books, 1986), page 385.

8. John Clarkson

1. *Detroit Free Press*, February 5, 1909.

2. John Clarkson is listed as a "jeweler" in the 1880 United States Census.

3. Earned run average was not a recognized statistic in 1884, but later researchers studied game scores and newspaper accounts and credit Clarkson with an ERA of 0.64 for Saginaw that season.

4. Frederick Ivor-Campbell and Robert L. Tiemann, editors. *Baseball's First Stars* (Cleveland, Ohio: Society for American Baseball Research, 1996), page 31.

5. *Chicago Tribune*, February 5, 1909.

6. *Ibid.*

7. *Detroit News*, February 5, 1909.

8. Doug Myers, *Essential Cubs: Chicago Cubs Facts, Feats, and Firsts* (New York: McGraw-Hill/Contemporary Books, 1999), page 352.

9. *The Sporting News*, April 6, 1963.

10. Adrian C. Anson, *A Ballplayer's Career* (Chicago, Illinois: Era Publishing, 1900), page 130.

11. A. H. Tarvin, "How It Became the Lucky Seventh," *Baseball Digest*, November 1944.

12. David Nemec, *The Great Encyclopedia of 19th-Century Major League Baseball* (New York: Donald I. Fine Books, 1997), page 291.

13. John Phillips, *Chief Sockalexis and the 1897 Cleveland Indians* (Cabin John, Maryland: Capital Publishing, 1991).

14. Myers, page 353.

15. *Sporting Life*, December 14, 1887.

16. *Sporting Life*, January 22, 1890.

17. *Ibid.*

18. *Sporting Life*, June 14, 1890.

19. John Phillips, *Cleveland Spiders Who Was Who* (Cabin John, Maryland: Capital Publishing Company, 1993).

20. *Ibid.*

21. Ivor-Campbell, page 32.
22. From an interview with Thomas Clarkson in *Sporting Life*, April 14, 1906.
23. Some modern researchers credit Radbourn with only 59 wins in 1884.
24. *Chicago Tribune*, February 5, 1909.

9. Elmer Flick

1. *Cleveland Record*, January 28, 1963.
2. *Chicago Tribune*, January 28, 1963.
3. *Cleveland Record*, January 28, 1963.
4. *The New York Times*, August 6, 1963.
5. The 1880 United States census found the four-year-old Elmer and his family on a farm near Elkhart, Indiana.
6. *Cleveland Record*, January 28, 1963.
7. Jonathan Taylor Light, *The Cultural Encyclopedia of Baseball* (Jefferson, North Carolina: McFarland & Company, 1997), page 266.
8. *The Sporting News*, February 9, 1963.
9. *The Sporting News*, January 23, 1971.
10. *The Sporting News*, January 23, 1971.
11. *Detroit Free Press*, June 25, 2002.
12. Franklin Lewis, *The Cleveland Indians* (New York: G. P. Putnam's Sons, 1949), page 52.
13. *Cleveland Record*, January 28, 1963.
14. *The Sporting News*, August 27, 1914.
15. *Cleveland Record*, January 28, 1963.
16. *The Sporting News*, January 23, 1971.
17. *The Sporting News*, January 23, 1971.
18. The other three were Freddy Parent, a shortstop for three teams from 1899 to 1911, Ralph Miller, who pitched for Baltimore and Brooklyn in 1898-99, and Charlie Emig, who pitched in one game in 1896 for Louisville. Elmer Flick was the next-to-last living 19th century position player.
19. *The Sporting News*, February 9, 1963.
20. *The Sporting News*, March 16, 1963.

10. Eppa Rixey

1. *Pittsburgh Post-Gazette*, December 4, 1994.
2. *The New York Times*, March 1, 1963.
3. *The Sporting News*, February 9, 1963.
4. *The Sporting News*, March 16, 1963.
5. J. C. Kofoed, "The Tallest Pitcher in the Game," *Baseball Magazine,* April 1916, pages 34–35.
6. Fred Lieb and Stan Baumgartner, *The Philadelphia Phillies* (New York: G. P. Putnam's Sons, 1948), page 111.
7. F. C. Lane, *Batting* (New York: Baseball Magazine Company, 1925), pages 53–54.
8. *The Sporting News*, March 16, 1963.
9. Lawrence Ritter, *The Glory of Their Times* (New York: William Morrow and Company, 1984), page 208.

10. Bill James, *The New Bill James Historical Baseball Abstract* (New York: Free Press, 2001), page 900.

11. Lee Allen, "It Wasn't Eppa Jephtha," *The Sporting News*, February 23, 1963.

12. Donald Honig, *The Cincinnati Reds: An Illustrated History* (New York: Simon and Schuster, 1992), page 71.

13. *The Sporting News*, March 16, 1963.

14. Lane, pages 169–170.

15. Allen, *The Sporting News*, February 23, 1963.

11. Jake Beckley

1. *The Sporting News*, July 4, 1918.

2. *The Sporting News*, in Jake's obituary, suggested that Beckley may have been up to five years older than his given date of birth would suggest. He was born in 1867 "according to his own statement, but other records give 1862 as the year of his birth." *The Sporting News*, July 4, 1918. However, the United States Census of July 1, 1880 lists his age as 14, which would indicate that he shaved, at most, one or two years off his age when he entered baseball.

3. Marty Appel and Burt Goldblatt, *Baseball's Best: The Hall of Fame Gallery* (New York: McGraw-Hill, 1980), page 27.

4. Lawrence Ritter, *The Glory of Their Times* (New York: William Morrow and Company, 1984), page 55.

5. Undated clipping from *The Sporting News* publication, *Daguerreotypes*, in the Jake Beckley file at the National Baseball Library, Cooperstown, New York.

6. John Phillips, *The 1898 Cleveland Spiders* (Cabin John, Maryland: Capital Publishing Company, 1997), page 46.

7. *The Sporting News*, July 4, 1918.

8. Fred Lieb, *The Pittsburgh Pirates* (New York: G. P. Putnam's Sons, 1948), page 37.

9. *Sporting Life*, May 19, 1906.

10. *Baseball Magazine*, July 1910, page 76.

11. *The Sporting News*, July 4, 1918.

12. Appel and Goldblatt, page 28.

12. Roger Connor

1. *Hartford Courant*, July 1, 2001.

2. A fifth future Hall member, Dan Brouthers, played three games for the Trojans in 1880.

3. *The Sporting News*, September 28, 1974.

4. *Sporting Life*, September 27, 1890.

5. *The Sporting News*, September 28, 1974.

6. Frederick Ivor-Campbell and Robert L. Tiemann, editors. *Baseball's First Stars* (Cleveland, Ohio: Society for American Baseball Research, 1996), page 38.

7. Mike Attiyeh, "Roger Connor: 19th Century Home Run King," Internet article at http://www.baseballguru.com.

8. *Sporting Life*, September 27, 1890.

9. *Ibid.*

10. One version of this oft-repeated story is found in John Phillips' *The 1898 Cleveland Spiders* (Cabin John, Maryland: Capital Publishing Company, 1997), page 27.

11. *New York Daily Mirror*, May 9, 1945.

12. *New York Daily Mirror*, February 3, 1950.

13. *New York Daily Mirror*, May 9, 1945. Parker wrote this article about two weeks after the Permanent Committee failed to include Connor among its 10 Hall of Fame selections.

14. Another Giant teammate, catcher Buck Ewing, was elected in 1939 as one of the Hall's 25 charter members.

13. Vic Willis

1. *Atlanta Journal-Constitution*, January 23, 1971.

2. Stephen Cunerd, "Vic Willis: Turn-of-the-Century Great," *Baseball Research Journal #18* (1989), pp. 55–57.

3. Nicholas Dawidoff, "A Fake Gem," *Sports Illustrated*, September 9, 1991, page 10.

4. *The Sporting News*, undated 1941 article in Vic Willis file, National Baseball Library, Cooperstown, New York.

5. Harold Kaese, *The Boston Braves* (New York: G. P. Putnam's Sons, 1948), page 93.

6. *Boston Journal*, July 2, 1899.

7. *The Sporting News*, 1941 article.

8. *Boston Journal*, July 2, 1899.

9. *The Sporting News*, 1941 article.

10. *Ibid.*

11. Undated 1995 clipping in Vic Willis file, National Baseball Library, Cooperstown, New York.

12. *The Sporting News*, 1941 article.

13. *Ibid.*

14. Undated 1995 clipping in Vic Willis file, National Baseball Library, Cooperstown, New York.

15. Some researchers and statisticians give Willis different totals in the won-lost column. Willis has been credited with as many as 249 wins and as few as 243 in different publications.

14. Willie Wells

1. *Austin Daily Texan*, February 9, 1998.

2. Bill James, *The Politics of Glory* (New York: Macmillan, 1994), page 185.

3. *Austin Daily Texan*, February 9, 1998.

4. *Austin Magazine*, June 1979.

5. *Austin Daily Texan*, February 9, 1998.

6. *Austin Daily Texan*, February 9, 1998.

7. *Austin Magazine*, June 1979.

8. *Ibid.*
9. *Ibid.*
10. *Washington Post*, March 9, 1997.
11. John Holway, *Black Diamonds* (Westport, Connecticut: Meckler Books, 1989), page 123.
12. Undated clipping from Willie Wells file, National Baseball Library, Cooperstown, New York.
13. Donn Rogosin, *Invisible Men* (New York: Atheneum, 1983), page 127.
14. Rogosin, page 107.
15. From http://www.pitchblackbaseball.com.
16. Article by John Holway at http://www.baseballguru.com.
17. *Houston Chronicle*, September 26, 1997.
18. *The New York Times*, March 23, 1997.
19. From the Willie Wells page at http://www.Negroleaguebaseball.com.
20. *Ibid.*
21. Holway, *Black Diamonds*, page 123.
22. Hornsby claimed that he quit the Mexican League due to the interference of league president Jorge Pasquel, who owned pieces of most of the league's teams and tried to manipulate game results to help certain teams at certain times. "I finally decided that I'd rather be a lamp-post in America than a general down there, so I quit," said Hornsby. Charles C. Alexander, *Rogers Hornsby: A Biography* (New York: H. Holt and Company, 1995), page 232.
23. Undated clipping from Willie Wells file, National Baseball Library.
24. *The New York Times*, March 23, 1997.
25. Undated clipping from Willie Wells file, National Baseball Library.
26. *Houston Chronicle*, September 26, 1997.
27. *Houston Chronicle*, August 4, 1997.
28. From the Baseball Hall of Fame website, http://www.baseballhalloffame.org.

15. Frank Selee

1. *The Record* (Bergen County, New Jersey), March 7, 1999.
2. *The Sporting News*, March 15, 1999.
3. Article by unknown writer, dated 1888, in *Silent World*, published by the Pennsylvania School for the Deaf. This was perhaps the earliest reference to Hoy's use of signs on the field.
4. Harold Kaese, *The Boston Braves* (New York: G. P. Putnam's Sons, 1948), pp. 55–56.
5. Frank G. Selee, "Twenty-One Years in Baseball," *Baseball Magazine*, December 1911, page 55.
6. Kaese, page 55.
7. *Spalding's Official Base Ball Guide*, 1896. Reprinted in *Extra Innings: A Documentary History of Baseball, 1825–1908* (Lincoln, Nebraska: University of Nebraska Press, 1995), edited by Dean A. Sullivan.
8. Kaese, page 89.
9. Kaese, page 105.
10. A. D. Suehsdorf, "Frank Selee, Dynasty Builder," *The National Pastime* (2000), page 40.
11. Selee, *Baseball Magazine*, December 1911, page 56.

12. *Chicago Tribune*, July 29, 1905. The *Tribune* report made it clear that Chance was the interim, not the permanent, manager of the Cubs for the rest of the 1905 campaign.

13. Hall of Fame web site, http://www.baseballhalloffame.org.

16. Bid McPhee

1. John Thorn and Pete Palmer, editors, *Total Baseball: The Official Encyclopedia of Major League Baseball, 2nd Edition* (New York: Warner Books, 1991), page 363.

2. *Cincinnati Post*, February 7, 2002.

3. Other sources claim that infighting between the leagues caused the cancellation of the series after only two games.

4. *Baseball as America: Seeing Ourselves Through Our National Game* (Washington, D. C.: National Geographic Society, 2002), page 252.

5. Eleven second basemen, all of whom wore gloves, have since tied McPhee's record.

6. *Cincinnati Enquirer*, July 16, 2000.

7. *The New York Times*, March 10, 1900.

8. Undated clipping from Bid McPhee file, National Baseball Hall of Fame Library, Cooperstown, New York.

9. Bill James, *The Politics of Glory* (New York: Macmillan, 1994), page 338.

♦ Bibliography ♦

Books

Anson, Adrian C. *A Ballplayer's Career* (Chicago, Illinois: Era Publishing, 1900).

Appel, Marty, and Goldblatt, Burt. *Baseball's Best: The Hall of Fame Gallery* (New York: McGraw-Hill, 1980).

Baseball as America: Seeing Ourselves Through Our National Game (Washington, D.C.: National Geographic Society, 2002).

Creamer, Robert. *Stengel: His Life and Times* (New York: Simon and Schuster, 1984).

Danzig, Allison, and Reichler, Joe. *The History of Baseball* (Englewood Cliffs, New Jersey: Prentice-Hall, 1959).

Deutsch, Jordan A., et al. *The Scrapbook History of Baseball* (Indianapolis: Bobbs-Merrill, 1975).

Grayson, Harry. *They Played the Game* (New York: A. S. Barnes and Company, 1944).

Holway, John. *Black Diamonds* (Westport, Connecticut: Meckler Books, 1989).

Ivor-Campbell, Frederick, and Tiemann, Robert L., editors. *Baseball's First Stars* (Cleveland, Ohio: Society for American Baseball Research, 1996).

James, Bill. *The Bill James Historical Baseball Abstract* (New York: Villard Books, 1986).

_____. *The New Bill James Historical Baseball Abstract* (New York: Free Press, 2001).

_____. *The Politics of Glory* (New York: Macmillan, 1994).

Kaese, Harold. *The Boston Braves* (New York: G. P. Putnam's Sons, 1948).

Lane, F. C. *Batting* (New York: Baseball Magazine Company, 1925).

Levine, Peter. *A. G. Spalding and the Rise of Baseball: The Promise of American Sport* (New York: Oxford University Press, 1985).

Lieb, Fred. *The Boston Red Sox* (New York: G. P. Putnam's Sons, 1947).

_____. *The Pittsburgh Pirates* (New York: G. P. Putnam's Sons, 1948).

_____, and Baumgartner, Stan. *The Philadelphia Phillies* (New York: G. P. Putnam's Sons, 1948).

Light, Jonathan Taylor. *The Cultural Encyclopedia of Baseball* (Jefferson, North Carolina: McFarland, 1997).

McGraw, John. *My Thirty Years in Baseball* (New York: Boni and Liveright, 1923).

Myers, Doug. *Essential Cubs: Chicago Cubs Facts, Feats, and Firsts* (New York: McGraw-Hill/Contemporary Books, 1999).

Nemec, David. *The Great Encyclopedia of 19th-Century Major League Baseball* (New York: Donald I. Fine Books, 1997).

Pietrusza, David, et al., editors. *Baseball: The Biographical Encyclopedia* (Kingston, New York: Total Sports Illustrated, 2000).

Phillips, John. *Chief Sockalexis and the 1897 Cleveland Indians* (Cabin John, Maryland: Capital Publishing, 1991).

_____. *Cleveland Spiders Who Was Who* (Cabin John, Maryland: Capital Publishing Company, 1991).

_____. *The 1896 Cleveland Spiders* (Cabin John, Maryland: Capital Publishing Company, 1995).

_____. *The 1898 Cleveland Spiders* (Cabin John, Maryland: Capital Publishing Company, 1997).

Ritter, Lawrence. *The Glory of Their Times* (New York: William Morrow and Company, 1984).

Rogosin, Donn. *Invisible Men* (New York: Atheneum, 1983).

Spalding, Albert G. *Base Ball: America's National Game, new edition* (San Francisco, California: Halo Books, 1991).

Sullivan, Dean A., editor. *Extra Innings: A Documentary History of Baseball, 1825–1908* (Lincoln, Nebraska: University of Nebraska Press, 1995).

Thorn, John, and Palmer, Pete, editors. *Total Baseball: The Official Encyclopedia of Major League Baseball, 2nd Edition* (New York: Warner Books, 1991).

Tiemann, Robert L., and Rucker, Mark, editors. *Nineteenth Century Stars* (Kansas City, Missouri: Society for American Baseball Research, 1989).

Ward, Geoffrey C., and Burns, Ken. *Baseball: An Illustrated History* (New York: Knopf, 1994).

Newspapers

Atlanta Journal-Constitution
Austin (TX) Daily Texan
Bergen County (NJ) Record
Boston Journal
Boston Post
Boston Record
Buffalo Evening News
Chicago Tribune
Cincinnati Enquirer
Cincinnati Post
Cleveland Leader
Cleveland Plain Dealer

Detroit Free Press
Hartford Courant
Houston Chronicle
New York Clipper
New York Daily Mirror
New York Journal
The New York Times
New York World-Telegram
Toledo Blade
Washington Post
Worcester (MA) Telegram

Magazines

Austin Magazine
Baseball Digest
Baseball Magazine
Baseball Research Journal

The National Pastime
Sporting Life
The Sporting News
Sports Illustrated

Internet sites

Baseball Almanac (*http://www.baseball-almanac.com*)
Baseball Guru (*http://www.baseballguru.com*)
Baseball Library (*http://www.baseballlibrary.com*)
Baseball Reference (*http://www.baseball-reference.com*)
The Dead Ball Era (http://www.thedeadballera.com)
National Baseball Hall of Fame and Museum (*http://www.baseballhalloffame.org*)
Negro League Baseball (http://www.Negroleaguebaseball.com)
The Sporting News (*http://www.sportingnews.com*)

♦ INDEX ♦